Praise for

The Electronic B@zaar

"Useful and instructive.

Some of this is to do with the historical perspective. This takes the reader back to both Gutenberg and the origins of double-entry book keeping, teaching ironical lessons along the way. Did you know for example that Johannes Gutenberg was actually a failed entrepreneur and that his printing press was one of the assets turned over to his creditors?

A bit more, though, has to do with Bloor´s shrewd eye how the e-world works in practice and the advantages that accrue from the average business´s decision to open a website or opt for electronic billing. Value, he concludes, lies in process, or rather process refinement. Whatever is on offer – however strong the brand – or proposition – is only as good as the systems that deliver it.

Many of the political ideas in the book – the role of the internet in undermining central goverment, for example – look seriously interesting."

The Sunday Times

To Rina Hands,
a lion of a woman and a teacher of men

The Electronic B@zaar

From the Silk Road to the eRoad

Robin Bloor

NICHOLAS BREALEY
PUBLISHING

LONDON

First published by
Nicholas Brealey Publishing in 2000
Reprinted 2000

36 John Street
London
WCIN 2AT, UK
Tel: +44 (0)20 7430 0224
Fax: +44 (0)20 7404 8311

1163 E. Ogden Avenue, Suite 705-229
Naperville
IL 60563-8535, USA
Tel: (888) BREALEY
Fax: (630) 898 3595

http://www.nbrealey-books.com
http://www.TheElectronicBazaar.com

ISBN 1-85788-258-X

Library of Congress Cataloging-in-Publication Data
Bloor, Robin
   The electronic b@azaar: from the silk road to the eRoad / Robin Bloor.
      p. cm.
   ISBN 1-85788-258-X
   1. Electronic commerce. 2. Business enterprises—Computer networks. 3. Internet
(Computer network) I. Title: Electronic bazaar. II. Title.

HF5548.32 .B59 2000
338´.064--dc21

00-020316

British Library Cataloguing in Publication Data
A catalogue record for this book is available from the British Library.

Printed in Finland by WS Bookwell

Contents

"In many ways the Internet more resembles an ancient bazaar than it fits the business models companies try to impose upon it."

The Cluetrain Manifesto, Rick Levine, Christopher Locke, Doc Searls, and David Weinberger (Perseus)

"The Linux community seemed to resemble a great babbling bazaar of differing agendas and approaches. The fact that this bazaar style seemed to work, and work well, came as a distinct shock. The Linux world not only didn't fly apart in confusion but seemed to go from strength to strength at a speed barely imaginable to cathedral-builders."

The Cathedral and the Bazaar, Eric S Raymond (O'Reilly)

Prologue

The electronic b@zaar is the rapidly developing electronic economy that is gradually absorbing all of the world's national economies. It is a huge and noisy market where traders from all parts of the globe sell everything from silk stockings to timeshares. In some areas of the b@zaar the customers haggle interminably with merchants, while in others business is conducted at lightning speed. Over here there is an auction taking place for electronic components, while in the far corner stocks and shares are traded through online brokerages in the blink of an eye.

In this area there are charity stalls, and just a click away you will find stalls that sell nothing at all—the stallholders wish only to have you join some political movement or other and they push leaflets at you as you walk by. In shady areas of the market illicit goods are on sale and people you had imagined were more respectable are queuing up to buy. As you drift past some of the stalls you witness price robots recording the prices of carpets and drapes and transmitting them to their masters, who are running stalls in yet another part of the b@zaar.

In a convenient cleared area, visitors to the b@zaar chat to each other for hours, telling of some highly unusual item they found in an obscure part of the market where they sell Japanese rain chains and Tibetan prayer wheels. If you listen carefully, you may hear of an extraordinary animated game of ray guns and aliens that 100,000 teenagers have suddenly discovered.

Rock music plays as you pass through the clothes emporiums with their 3D displays and virtual changing rooms. At the healthfood stall you hear new age music, Peruvian pipes mixed with the sound of a waterfall. There are food halls and showrooms stretching to infinity, but any one of them is as close as you want it to be—just a few clicks and you're there.

And so economic life goes on in the brave new wonderful world of the electronic b@zaar...

A PRACTICAL FOUNDATION

The primary purpose of this book is to explain the internet: what it is, how it evolved, what its economic impact will be, and where it will finally lead us. As such, it may at times give the false impression that it is a "theoretical" work. However, it is not really theoretical at all. The ideas and models explained in the book derive from the practical material used by Bloor Research consultants in their various assignments.

Bloor Research has two distinct lines of business. The first is to analyze and validate information technology in all its forms. As such, it has an IT analysis arm and could be classified along with fairly well-known American IT analysts such as the Gartner Group and Forrester. The second is to assist its corporate clients in building computer systems and websites. The models and ideas in this book are used as practical aids in both these lines of business.

Bloor Research itself spent much of 1998 and 1999 transforming its own business to conform to a web-driven model. It set up several new websites, the most notable being IT-Director.com and IT-Analysis.com. Many of the ideas presented in this book represent practical lessons learned or ideas proved by the team carrying out that work. The first of these websites, launched in April 1999, has proved to be a success, going into profit within six months and attracting hundreds of thousands of visitors per month. It has been described by some of its users as "the best English language IT information source on the web." The second site, IT-Analysis.com, was launched in July 1999 and is also showing traffic growth at the rate of 15 percent a month. At the time of writing it is not yet profitable.

I have also set up a website for this book: TheElectronicBazaar.com. Its primary function is to provide complementary reference material. Thus throughout the book I illustrate specific ideas by referring to websites that employed those ideas. On TheElectronicBazaar.com you will find links to those other sites—by following those links you will be able to judge the practical implementation of the ideas. The reference links are laid out under the chapter headings and appear in the same order as in the book. As far as I am aware, this is the first book to provide such a reference.

The website also offers a community area where readers of the book, or passing surfers, can make comments or post ideas.

THE FOLLY OF THE DECKCHAIR PROJECT

If your business is not already directly and actively using the internet and consequently undergoing a major transformation, I have something to tell you:

In all probability you will read this book and not use it.

You may enjoy some of its contents and it may cause you to stop and think at some points. It may even provide you with some ideas that you can employ. However, it is unlikely in the extreme that it will cause you to act. But you need to act and you need to act today, if not sooner.

Your ship is on a collision course with an iceberg.

You need to act now, but you won't. Instead, you will get completely embroiled in an important scheme concerning the arrangement of deckchairs on one of the upper decks of your unsinkable luxury liner.

Do you smell ice in the air, or is that just a fresh northerly breeze? Never mind.

As your Titanic sinks you will be able to comfort yourself in the knowledge that, with your exciting new deckchair arrangement, at least another 10 passengers would have been able to take the sun on the starboard side of the ship in the mornings.

Icebergs are very large and nine-tenths of them are invisible. This is also true of the internet. Nine-tenths of it is invisible. Icebergs may melt, but the internet does not. It just grows. It is growing as you read these words. It is not going to go away, it is going to grow away.

If you don't use it, embrace it, and immerse your business in it, then the internet will one day take your customers away from you and your business will die. It may already be doing this.

You have been warned. Now do something.

The internet has already arrived. The greatest danger that it poses to businesspeople is that they remain in denial about what is happening and continue to pretend that nothing new is going on. It may seem strange to readers of this book who have embraced the internet that it is necessary to point this out. After all, millions of people in all the advanced economies now use the internet and since 1998 the old media—television, radio, and the published word—have been inundated with adverts for websites and awash with URLs.

Nevertheless, market research carried out during 1999 for PeopleSoft and IBM by TBC Research, based on interviews with 100 senior managers in Europe's top 1,000 companies, showed a surprising level of complacency. In the survey, only 13 percent of those questioned viewed ebusiness as a high priority. Most saw it as being only of medium priority, and when asked to identify the biggest challenge facing their organizations over the next 10 years, only 2 percent cited ecommerce. If this is the view in large European companies, then the level of complacency in smaller organizations is likely to be higher still.

Therefore, let me quickly confront 10 denial statements—propositions that I have heard too many times—in the hope of collapsing them.

Ten denial statements

The internet will not affect my business
True perhaps for buskers and beggars, but otherwise not so. The internet will pervade your business—the sooner the better.

The internet is overhyped
It is not, it is underhyped. It is deeply underhyped. It is dangerously underhyped. Its overall effects, particularly in business-to-business transactions and in politics and society more generally, have only just begun to be visible.

We are manufacturers, so we will not be greatly affected

Wrong. Manufacturers of all kinds will be affected. Manufacturing will change in many ways. Even the business of manufacturing widgets will change.

We are not retailers, so we won't be affected much

Every organization retails something in some way. The internet creates a new channel and alters the groundrules for the most fundamental transaction a business executes—the buy/sell transaction. The way the whole economy works is changing. You *will* be affected.

Only certain areas of retail will be affected

The internet will have the least impact on retailers selling goods or services that you have to collect and consume in person: restaurants, coffee shops, and hairdressing salons. However, it will still affect the marketing of such businesses and it may also alter their business model, as the whole area of retail is set to change.

We've created a website and we can take orders online, so we are an internet business

Wrong. Examine every business process you have, from sending paper mail through to procuring paperclips, and see how you can use the internet to make it more efficient. The depth of information on the internet is extraordinary. There are ideas and information that can assist in carrying out almost any business process. There are communities of self-interest that reward involvement. You can consult the internet almost in the way that you might consult an adviser.

In moving on to the web, you have to cannibalize your traditional business and I can't afford to do that

Then sell up and get out. This is the wrong way of looking at things. A very large percentage of the whole spectrum of traditional business transactions is heading for the web and they will not be prevented from moving there. A company should seek to recapture this business when it moves and perhaps capture new business too. Be aware that the web itself usually increases the level of business in two ways: Prices tend to fall, stimulating demand, and wider coverage increases the potential customer pool.

We don't have the necessary expertise to run an internet business

Then get it at once. Educate yourself and hire some help. And don't get the idea that there are any real internet experts out there. Internet veterans only have five years' experience and half of it is probably useless. Hiring some bright kids would be a good idea.

Some of my market may migrate to the internet, but not all of it will. I can concentrate on the part that remains in the realm of bricks and mortar

Quite so. The internal combustion engine was always going to affect the horse-drawn transport industry, but it didn't destroy it. There is no denying that it still exists in some places. In New York, by Central Park, you can see horses and carriages making an excellent profit from the tourist trade. Get real.

The internet is just a fad

Dream on.

1

From the Silk Road
to the eRoad

The world is experiencing a complete transformation, from bricks-and-mortar to electrons. My hypothesis is simple:

> *We have been living in an economy that is driven by paper-based information founded on paper money. We are moving to one where the market, money and all its supporting information systems are completely electronic.*

The Silk Road was the international trade route for the civilizations of Eurasia for 18 centuries. It ran over the roof of the world, from China through Central Asia to Asia Minor, starting at Yumen near to the Jade Gate at the northwest end of the Great Wall of China. From there, it passed through the southern reaches of the Gobi desert to the Tarim oases, then through Tashkent, Samarkand, and Bokhara, turning south of the Caspian Sea into Iran and on to Damascus.

It was once the world's main trading route, opened by China under the Han dynasty in the third century BC to enable trade with Athens and Rome. As trade flourished, each nation or settlement along the Silk Road took care of its maintenance, garrisoning the highway, protecting caravans and collecting tolls. From China came silk, tea, porcelain, and spices, and in return went wool, gold, silver, and gemstones, carried over dusty roads on the backs of camels. At points on the road there were well-known bazaars where European, Arab, Persian, and Indian traders exchanged goods with the nomad merchants who then traveled back to China to pass merchandise to their Chinese clients.

A web of minor trade routes evolved at both ends of the Silk Road, with goods eventually passing through the whole of Arabia and into Europe.

In 1490, a Portuguese adventurer called Pero da Corvilha reported, on his return from a mission to the East, that pepper and ginger were grown in India and that cloves and cinnamon were brought to Arabia from islands further east. More significantly, he also circulated important navigational information gleaned from the crews of Arab trading ships. Exciting possibilities were discussed in the courts of Portugal and Spain. European galleons could carry large cargoes and move quickly. If another route could be found to the East, the multitude of middlemen on the Silk Road and throughout Arabia would be disintermediated. It might no longer be just spices and silk that came to Europe from mysterious India and distant China. Suddenly, the hunt was on for a sea route to the Indies.

Once Magellan had rounded the Horn, the days of the Silk Road were numbered. The merchant states of Europe quickly established a global highway across the seven seas and policed it with their navies, dividing up the world among themselves. Just as the Silk Road spawned a web of subsidiary trade routes, so did the global trade routes over which the European nations originally presided. A lucrative trade grew in coffee, cocoa, sugar, and other commodity crops and, following the Industrial Revolution, an international trade developed in copper, tin, petroleum, and other raw industrial commodities. The eighteenth, nineteenth, and twentieth centuries brought successive revolutions in transportation; roads, bridges, canals, railways, steamships, airplanes. People could move further and faster and so could goods. The network effects of the Industrial Revolution were evident as trade exploded both nationally and internationally, enabled by a whole spectrum of trading routes.

Then, toward the end of the twentieth century, something quite surprising happened—surprising because nobody had expected it or predicted it. A new and very powerful trading route suddenly emerged out of the West Coast of the United States, growing at an alarming speed and connecting directly to the developed economies of Europe and the Far East. Some of the more perceptive businesspeople of the day recognized it immediately for what it was. They saw at once that it would disintermediate many of the large established businesses in the major economies of the world and they quickly invested in it.

But many took longer to recognize this fact, and remained confused and bewildered by it.

This was and is an electronic trading highway, an eroad, a pervasive electronic web with strands spreading out to every corner of the planet. It has already become the road to the future. It has not yet pulled the economies of the world under its control. But it is rapidly doing this and it will not be stopped. It is destined to connect every commercial enterprise from San Francisco to Vladivostok, from the smallest trading post in Tierra Del Fuego to the souks of Istanbul and all points in between. It has existed so far for less than a decade and yet it is already clear that it is destined to become the primary trading route for the whole population of the planet, usurping the current trading mechanisms or at least altering them beyond recognition.

THE INTERNET IS DISRUPTIVE

Since the resolution of the Second World War, the economic environment has been reasonably kind. It is true that there have been good times and bad, and it is also true that many companies that were once powerful and dominant have faded and died. Nevertheless, the economic climate has been temperate.

The internet is causing a far more fundamental change in the economies of the world than anything that has happened in the past two centuries. It is certainly far more disruptive than the oil crisis of the 1970s, a point illustrated by some useful comparisons:

@   The oil crisis was inflationary—it drove prices up. The net is deflationary. It is driving prices down.

@   The oil crisis affected all businesses, but mostly indirectly through inflation. The net will affect all businesses. It will affect every business indirectly, through the force of deflation—and it will affect the vast majority directly.

@   The oil crisis redistributed wealth to the oil producers. The net will redistribute wealth to the internet generation of companies.

@   The oil crisis destroyed a number of businesses. The net will destroy a very large number of businesses.

3

@   The oil crisis altered the balance of power in the world. The net will also alter the balance of power in the world.

It is of the utmost importance that the business executive and the entrepreneur understand the economic revolution that the internet is delivering. You may already believe that the net will bring great change because it has already grown in a very remarkable fashion, but "you ain't seen nothing yet."

THE GAUNTLET THROWN DOWN

The internet is going to rearrange the economic landscape. Our odyssey through the electronic economy will encounter the same factors again and again. We will summarize these challenges now, before providing the means to develop a proactive response.

The seven distinct challenges are as follows.

Information freedom and globalization

Ignorance has died. The customer can know just about everything that it is possible to know about buying a particular product. In the electronic economy, the customer will be well informed and hence commercial strategies based on deceiving the customer can no longer stand. The customer is also global—or if not, then only because the delivery of goods or services causes insuperable logistic problems. With global customers you are also subject to laws of which you may not even be aware. Consumer laws vary significantly from one country to another.

More efficient markets

The electronic economy will turn inefficient markets into efficient markets. The consequences for some companies may be profound. For example, they may discover that the goods they currently retail and distribute can only now be sold at auction. Perhaps their chain of retail stores is suddenly a wasting asset that is destined to turn into a liability. For some manufacturers the route to market, the channels themselves, will be rebuilt.

Any study of efficient markets reveals very quickly that they can be brutal. Farm produce, for example, is mostly sold in an efficient market. Thus, the farmer can have a good harvest, but the price falls to a point where he loses money. The next year, he may have a poor harvest and also lose money even though the price is high.

Customization

In efficient markets, the price is not at all sentimental about the efforts of the producer. Therefore, most producers avoid such markets and do so by differentiating their products and by branding. In the electronic economy, this naturally leads toward customization as the obvious counter to efficient markets.

Lower transaction costs

The internet is lowering transaction costs and this will have a wider effect than many commentators suppose. In order to understand this, we need to take note of the fact that both a supply chain and a value chain consist of an aggregation of transactions. In the electronic economy, it is not just the transaction cost of buying the end product that is falling, it is the cost of each sub-transaction in the whole process that creates the product and makes it available. For the foreseeable future, the trend in transaction costs is continually downward. This factor can suddenly open up new, unexploited markets. For example, one of the remarkable consequences of the popularity of electronic auctions is that it is promoting the sale of secondhand items that would never otherwise be sold.

New entrants to established markets

Typically, new competition enters a market against a dominant competitor by picking a niche and expanding from it, just as Canon did in competition with Xerox by picking on low-cost copiers. The general altering of transaction costs creates many opportunities for new players to enter established markets. The internet is also allowing new entrants. They are young, aggressive companies with new ideas, and often with good management. Established companies will find them tough competition, just as Barnes & Noble has found Amazon tough to compete with.

The exploitation of information technology

A market always has a context. The competition in retailing, once it moves beyond price, is based on the layout and the ambience of retail outlets—the shopping experience. This is so no matter whether we are talking of a super-market or a tailor or a record store. Soon the shopping experience will have its foundations in the web. This means that the retailing aspects of any business may become completely software driven. If you travel through the web and visit the websites that are successful and those that are not, you quickly realize that it is all about website design and marketing, which are highly software depen-dent. The context of most markets will become software.

Mergers and acquisitions

The final factor to consider is the inevitability of mergers and acquisitions. The lowering of transaction costs, higher level of automation, and the global market that the internet is bringing are going to increase the maximum "efficient size" of an organization. In other words, information technology will make it possi-ble for an organization to be much larger in terms of number of customers or volume of product sold. Consider AOL or Yahoo!. Both have more visitors to their websites in a month than most countries have citizens.

There will be many mergers and acquisitions. Some will simply be the successful organizations feeding on the unsuccessful ones to acquire the economies of scale. Such mergers will demand a genuinely flexible IT capability.

Small companies are born on a daily basis. Some die almost at birth and others in their infancy. However, some grow to adulthood acquiring great finan-cial health and prosperity. The whole process takes place according to a process of natural selection—the survival of the fittest.

In truth, many companies fail because they no longer understand the prevailing business environment. Because they have ceased to understand, executives make bad decisions and eventually, often very quickly, the consequences come to visit them, like Nemesis, the goddess of retribution and the daughter of night.

Considering the situation of the individual business in respect of all of these issues, the prospect is daunting. As the electronic economy grows, there will surely be a culling of businesses: large, medium, and small. For all businesses there is a growing imperative to understand how they can survive and prosper in the next 10 years. It is the goal of this book to provide that understanding.

THE BIRTH OF THE PAPER ECONOMY

The challenge has been plainly laid out, but in order to work out where to go from here we need to gaze back in history and look for some parallels. It is important to find our "source of the Nile"—the origin of the modern economy. And when we find it we discover, perhaps unsurprisingly, that we are looking at the origin of information systems.

In 1973, French economist Georges Anderla undertook a project on behalf of the Organisation for Economic Cooperation and Development (OECD) and mapped out "the information explosion." Taking what he estimated to be all the information possessed by humanity at AD1 to be a single unit, he made assessments of the increase in its size up to the current era. According to Anderla, it took until AD1500 for this amount of information to double. This was the point when printing technology came into commercial usage. It took only a further 250 years for it to double again to four units, and a further 150 years to double again, so that by 1900 there was, in theory, eight times the amount of information that had existed at AD1 (see Figure 1).

It doubled again in 1950 when computer technology first came into use. At this point the graph heads for the stars, with the amount of information doubling in the following ten years, and then again in the seven years to 1967, and finally again in the six years to 1973 when the study was completed. This gave a final total of 128 times the amount of information of AD1. If the graph were

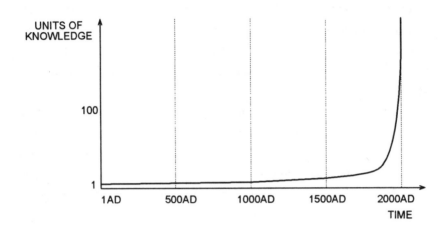

Figure 1 The information explosion

continued now it would go off the page, through the roof and into the stratosphere.

Anderla's assessments were based only on information that he deemed to contribute to humanity's fund of knowledge, so the graph does not provide a true picture of the volume of all information, only information judged to be of a high quality. A similar graph that took in all data would have the same shape and it would also head for the stars, but at an even faster rate. There is in the British Museum in London a set of 263 huge volumes, which contain references to all printed work of which the British Museum is aware—in theory, all published work. Each page simply lists the titles and details of author, publisher, publication date, and so on. Each volume is itself huge and the whole set took 10 years to assemble, with work beginning in 1956 and being completed in 1966.

Naturally, the volume of information referred to by this immense work of reference is only a fraction of all the information that exists now—many more books have been written, the number of newspapers and magazines has exploded, and now there are websites at least a billion words are being added to the web each day. Added to this is the ever-increasing volume of images, video, and sound that is being recorded. This is one mighty heap of data.

It is quite clear when looking for the origins of Anderla's information explosion that we will have to go back to the Middle Ages where it is clear that something happened. The evidence suggests that what happened was book-keeping. Let me try to explain.

FROM EMPERORS TO ACCOUNTANTS: THE MISTY BIRTH OF INFORMATION SYSTEMS

Genghis Khan had a distinctly controversial view of what happiness was. He is reported to have said: "Happiness lies in conquering one's enemies, in driving them in front of oneself, in taking their property, in savoring their despair, in outraging their wives and daughters." From about 1206 onwards, he blazed a trail of his peculiar brand of happiness all across Asia as far as the borders of Europe, leaving destruction in his wake. His legacies were a vicious empire larger than either Julius Caesar or Alexander the Great ever dreamed of and a plague that swept through Asia and Europe.

In 1347, Genoese trading ships that plied their trade in the Black Sea area introduced the plague to Italy. From here it spread across Europe almost like a forest fire, inflicting far more damage than it had done in Asia. The Europeans of the day had no natural resistance to this disease and it cut their numbers in a merciless fashion, killing an estimated one in three of the whole population. Appalling though such a death rate might seem, it was worse still in the centers of commerce—the crowded towns and cities of Italy, France, and northern Europe that were teetering on the edge of prosperity when the plague first struck. In these fertile areas the Black Death took hold with a pitiless vengeance, sweeping through the crowded slums, bringing the economy to a grinding halt, and prompting the wealthy to flee to the countryside.

Time passed, and across the European landmass four new cultures gradually emerged as the Mongol empire crumbled and the disastrous effects of the Black Death wore off. In the East, Chinese rule was restored and Chu Yuang-Chang proclaimed himself the first emperor of the Ming dynasty. In Chinese Ming means "brilliant." Moving west from China, the Mughal Empire was established in India, by a Mongol called Babur, who was more intent on founding a well-ordered empire than roaming the world in an orgy of destruction.

The Middle East saw the growth of the Ottoman Empire throughout the fifteenth and sixteenth centuries, which reached its height in the sixteenth century under Suleiman the Magnificent, who rebuilt Jerusalem and beautified the city of Istanbul.

Finally, in Renaissance Europe there was also a recovery of civilization, beginning with a cultural explosion in the wealthy trading state of Florence. However, the European situation was significantly different. Florence was not a great empire, even if it was a wealthy and powerful trading state. Unlike the Ottoman, Mughal, and Chinese empires, where an emperor presided over the restoration of order and the cultural explosion that followed, the man who initially financed the Renaissance was not an emperor at all but a banker called Cosimo Medici. Some of us might be surprised to read the following description of the education and training of the son of Donato Velluti, a Florentine lawyer who died in 1370:

> *I sent him to school. Having learned how to read, and possessing good intelligence, memory, and talent, as well as sound ability in speech, he applied himself and made good progress. Then I sent him to learn mathematics and in a short time, he became proficient. I withdrew him from school and sent him to Ciore Pitti's shop, then to Menente Amidei's ... He was given an account book of debits and credits, and managed it as though he were a man of forty.*

That accountancy was alive and well in fourteenth-century Florence has great significance. The name of its inventor is not known, indeed all that is known is that the idea was quickly taken up by the merchants of Genoa and Venice who controlled the trading routes of the Mediterranean. It then spread throughout Europe to all the other centers of commerce and the first book on the topic was published in 1494, written by the Venetian monk Luca Pacioli. Pacioli's book summarized the principles of accounting, which have remained largely unchanged for centuries.

If we were to write a history of computing, we would almost certainly begin with Babbage and proceed quickly to the code-breaking machines of the Second World War. However, if we were to write a history of information systems, we would be obliged to begin elsewhere. We would have to start with the first records of double-entry bookkeeping of an unnamed accountant found in Genoa and dating from 1340.

The importance of accountancy becomes clearer if we consider a simple manufacturing operation. The manufacturing process combines labor and the skillful use of tools to make a product from raw materials. The consumer exchanges money for this, which feeds back into the system. This money then pays for labor and raw materials, replenishing worn-out tools and, hopefully, leaves a surplus called profit.

What this produces is a regulated feedback system. If insufficient money comes in, then either costs will need to be cut or the operation ceases. If there is profit, then the owner of the system can take it as a reward or can invest in growth, or, more likely, do both. Systems such as this are difficult to manage, primarily because none of their major elements is static. The cost of raw materials and labor can vary considerably. This means that the price of the final product is difficult to hold constant. If the price varies, then it is likely that demand for the product will change; but even if the price remains constant, demand for the product may not. Thus, the inflow of money is unpredictable.

There is no way to manage such a system without being able to allocate money to various real or potential future costs. The valuation of stock-on-hand and the depreciation of tools need to be taken into account. Variations in income and demand have to be examined and interpreted.

In other words, an information system is required, without which there will be a definite limitation to the size of organization that can be managed. The invention of accounting offered such a system and, in doing so, provided the basis for the Industrial Revolution that was to occur centuries later.

The accounting system was the first information-processing system that came into common usage and much of what has since happened with the organization of commerce stands on this foundation. Thus, the accounting system was the first target for automation as soon as business machines or computers became commercially available. An accounting system appears to have made both the Renaissance and the Industrial Revolution possible. Indeed, it is arguable that previous advanced cultures never got to the point of industrialization simply because they lacked accountancy.

A FAILED ENTREPRENEUR, A NEW INFORMATION TECHNOLOGY

Accountancy on its own did not provide the foundations for the information economy that we now live in, even if it helped considerably. For information systems to be effective, there needs to be a means of distributing information reliably. This was provided by Johannes Gutenberg, a diamond polisher from Mainz and a failed entrepreneur.

In 1455, Gutenberg found himself in court for the non-payment of debts. The business that he had been building had clearly been under-capitalized and had failed to provide enough revenue to support itself. Consequently, the creditors had decided to pull the plug and grab the assets while there still were any. These assets were the world's first printing press.

Even though he was later ennobled by the Archbishop of Mainz for his efforts and his name is written into history, Gutenberg may well have felt under-rewarded. By 1500, forty-five years after it was first printed, millions of copies of the Gutenberg Bible had been sold, mainly to the church and for a good profit. Gutenberg had invented the ability to distribute information cheaply. From our perspective, he had invented an information technology.

Although it took a long time, the printing press extended the reach of information dramatically, encouraging literacy and eventually promoting the whole idea of education as a right. The printed word could spread ideas and detailed information far faster than had ever previously been possible. It made censorship far more difficult, it empowered thinkers, and it pulled down governments. But in reality only one thing had changed—the cost of distributing information had fallen dramatically and this increased the level of access.

The role of printing as the basis for information systems is rarely highlighted, but it was vitally important in the formation of the modern economy. Printing provided the basis for the creation of distributed information systems and as time passed many such systems came into existence.

THE BASIS FOR INFORMATION SYSTEMS: PUSHING PAPER AROUND

An information system does only five distinct things and all information technologies of any kind can be classified as belonging to one of these five activities or a combination of several of them. An information system:

@   takes data in
@   processes or transforms data
@   stores data
@   moves data around
@   puts data out.

Data input

There is little point in assembling large amounts of information unless it can be preserved and shared. Prior to printing, the amount of effort that humanity as a whole devoted to this activity was small; large-scale efforts, such as the Domesday Book, were few and far between.

Once printing became an established technology, this changed and various data-gathering exercises started to occur. For example, life insurance was based on the work of Englishman John Graunt. He gathered information on births and deaths from parish registers. From this it was possible to estimate a person's life expectancy and to monitor any changes in circumstances that might have an impact on general mortality trends. Measuring the size of a nation's population and the use of such information to plan taxation and expenditure now made sense.

Data processing

The value of accounting, apart from keeping the figures accurate, is its ability to classify expenditure so the use of money can be analyzed. The invention of printing made useful and productive analyses of information possible in many areas.

In 1656, Rome attempted to rally its influence in the face of heavy desertion to the various Protestant sects that were flourishing across Europe.

The Council of Trent, in Northern Italy, was convened and met on and off for several decades. Among other things, it decided to standardize the form of the Catholic service and prayer book, so that everyone was literally singing from the same hymnsheet. It also established a list of prohibited books.

As part of the standardization effort, a new Bible was commissioned that augmented the basic text, so that the whole could be more easily understood. The new Bible's appendices included various treatises on biblical coinage, weights and measures, languages, maps of the Holy Land, and so forth. This work was very popular in its time and the writers and researchers who were involved in the effort went on to other similar work on texts from Latin and Greek. Thus began a new effort on the classification of knowledge, which spread quickly. It helped to invigorate the existing universities and saw the establishment of many new universities, colleges, and academies across Europe.

Standardization also saw the emergence of the dictionary, foreign language dictionaries, and the encyclopedia. The whole of learning was broken up and classified. Eventually, but only after centuries, the Dewey Decimal system became a common standard for the classification of books by content.

Data storage

It is difficult to overemphasize the improvement to data storage that print technology gave. First of all, information began to be accumulative. Prior to the printed word most information, including a great deal of important information, was forgotten or lost.

Thus it is not surprising that Georges Anderla could represent the growth of human knowledge as a curve that only began to rise significantly with the invention of print.

It is an undeniable fact that the Roman Empire, for example, had far superior road-building technology and sanitary technology than ever existed in the Dark Ages or the Middle Ages. This information was forgotten or destroyed. Almost all the important technological discoveries occurred in the last 500 or so years and even then, most happened in the past 100 years. What distinguishes the final 500 years is that humanity ceased to suffer from amnesia once printing was invented.

There is also another point worth making here. Printing technology enabled paper money—it enabled the storing of "value" on paper. The great trading cities of seventeenth-century Europe, particularly London and Amsterdam, began to abandon barter-based trading for paper-based trading. The exchange of precious metals or valuable coins for goods and services was slowly superseded by the exchange of "paper title" for goods and services. Paper money and all the economic structures for exchanging it and processing it were born. The switch between systems was not achieved quickly and many of the sophisticated economic mechanisms that we are now familiar with took decades or even centuries to develop. However, a revolution took place.

Data communication and distribution

One aspect of printing is the fact that it makes information far more portable. Compare the town crier with the newspaper. The newspaper has greater potential reach, greater flexibility as to when you can receive the information, and much less opportunity for random distortion.

What is perhaps less obvious is that the ability to distribute information in a printed form increased the power of the individual citizen. Prior to printing, the only realistic form of government was some type of monarchy where power was vested in one family who was, hopefully, surrounded by an educated elite to advise in various worldly matters. Once information was distributed, such a structure could no longer hold. It was abandoned as a meaningful form of government in the founding of the United States and has since been in decline.

The court used to be the central hub of power, knowledge, and wealth. When information and hence knowledge began to circulate, power and wealth traveled with it. This did not happen quickly, because literacy did not rise particularly quickly, but it happened all the same.

Data output

Printing is all about data output and hence the fact that a whole spectrum of published products quickly emerged after Gutenberg is not surprising. Neither are the literary traditions that sprang up so quickly in all the European centers of culture.

Some of the books and pamphlets that circulated had a dramatic impact and changed the world. Here we can list, among other works, Thomas Paine's

The Rights of Man and *The Age of Reason*, Jean Jacques Rousseau's *Social Contract* and Karl Marx's *Das Kapital*. Such books might have been banned, if it had been possible to suppress them, but print technology makes such suppression difficult.

Often, publishing was of extreme commercial importance, as for example with navigation maps. Maps could make the difference between accurate and inaccurate navigation, and thus reduce the incidence of shipwreck, which was highly expensive. As maps and navigation techniques improved, the costs of maritime trading reduced and trading economies prospered.

As a form of publishing, advertising arrived late on the scene. It provided a means of subsidizing magazine publishing and eventually became the prime source of revenues for some types of publication. But this only blossomed when capitalism was in full swing and many companies were vying for the attention of a population of consumers.

Also fairly late on the scene was packaging information—information added to a product for presentation purposes, for legal reasons, to provide a "guarantee" and service information, or simply to be informative. With food, there are now regulations about declaring the ingredients and the weight. With packaging comes the whole idea of branding. A brand is an absolute necessity for an advertised product as it links the product to the advert, but it can also be an extraordinary signature of "value," so nowadays the brand image is incorporated into the packaging process. A brand is also an interesting information artifact. Suddenly, a specific word has value of itself. The most valuable word in the world is hyphenated—it is Coca-Cola. Of very similar value are the words McDonald's and Yahoo!.

It became possible to store information in filing cabinets and access it when needed. Special documents could be designed for moving information around and so on. This kind of system took centuries to evolve, but eventually order forms, requisitions, delivery notes, card files, memos, and all the paper artifacts of early office systems evolved.

The five aspects of an information system were not just employed, they were brought into a harmony that circulated information efficiently throughout an organization.

Accountancy and printing: the foundation of the modern economy

Taken together, it is clear that the information system of accountancy and the information technology of printing are the foundation of the modern economy. From them everything else emerges.

It soon becomes obvious that computer-based information systems were not a wholly new phenomenon that was born when the computer was created. In reality, the building of early computer information systems usually involved the transfer of paper-based systems to an electronic medium. The electronic medium came into existence long before the computer—the electronic infrastructure that now makes up the internet began with the invention of the telegraph in the nineteenth century. Then followed the invention of telephone and radio.

The first digital computers were built during and just after the Second World War for military applications. The commercial computer market evolved from post-war military projects, with the US quickly gaining market dominance. The early giants of the business machine market, IBM, NCR, and Remington Rand, all became involved in developing commercial machines, and IBM quickly established itself as the dominant player across the globe.

THE DOG BEGINS TO WAG THE TAIL: THE MOVE TO ELECTRONIC TITLE

It is important to understand that the new electronic technologies were first put at the service of the paper economy to make paper information systems and a paper-based economy more efficient. Companies in the financial sector were the early adopters of computing and the primary application transferred to the computer was the accounting system.

The uptake of computer technology mirrored the events of many centuries earlier, but it all happened at 20 times the speed or faster. First, computers became accounting machines and then they became printing machines, with banks and insurance companies automating the production of the paper artifacts for the paper economy.

When the 1980s arrived, the computer was beginning to inveigle its way into all areas of an organization; by the early 1990s PCs were becoming ubiquitous in business. The killer applications that caused the spread of PCs were the spreadsheet and the wordprocessor—accounting and printing were yet again driving the technology.

For a long time, the shadow of the coin-based economy hung over the paper-based economy. Indeed, it was not until the 1970s that the world economy severed the link between the value of money and the value of gold.

In the seventeenth century, the introduction of paper money led to the splitting of the act of buying or selling into two parts. First, there was the trade, when agreement to do the transaction was reached, and then there was settlement, when the exchange of money and goods was resolved. Even now, when we buy goods using a credit card or a check it takes days for the transaction to be settled and the money to pass from buyer to seller. This pattern of "trade and settlement" is due to change, however. With electronic money, settlement will be instant.

The historical revolution that began on the academic computer networks of the early 1990s will not be over until electronic money is issued and widely used. Currently, the paper economy and all its rules and regulations govern the infant electronic economy. The tail is wagging the dog, but soon it will be time for the dog to wag the tail.

A far-reaching economic change is in progress. The exchange of paper title for goods and services is being replaced by the exchange of electronic title for goods and services. Electronic money and all the economic structures for exchanging it and processing it are being born. When commentators write about the phenomenon of the internet, they usually point to the remarkable things: the extraordinary growth rate in users or websites, the amazing IPOs of various internet companies, the exponential growth rates of some of the net-based businesses, the new business models that are emerging, and so on. These may well be interesting in their own right, but they are all symptoms of a single fundamental change that technology is delivering to us—the move to electronic money and electronic title.

The speed of evolution of the paper economy could be described as leisurely, if not painstakingly slow. In contrast, the speed of evolution of the electronic economy is extraordinarily fast and unprecedented.

THE FOUR HINGES

"In order to understand a door, it is only necessary to understand the hinges," as the saying goes. In analyzing the electronic economy, we have identified four hinges—the four fundamental mechanisms that are making the whole thing work and that need to be understood in order to gain a complete picture. These hinges open the door to the future for the businessperson and the entrepreneur.

The hockey stick curve

The first hinge is a new model of market growth.

The growth and saturation of markets have long been objects of study. They have been roughly represented by many commentators as a normal distribution, the familiar bell-shaped curve.

However, this curve does not provide a valid model for the growth of internet markets and internet companies. Because of this, various internet growth patterns are modeled using a different curve that has slightly different characteristics. This is the "hockey stick curve," so called because it is roughly shaped like a hockey stick, the length of the hockey stick corresponding to a phase of massive growth.

The hockey stick curve can be observed as the growth model for a whole series of internet businesses, including well-known names such as Amazon and eBay. Once the bend in the hockey stick has passed, the business accelerates like a rocket, leading to unprecedented growth statistics. Take, for example, the fact that on its website, online stockbroker Charles Schwab experienced an increase in traffic of a factor of six in a period of a year from the first quarter of 1998 to the first quarter of 1999. In the same period, its level of trading rose from roughly $2 billion per week to about $2 billion per day (on weekdays).

Publish–subscribe

The second hinge is a series of mechanisms (email, the website, the multi-user domain (MUD) or community, and the search engine) by which electronic interaction occurs in the electronic economy.

In the bricks-and-mortar economy, customers and companies interact in a particular and well-defined way. However, the modes of interaction in the electronic economy are slightly different, and the consequences of this are profound. The fundamental difference is that in the bricks-and-mortar world the individual relates in a one-to-one manner in many situations, and organizations tend to relate in a one-to-thousands manner. In the electronic economy, the customer is suddenly given the power to relate in a one-to-many manner and the organization can respond in a more refined one-to-many manner. This arrangement is described as publish–subscribe, where one party publishes information and the other subscribes, if he or she wishes to do so.

In respect of email, joke-of-the-day.com is an advertising business that simply emails a joke to subscribers every day. There are literally millions of examples of websites with varying degrees of sophistication, from Amazon with its single-click purchase to Boo.com with its three-dimensional dressing room for clothes buyers. Perhaps the best example of a community-based website is The Well as it was, in the early days of the web, a very influential site where many individuals floated ideas and exchanged views. However, there are also sites, such as the health site WebMD.com, which use the community mechanisms (the bulletin board or MUD) as a business mechanism. Finally, websites like AltaVista and Ask Jeeves are based entirely on the search engine, a mechanism that allows an individual to identify multiple sources of information at once.

The force of automation

The third hinge, the force of automation, is a fundamental force of change and is very important within the electronic economy.

A simple example is provided by the recent innovation of soft drink machines in Finland selling Coca-Cola. You can buy a can of drink in one of two ways. Either you put money in, or you can dial a telephone number displayed on the machine using a mobile phone. The number dialed is answered by a computer, which contacts the drinks machine over the internet telling a local embedded chip to release the selected can of drink. The computer then automatically sends a bill for the drinks can to the mobile phone service, which adds the charge to your mobile phone bill.

This is a very slick idea that will work well in areas such as Scandinavia, Hong Kong, or Italy where mobile phone penetration among the population is very high. For the idea to work, various new technologies had to have come into usage: embedded chips that are able to communicate, mobile phones, and the internet. This is the force of automation in action, creating new business opportunities by virtue of the deployment of new technology.

The trading model

The final hinge, and one that offers a background for all the others, is a simple model of a market, the pattern of the buy/sell transaction. One of the main areas of change that the net introduces is that it alters the way in which markets behave. The trading model provides us with the capability to understand how the net changes the picture, because it charts the information flows between all the players in a market. Think of the internet as a large market, an electronic b@zaar with many stallholders selling a range of similar or even identical goods, and a large number of buyers haggling with the sellers to agree a reasonable price.

It cannot have escaped many people's notice that auctioning, which is a fairly marginal activity for selling goods in the bricks-and-mortar economy, is a massive and very popular way of selling goods on the internet. There are now businesses worth billions of dollars, such as Priceline and eBay, that handle the auctioning of hundreds of thousands of items every day. Some manufacturers are also using auctions as a selling mechanism, occasionally just to dispose of unwanted inventory but sometimes as a genuine channel to market.

We could ask why this is—and we might come up with many justifications, such as taking part in auctions is fun, auctions nearly always ensure that goods get sold, people can get bargains, and so on. In reality, these are just details. Auctions work very well on the web because the internet allows information to flow efficiently between sellers and buyers and it can connect together millions of people at once. The popularity of auctions and other forms of market making become far easier to understand if you understand the trading model.

All of the world's economies are being quickly pulled into the electronic b@zaar. The very nature of buying and selling is changing dramatically and every one of us will have to adjust to it at every level—as an employee or businessperson and as a consumer and a citizen of the planet. We are all, whether we like it or not, becoming part of the electronic b@zaar.

2

The Mad Hatter's eParty

Cyberspace. A consensual hallucination experienced daily by billions of legitimate operators, in every nation, by children being taught mathematical concepts . . . A graphic representation of data abstracted from the banks of every computer in the human system. Unthinkable complexity. Lines of light arranged in the non-space of the mind, clusters and constellations of data. Like city lights receding. . .

This is how cyberspace was described in the dark and powerful science fiction novel *Neuromancer*, by William Gibson. It is where the word "cyberspace" was invented. With great foresight, the book, written in 1984, depicts a fully connected world and also predicts the idea of virtual reality. The prefix "cyber" derives from the word cybernetics, the interdisciplinary science of communication and control systems, which in turn derives from the Greek word *kubernētēs*, which has the original meaning of "steersman" or "governor." Etymologically it is a misleading hybrid, but Gibson's word persisted and entered the English language.

His surreal vision of cyberspace remained in the realm of fiction, but in some ways it wasn't too wide of the mark as, from the very beginning, the real cyberspace seemed to embrace the surreal. Life was not imitating art, it was competing with it, as a brief tour through some of the murkier regions of cyberspace quickly demonstrates. The internet is a huge network that is frequented by every kind of individual you can imagine, from the altruist to the madman and all stops in between.

For example, Steven J. Slickpicklehamburger is the curator of the Air Sickness Bag Virtual Museum. His website lists air sickness bags from his collection, giving "vintage, donor information and much more besides," should you actually want it. Other sites are disturbing, like the one that focuses on different ways of killing tortoises and turtles. There are also some bizarre information services. If you care to visit www.sorabji.com/livewire/payphones/, you will be shown a list of randomly selected payphone numbers from across the world. Just dial any one of them and wait until a passer-by picks up the receiver. You can then have a truly random conversation with someone you have never met before.

Some of these websites are nothing more than bizarre graffiti scrawled on the fabric of the internet, but the phenomenon is easy to understand. Geocities (www.geocities.com), currently the largest online community, provides all subscribers with an email address and a home page. Naturally, many subscribers use their home page simply to have some fun, or play student jokes, or make a gesture that they believe to be meaningful. If you can think of a strange enough theme for a website then you may even be rewarded by a horde of visitors—until the novelty wears off. Some websites have a visitors' book where you can leave a message and the statistics they give indicate that they attract a respectable number of visitors, often in the thousands.

The Geocities idea of a free website was extensively copied by many internet service providers (ISPs), the companies that provide access to the internet. The cost of computer resource to the ISP is minimal and web users like the idea of having their own site. There are a number of family sites out there, with photographs, pertinent family details, and even extensive family trees. If the space to do this is provided at very low cost, and it is, then people will use it.

We can witness the same strange phenomenon with usenet groups. The usenet is an integral part of the web. It is a vast community facility of bulletin boards that is divided up under a huge variety of topics. Log on to www.dejanews.com and take a look. You can get involved in discussions on anything from politics to pumpkin pie. And naturally, among the thousands of usenet groups there are a number of "fun" groups, including some devoted simply to telling jokes (rec.humor) or delivering insults (alt.flame). If you'd specifically like to be insulted, then try news.admin.net-abuse.misc: the visitors to that newsgroup specialize in insults. There are also grievance groups like alt.aol-sucks for people who dislike AOL or perhaps make a hobby out of disliking that company. Some of the usenet groups are long-running jokes that have seen better days, such as alt.fan.tonya-harding.whack.whack.whack. Alt.tasteless is devoted to ill-mannered, abusive, and completely tasteless behavior. In 1994, some of the alt.tasteless tribe invaded rec.pets.cats posting dubious remarks and jokes about cats, but such behavior is quite rare.

CYBERTALK

As is now well documented, cyberspace emerged from a suggestion to the US Military by the Rand Corporation to network all its defense computers together allowing them to back each other up, and allowing communications to take many possible routes, so that the whole network would operate if even a fairly large number of its nodes were destroyed by nuclear or conventional attack. So at its birth, cyberspace was a communication and control system, a military network called ARPANET. This network grew to include the National Science Foundation Network (NSFNET), which linked in research agencies and universities, and thus it became international.

The World Wide Web was proposed in 1989 by Tim Berners Lee who was working at CERN, the European Centre for Nuclear Research, and it was born in 1990. Berners Lee was responsible for an initiative to link documents together between all connected sites using weblinks (hypermedia techniques) so that global information sharing was possible. It was a brilliant idea. By 1994, the idea of a website had solidified and there were approximately 500 websites in existence. Thus the year 1994 is normally taken as the birth of the internet – the global inter-network.

By the start of 1995, there were nearly 10,000 websites and 10 million web users. Then in its final formative act, the internet absorbed all the alternative networks—CompuServe, MSN, Prodigy, and AOL—which could no longer afford to be separate.

The electronic signpost

The internet has done what many victorious technologies previously did. It has introduced a whole new set of words and terms to the language. As an aid to the less web-familiar reader, I will explain a few of these as we chart and explain the internet's history. Let us begin at the beginning with the technically oriented terms of IP, URL, http, weblink, IP address, and browser.

Tim Berners Lee's original conception was academic in its orientation. The idea was to enable documents to link to each other in the way that academic works are often cross-referenced. It is highly unlikely that he had any notion of what he was starting when he first came up with the idea. Creating links over a computer network demanded that each linked document should have an address, so that other computers could find it. At the technical level many computers already had *IP* addresses, which identified the computer itself. IP stands for Internet Protocol, which amounted to a series of numbers that the TCP/IP protocol (a set of formal rules describing how to transmit data) could use to find a specific computer within a large network. There were other protocols and other types of addresses, but by 1990 TCP/IP had become the dominant standard.

The IP address was fine for computers talking to computers, but less than memorable for people trying to find documents. Thus the *domain name* was invented, representing a location on a computer—in reality this is a convention for attaching a description to the IP address. The full document address was referred to as a *URL*, standing for Universal Resource Locator, and it took the form:

http://:www.name.type.country/localbit/file.html
for example: http://www.mycompany.co.uk/mydocs/thisdoc.html

Let me explain this address or signpost bit by bit.

The "http://" part tells the computer that the address is a URL, where the http actually stands for HyperText Transfer Protocol. (It's pretty obvious that computer people were responsible for this.)

The "www" tells the computer to go and look this address up via the world wide web, as the address is not local to that computer.

The "name," "type" (e.g., co, org, gov) and "country" (e.g., .uk for the UK, .sa for South Africa) refer to a specific domain. It is easiest to think of this as a specific computer rather than a domain. To confuse matters a little, the US chose to allow the creation of a series of domain names that were not qualified by country (.com, .net, .org, and so on), even though the US itself has the predictable country designation of .us.

Early internet entrepreneurs quickly came to the conclusion that having to type the country would irritate web users—after all, a few extra characters would exhaust the typing fingers, wouldn't they?—so they quickly coalesced around the .com designation. Non-US entrepreneurs quickly followed suit and suddenly having a .com domain name was *de rigueur*. Clearly, the addressing scheme was failing from the off, but within a few months it was too late, because the .com domains had suddenly acquired value. This was a gold rush and claims had been staked.

The final part of the URL, "/localbit/file.html," refers to a specific computer file, but note the .html suffix—it means that the file is stored in *HTML* format. This stands for HyperText Markup Language, which is not a language at all but rather a set of instructions that can be embedded in a string of text and images in order to specify how it should appear on screen.

Unless you actually intend to build web pages yourself you don't need to know any more about HTML than this, except for one fact: that HTML allows you to embed the addresses of other documents that might be anywhere else in the world.

When you embed such an address it appears as a link on a web page; when you click on the link, the computer takes you directly to the document, which is usually itself a web page. This is quite a clever idea. It turns all the websites everywhere and all the documents they contain into a single massive information lump through which you can navigate.

All you then need—aside, obviously, from a computer and an internet connection—is a piece of software that allows you to follow the links. Such software is called a *browser*.

Netiquette

The early spirit of the internet reflected the behavior of its pioneers. In the main they were a mixture of hobbyists and academics, and they included a few journalists who discovered early on that the internet was an excellent information source. They quickly became an interactive social group that evolved its acceptable behavior or *netiquette*.

The early interactions that could take place on the web consisted of email and the posting of messages, letters, and debating points on a bulletin board. Both of these capabilities are parallels of non-electronic activities— exchanging mail and posting notes on a real-life noticeboard. In the electronic versions, however, there are some very important differences.

@   With email and bulletin boards, a full record of what has occurred can be kept. With email it is a personal decision as to what to keep. With a bulletin board it may depend on the sysop (systems operator), the individual that "moderates," as to what is kept in the archive, but it is possible for everything to be kept.

@   Email and bulletin board items are typed, so the message is very bare. It is not possible to guarantee the way it looks to the reader and it is very difficult to enhance its presentation; although it is now possible to use HTML to style emails, not every recipient may be able to receive them in this format. Thus the presentation of the message is in its content. When read, email and bulletin board items are often more stark than the author intended.

@   Online activity can be anonymous. You don't have to declare who you are.

Taken together, these points helped to shape the nature of early internet use. The lack of graphical capability gave rise to a set of conventions for writing messages. The use of capital letters was taken to signify SHOUTING, and tended only to be used when someone wished to convey annoyance or something stronger. Two conventions were adopted to indicate the emotional tone of a sentence. The combination of characters :-) looks roughly like a smiley face on its side and indicates a smile. Similarly, :-(represents a sad face and ;-) indicates a wink. These conventions are referred to as *emoticons* (i.e., emotional icons). They add spice to the written word and are often employed in an ironic manner. They are still used extensively in emails.

The fact that all information can be preserved is extremely useful and powerful. A discussion group can form around a specific topic and a debate will arise. If the topic of discussion is compelling it may attract some very bright minds and the whole interchange will be recorded and be available for others to read, possibly for ever. The discussion can be pursued until no one has anything further to add, and it occurs at times convenient for participants.

Bulletin board debates of this sort require a moderator to archive the conversations that have occurred in an accessible manner and part of this process involves the creation of a *FAQ* (frequently asked questions) list. This is simply a fast introduction to the topic under discussion that records the main questions that were asked in the early life of an online discussion. Netiquette demands that anyone entering a debate should at least read through the FAQs and scan the archived entries so that they don't post irrelevant messages. Debating is just one of the possible activities of a bulletin board. The most common activity is simply to post news or gossip.

The various bulletin boards that existed on the net soon became united under a formal structure and they are now referred to as usenet newsgroups. Like websites, they have distinct addresses, such as rec.music.reviews or alt.politics.democrats or alt.support.stop-smoking. (Rec stands for recreation, alt stands for alternative, as in alternative medicine, but in reality alt simply indicates a free-form forum.) Many of these groups are intended only to be current and thus they delete postings after four days or so. Usenet newsgroups are open to everyone and you can organize to have new postings to a newsgroup emailed to you direct.

A newsgroup is an example of a *MUD*, an acronym that stands for multi-user domain. It is a structure that brings together a group of individuals with a common interest. Originally, the only means of interaction was via posting a submission, so the interaction was not "live," which mitigated in favor of debates and the posting of news and gossip. True live interaction with multiple participants became possible fairly recently (using internet relay chat (IRC) software) and this operates in favor of group meetings, group socializing, and group working.

Multi-user domains are also sometimes referred to, in a lighthearted manner, as multi-user dungeons, connecting them with the popular role-playing game of Dungeons and Dragons. The connection is meaningful, because participants in MUDs often choose to be anonymous. Indeed, the practice of adopting a different persona for such cyberenvironments is frequent enough for a word, *avatar*, to have emerged to describe the cyber persona. If you want to put your opinions forward as "St Ziggy from the planet Truthquest" then you can, but you may have to cross swords with other avatars: "Quicksilver, Lord of Deception" or "Razorsharp, the Intellectual Samurai," perhaps.

The technology of the net lends itself to anonymity and playing in this manner. We can normally recognize people by their looks and by their voices and by their handwriting. It is not so easy (but in some instances possible) to recognize people from their writing style. By interacting in text we give very little of ourselves away and it is possible in this medium to remain anonymous even among people you know. The freedom that this provides is widely enjoyed. Some "netizens" who are particularly enchanted by the possibilities long for the time when MUDs will be populated by full-color animated 3D avatars with faces, figures, and voices chosen from Hollywood stars or historical figures. This time will come.

The usenet mechanisms encourage anonymity, as you are not obliged to post items under your own name and it is also possible to conceal your email identity in various ways, from configuring a false email ID on your own computer through to using a remailer service, which forwards mail on your behalf but conceals your details. There are no mechanisms to guarantee your anonymity absolutely if someone chooses to pursue you for legal reasons. Thus there is no absolute protection for those who wish to perpetrate antisocial or criminal behavior. However, at the moment the web is growing so quickly and is so poorly policed that a significant level of antisocial and criminal behavior does go unchallenged.

Spam and scam

Having fun on websites or in usenet groups is quite different to executing pranks with email. Email is personal—with it you demand someone's time and attention, so they can get justifiably irritated if they receive unsolicited rubbish, whether it is a joke or an advert. The term *spam*—after the famous Monty Python "spam" sketch—has emerged to describe junk email of all types, and it has become a genuine problem.

Spam was born on April 12, 1994, when Laurence Canter and Martha Siegel posted an advert on the approximately 10,000 newsgroups that were in existence at the time. They were advertising a paid-for service that claimed to help you get a green card in the US Government's regular Green Card Lottery. They managed to annoy a good proportion of the population of newsgroup users. This was not simply because they posted an advert, but because they flooded all the usenet groups with it in an antisocial manner.

The negative reaction was massive and continued for months. It consisted of huge numbers of complaining emails to Canter and Siegel and to their Arizona ISP. The sheer volume of complaints repeatedly crashed the ISP's computers and thus threatened its business. Netizens also wrote volumes of letters to newspapers and congressmen.

Nowadays, if you want junk email it is easy to come by—just add your name to an electronic mailing list. Some lists are run responsibly and some are not and you discover which by experience. Also note that replying to an email advert that invites you to "reply if you want to be removed from the list" actually validates that your email address is active, so your reply will not necessarily have the desired outcome.

It is hard to get off some lists and it is hard to know how some spammers obtain their email lists. For example, at Bloor Research, one of the staff received an advert for an "adult website" direct to her personally at her company email address. She was the only person in the company to receive the email and she never, to her knowledge, gave her email address out to anyone other than business contacts. The email was a widely distributed advert for a pornographic website. We can only presume that someone added her to a doubtful email list as a joke, but we can't know for sure.

Apart from adverts, other kinds of spam are sent to email lists. Take, for example, the following request for electronic immortality:

Subject: My dying wish
My name is Anthony Parkin, and you don't know me. I'm 7 years
old, and I have leukemia. I found your name using gopher, and I
would like for you to carry out my dying wish of starting a chain
letter. Please send this letter to five people you know so I can live
forever.
Thank you very much.

This email has been traced and is known to be a hoax, but it may still be circulating out somewhere on the internet. There are also other such emails that may be naïve attempts at fraud. Try this for size:

Hello everybody,
My name is Bill Gates. I have just written an email tracing pro-
gram that traces everyone to whom this message is forwarded. I am
experimenting with this and I need your help. Forward this to
everyone you know and if it reaches 1,000 people everyone on the
list will receive $1,000 at my expense. Enjoy.
Your friend, Bill Gates.

This will remind most readers of the chain-letter scam that fraudsters have used for years to try to separate people from their money. Anyone who believes that Bill Gates or anyone else is suddenly going to start sending bags full of dollars to random email users should immediately write and explain why to seriously.credulous@gullible.com.

A few weeks after receiving the email, you may receive another email from Bill Gates thanking you for participating and inviting you to send credit card details, by responding directly to the email, so that you can claim your $1,000 "compensation" prize, freely given to some of those that took part in the test. Anybody willing to send their credit card details casually and randomly to an unknown email address would be well advised to send them also to florida.swampland@excellent.prices where, we understand, there are some great real-estate deals available.

For the record, this hoax has also appeared in another incarnation promising free merchandise from Nike for randomly selected participants. There are other variants of the Bill Gates version with elaborate stories explaining in deep technical detail how the email chain will test some new Microsoft product. It is doubtful whether it generated much of a return for its perpetrators. There has been one web scam that did, however, and it was very cleverly conceived.

The web site www.sexygirls.com no longer exists. It went out of commission in February 1998, but not before it had been visited by a fair number of internet users (the actual number is not known). It was a porn site, but unlike other such sites it claimed not to charge for looking at its images. It asked visitors to download a "plug-in" that could then be used to view its photographs. And, as good as its word, you could view its adult material once you had downloaded the plug-in. However, this plug-in had other functions. When it executed, it disconnected you from the net and reconnected you through a telecoms hub in Moldova without your being aware. It also directed all your internet access through this hub from then on. The hub charged you at a rate of $2 per minute.

It is believed that the Moldovan telecoms operator was kicking money back to the perpetrators of the scam. As sexygirls closed down they set up other websites, including a fake Beavis and Butthead site, but within a few months they disappeared from view. The scam had worked. Those who complained may eventually have their money refunded, but there were undoubtedly many victims who were not overanxious to complain for "domestic reasons"—they had been mugged in the internet's red-light district.

Portals, hortals, and vortals

Internet entrepreneurs were active almost from the birth of the net in 1994. As well as being the year when spam was born, this was also the year that Amazon.com was founded. It took about three years before undeniable evidence began to emerge of the commercial potential of the web. At the end of

1997, surveys were suggesting that the figures for commercial internet trade were at the level of about $9 billion, of which business-to-business trade was $7.5 billion.

In those days a fair number of internet skeptics still existed, but when the figures for 1998 suggested that the level of trade had risen to $77 billion, their numbers began to thin out. By then, new websites were appearing at the rate of one a minute and the number of people buying goods over the internet was doubling every nine months. The early academic character of the net was being submerged as its population grew. As the character of the net changed, more terminology appeared.

1997 was the year that IBM stole the letter *e*, in what is now being fêted as its most successful ever advertising campaign. It took the @ character and stuck an *e* in the middle, theming its ad campaign around the word *ebusiness*. The ubiquitous *e* originally came from email, but a fair number of prominent websites, such as E*Trade, eToys, and eBay, had adopted it. IBM was clever enough not to trademark the word ebusiness, which it could have done. It let anybody, even competitors, use it freely.

And so the "etendency" was amplified and we began to see a whole host of websites appear, such as e-Steel, First-e (an internet bank) and eCircles (a community-based web business). They all leapt on to the ebandwagon. By early 1999 it was almost impossible to find any domain name consisting of an English word with a *e* in front of it that had not already been registered. Even eieio (as in "Old Macdonald had a farm, E-I-E-I-O") had been claimed. The words etailing, ebusiness, and ecommerce are now part of the language.

The word *portal* was hijacked in about 1997. There was a need to describe those websites that were leaping-off points for web users. They were primarily search engine sites such as Yahoo!, Excite, and Lycos, but there were also other sites that provided lists of useful weblinks. Such sites acted as navigation points to web users and could thus earn a respectable living by pushing banner ads at their customers.

The search engine portals employ "spiders" or, if you like, "robots"— either word will do. These are software programs that are permanently searching for completely new websites or for new information on frequently used sites, such as news sites. When they find new information they index it and add it to the considerable database that the search engine keeps. However, even though the whole operation is highly automated, estimates suggest that the best coverage of the web (which is probably provided by the AltaVista engine) is no better than about 10 percent.

Once a good number of portals (Netscape, Yahoo!, Lycos, Infoseek, Excite, AltaVista, and so on) had been established, the market began to look somewhat saturated. New entrants into the portal market naturally began to target specific industries—telecoms, farming, steel, and so on—in order to differentiate themselves. Examples include Altra Energy (altranet.com, for the energy industry) and PlasticsNet.com. These vertical portals provided links that were useful in the context of the particular industry and came to be known as "vortals." This naturally gave rise to the idea of a "hortal" (a horizontal portal), which, as you might guess, stands at right angles to a vortal. A hortal deals with natural subgroups of the populace, such as accountants, computer programmers, women, gays, and so on. Examples include Women.com and IT-Director.com (for computer executives).

Because of their sensible concentration on a specific information area, vortals and hortals started to acquire more and more depth and some began to offer useful services to their visitors. This led to some sites specializing in helping or even automating procurement in specific vertical markets. They became sites where business was carried out rather than navigation sites that people passed through on their way to somewhere else. As these sites were no longer just specialized portals, commentators began to refer to them as *hubs*. The hubs themselves naturally split into horizontal and vertical. Some are industry specific, such as e-Steel or PaperExchange, and some are cross-industry, such as MRO.com (maintenance, repair, and operating procurement) and YOUtilities (energy management).

And so it came to pass that some of the vortals evolved into vertical or horizontal hubs. In one way it would have been better if all of them had. The terms vortal and hortal are linguistic atrocities, but nevertheless they stand a fair chance of entering the language.

THE WHITE BICYCLE INITIATIVE

The "white bicycle" idea emerged in the flower power days of the late 1960s in Amsterdam. Citizens, particularly students, were invited to paint their bicycles white and share them in a communal manner. You would thus be able to walk around Amsterdam, see a white bicycle, and take it to ride to wherever you wanted to go. You would then simply leave it parked in a convenient place for someone else to use. The idea was popular and even gave rise to a pop song called *My White Bicycle*. Most of Amsterdam's white bicycles ended up in Calcutta, on the black market, having been stolen *en masse* by a gang of international thieves who were quick to spot a business opportunity.

It seems obvious and just to some idealists that information should be free, and from the early days of the internet there has been a growing belief that perhaps it will be—by fiat. Information has the beguiling property that the cost of duplicating it is very low, and this cost is also declining. With the growth of the internet we have witnessed what appears to be an extraordinary level of generosity on the part of educational establishments and commercial operations, freely providing massive amounts of information that was once reasonably expensive or difficult to obtain. We have also seen the emergence of the open source software movement, which appears to be making a business out of giving software away.

The idea of free information contains a certain element of white bicycle thinking, but nevertheless it is a popular concept and some of the phenomena that surround it deserve attention. They have political as well as economic implications. The freedom of information is, after all, a pillar of the American Constitution and an article of faith in most modern democracies. However, free information and freedom of information are quite different things.

Enter the new frontiersmen

Cyberspace is in some ways very similar to the pioneer settlements of late nineteenth-century America, from which the image of the Wild West sprang. It is not lawless, but neither has the rule of law been properly established. It is a vast country. By the end of 1996 its population was roughly 10 million, but a year later it was 50 million, and then by the end of 1998 it was in the 100 million region. At the time of writing the estimates put it at 200 million and it will probably continue to grow at breakneck speed.

The net was political at birth, with a web-oriented political movement emerging in the very early days of the usenet newsgroups under the name of the Electronic Frontier Foundation. It is best introduced with its own words from its website:

> *EFF, the Electronic Frontier Foundation, is a non-profit, non-partisan organization working in the public interest to protect fundamental civil liberties, including privacy and freedom of expression, in the arena of computers and the Internet. EFF was founded in 1990, and is based in San Francisco, California, with offices in Washington, DC, and New York City.*
>
> *The vast web of electronic media that connects us is heralding a new age of communications. New digital networks offer a tremendous potential to empower individuals in an ever-overpowering world. However, these communications networks are also the subject of significant debate concerning governance and jurisdiction.*
>
> *For, while the free flow of information is generally a positive thing, serious problems arise when information flows free— problems such as how to protect children and undesiring adults from exposure to sexually explicit or potentially offensive materials; how to protect intellectual property rights; how to determine which country's laws have jurisdiction over a medium that is nowhere and everywhere at the same time; how best to protect privacy while still permitting recovery for harm; how to ensure that legislators, access providers, intellectual property holders and disgruntled network users do not stifle disagreeable or controversial speech. While well-established legal principles and cultural norms give structure and coherence to uses of conventional media, the new digital media do not fit so easily into existing frameworks.*

The Electronic Frontier Foundation was created by John Perry Barlow, Mitch Kapor, and John Gilmour. These three had quickly come to the conclusion that "Cyberspace should be its own sovereign state," and the Electronic Frontier Foundation was established to give this idea a chance, if not directly to promote it. John Perry Barlow was already notable before the existence of the EFF, as a lyricist for the legendary 1960s rock group, The Grateful Dead.

In an interview in *Digerati*, a book by John Brockman, he is quoted as saying:

> *The EFF defends the borders of cyberspace against hegemonic incursions by various power sources of the terrestrial world. The problem is that most of the major foci of power in the terrestrial world are artifacts of the Industrial Revolution. The nation-state was created to serve the needs and purposes of industry.*

He also states, perceptively:

> *The pornography issue in the United States is nothing but a stalking horse for control. What we have here is the attempted governance by the completely clueless in a place they've never been, using tools they don't possess. When I go to Washington I feel like Tom Paine must have felt when he visited the court of King George in about 1770. The audacity of these people to claim moral right to govern an area where they've never even been is stupefying.*

This may or may not be the stuff on which revolutions are built, but it is certainly thought provoking. It doesn't take too much pondering to conclude that many of the mechanisms of government don't work too well in cyberspace. Indeed, the whole process of national and global government will ultimately have to be rethought as a result of cyberspace—like it or not. The Grateful Dead connection may conjure up images of a hippie-based tree-hugging movement dominated by marijuana-flavored ideals, but this is a misconception. The EFF board of directors consists mainly of IT luminaries and entrepreneurs, including Esther Dyson (the leading light of EDVenture Holdings), Lisa

Gansky (of GNN), Roel Pieper (until 1998 a senior executive of Compaq), and Tim O'Reilly (of O'Reilly and Associates).

The web has already raised a number of civil liberty issues. The most interesting involved the Church of Scientology, and took place on alt.religion.scientology, a usenet newsgroup, in 1994. This particular newsgroup had attracted, as some newsgroups do, a mix of individuals, both strong supporters and severe critics of the topic in question. The Church of Scientology has a long record of taking legal action against individuals or groups whom it deems to be harming its interests, and in this case a virtual skirmish broke out in cyberspace that eventually had to be resolved by law, in a way that drew some of the legal boundaries of cyberspace. This began when Dennis Erlich, an ex-scientologist and antiscientologist, joined the party. Erlich was of the opinion that the Church of Scientology was an evil and dangerous organization.

In December 1994, messages began to disappear from alt.religion.scientology that had not been officially canceled, but nobody was taking responsibility. It later became clear that the cancelations were unauthorized and at least some of the canceling activity was traced back to a scientologist. The Church of Scientology later requested that alt.religion.scientology be removed from all sites because, among other things, scientology was a trademark and the newsgroup was being heavily abused with "trade secret and copyright violations" taking place. This request was ignored and the Church of Scientology went to the courts.

As we have mentioned, it is possible to remain anonymous and difficult to trace on the net by the intelligent use of false names, anonymous remailing services, and the simple expedient of setting up disguised email accounts with ISPs. An anonymous poster with the pseudonym of Scamizdat had been posting collections of scientology documents, including some that were covered by copyright. By filing complaints, the Church of Scientology succeeded in having a remailing service in Finland raided by the Finnish police to obtain the name of an anonymous poster who had signed himself "-AB-". It then filed a complaint in San Jose, California, against Dennis Erlich, Tom Klemesrud, the sysop of the bulletin board that Erlich used, and his ISP (Netcom), and the Federal District Judge issued a restraining order. A legal battle ensued.

On being notified of the details of the case, the Electronic Frontier

Foundation took the view that there was an issue of cyberfreedom to be fought and found defense attorneys for Ehrlich. The actions against Netcom and Tom Klemesrud were settled out of court in 1996, but the case against Erlich is still awaiting trial. Tom Klemesrud was reportedly unhappy that his insurers had chosen to settle out of court, as he claimed that he would have preferred to have the case heard so that the outcome could set a precedent for other individuals in his position. Netcom had settled simply as a business expedient, and has taken practical steps to protect itself against its more anarchic customers. Copyright violation is not something that a commercial organization is likely to support, irrespective of the justification.

In any event, Erlich was not Scamizdat and the latter is still in action, not yet having been tracked down by the Church of Scientology. There are also a whole series of individuals across the world who are even now pursuing the same policy of revealing copyrighted material. Their point is an intriguing one: the detractors of the Church of Scientology believe that nobody would be interested in joining it if they knew some of its inner teaching, which they maintain is only revealed once the church has softened up the suggestibility of the individual who joins. Thus they believe that the Church of Scientology is using copyright protection as a form of censorship. So far, the scientologists have not been able to stamp out the campaign to violate their copyright. Indeed, one individual in Sweden, Zenon Panousis, turned some of the "copyrighted" papers over to the Swedish Parliament, thereby making them a public document under the Swedish constitution. At the time of writing, I checked to see if the copyrighted information was still available on the net—it is.

According to John Gilmour, "The net interprets censorship as damage, and routes around it." The scientology incident seems to illustrate the phenomenon.

LINUX'S WORLD

John Perry Barlow has suggested that "intellectual property is an oxymoron." This is in some ways an astute observation, in the sense that information realizes its maximum value via being widely shared, whereas property usually acquires its value via single ownership. However, the establishment of intellectual property was one of the foundations of the Industrial Revolution and the law of patents is there to protect its value. Information is usually something that is paid for. Barlow's words could also be interpreted in another way. He might just be saying that "intellectual property is theft."

The argument for free information walks hand in hand with the argument for free software, and the background facts are similar. There is a certain amount of free software, generally referred to as freeware. Some of it is very useful and some of it less so. The free software movement has its origins in the fact that an immense amount of useful software is written, but not all of it is useful enough, or general enough, to be turned into a viable commercial product. Academia is often the source of free software. In the 1980s, some computer user organizations began to provide "contributed libraries" of software, which consisted of small programs that one of their members had written. A small fee was paid for the cost of maintaining the library, but its contents were free.

The PC wave expanded the idea and "shareware" emerged. Individual programmers who did not have the inclination or the time to start up their own business provided software as shareware. Such software could be used for free, but the user was invited to send a small fee to the author. If the software was useful then it could generate a sizable income for the author and many users would pay. The emergence of the web added a new and surprising twist to the whole free software movement. Strange as it may seem, free software may be a more realistic possibility than free information.

If you have a deep interest in the development of software, there is a well-written essay entitled "The cathedral and the bazaar" that has been posted on a number of websites including that of its writer, Eric Raymond (http://www.tuxedo.org/~esr/writings/cathedral-bazaar/cathedral-bazaar.html). He is the prime author of a free software product called fetch-mail, and the essay describes an innovative method of developing large software products. It distinguishes between two radically different developmental methods, describing the first as the "cathedral approach," which involves groups of software developers hand crafting a solution under the close direction of a project manager and usually as part of a very large team. This is the traditional method by which software is built and all software used to be developed according to some variant of it. The problem is that it can take a long time and often produces a product that is very ornate but not necessarily very practical; rather like a cathedral, some would argue.

The alternative, and a very new approach indeed, is—like our trading model—compared to the activity of a bazaar. Here the software development is carried out as if in a marketplace with a whole multitude of developers busily in action in an apparently uncontrolled manner. This method of development was invented, or perhaps it would be more accurate to say evolved, by Linus Torvalds, the prime author of the increasing popular version of UNIX called Linux and a modern-day software hero.

"The cathedral and the bazaar" explains the difference between the two methods:

> *Linus Torvalds' style of development—release early and often, del-*
> *egate everything you can, be open to the point of promiscuity—*
> *came as a surprise. No quiet, reverent cathedral-building*
> *here—rather, the Linux community seemed to resemble a great*
> *babbling bazaar of differing agendas and approaches out of which*
> *a coherent and stable system could seemingly emerge only by a suc-*
> *cession of miracles.*

The rest of the essay goes on to claim that the bazaar development method not only works, but is far superior to the cathedral method in a number of ways; in particular, it is faster and it produces better software. The method consists quite simply of opening up the development project to the whole world and allowing a multitude of volunteer programmers to contribute collectively to the development. It requires intellectual leadership and constructive cooperative behavior. It also depends to some extent on the existence of the internet, as this creates an environment where hundreds of programmers can cooperate in a meaningful way.

Given the right leadership and organization, the bazaar method of developing software does deliver. Apart from fetchmail and Linux, it has also delivered the Apache Web server and the GNU compiler. All of these products are very widely used and all of them are free. It could also be argued that some are the best products of their kind available; certainly, many users would argue that Linux and Apache are "best of breed."

So while the Microsofts and IBMs of this world keep their source code secret, there is a software movement that opens its source code to the world for free. The source is referred to as copyleft rather than copyright; it is subject to free usage on the basis that whatever you add to it must be made available for all other users. There is a well-written contract for the use of such source code, referred to as the GPL.

Four organizations—Caldera, Red Hat, SuSE, and TurboLinux—provide commercial versions of Linux. Their businesses are based on adding value to the free product by providing support and complementary software components. Linux and Apache stand as visible proof that the free software movement is not just another white bicycle initiative. As Eric Raymond says in "The cathedral and the bazaar":

> *The Linux world behaves in many respects like a free market or an ecology, a collection of selfish agents attempting to maximize utility which in the process produces a self-correcting spontaneous order more elaborate and efficient than any amount of central planning could have achieved...*
>
> *Perhaps in the end the open-source culture will triumph, not because cooperation is morally right or software "hoarding" is morally wrong, but simply because the closed-source world cannot win an evolutionary arms race with open-source communities that can put orders of magnitude more skilled time into a problem.*

Perhaps so, perhaps not. What is undeniable is that some open-source products have become very fashionable and are being used extensively in the computer departments of commercial businesses. At the time of writing, Apache has 53 percent of the web server market—not just ahead of the competition, but massively dominant. Meanwhile, there are over 9 million Linux installations and its market share is growing fast. Pundits are now predicting, probably correctly, that Linux will bring Microsoft's Windows-based empire crashing to the ground.

The info pyramid

In order to understand what is taking place, it will help if we look at a simple model, which we can call the info pyramid. This expresses the self-evident idea that there are degrees of refinement of information. The info pyramid is, as illustrated in Figure 2, a simple four-layer affair.

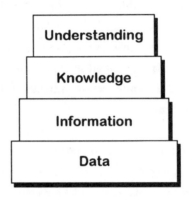

Figure 2 The info pyramid

As the diagram implies, data are not information. Data consists of raw facts that are not organized. You can have data about something, say a cup. You can note its height, its volume, its shape, the design on it, and so forth. When you organize it together you get information. What the organizing of data does is to add context.

Just as data are not information, information is not knowledge. There can, of course, be gradations of information. One organization of information may be more efficient than another and one collection of information may have greater volume than another. So one book on astronomy may be more accessible than another and one may have more depth than another. But to get to knowledge we have to add the idea of "how."

Using this definition, we can claim that it is not possible to store knowledge in books, even though, paradoxically, it is possible to store information *about* knowledge in books. Knowledge involves "knowing the process." And so it is possible to store knowledge in a computer and, of course, have the computer act on it. All software could be defined as stored knowledge of a kind, because it is stored process and, when it is run, it exhibits intelligence. In the world of computing, the field of artificial intelligence covers software that is explicitly aimed at being a repository for knowledge and can, if properly constructed, display the knowledge of, say, a doctor or a lawyer. As with information, knowledge can be organized well or badly and it can be shallow or have great depth.

Finally, to get to understanding, we have to add "why." Knowledge is something that can be stored in people or in computers, but understanding can only be stored in people. Thus in terms of exhibiting intelligent behavior, a computer may eventually be able to equal a human, but in terms of flexibility, which understanding confers, the computer will never match us.

We can explain this by an example. "USA 4 Canada 3" is data. It is no more than a collection of words and numbers, and its meaning is uncertain. We might see it accidentally on a television screen as we walked past a shop and it would tell us very little. However, if we knew that an international ice-hockey match had been played that day, we could probably set the phrase in context and know, without anyone telling us, that this was the result of that match. The data has acquired meaning by our making a connection, and it has become information.

Knowledge does not result simply by putting some data in context. We might claim that we had knowledge if we had watched the match and thus had much more context, and perhaps knew that one team was unlucky, or the other played above itself, or one had key players missing, and so on. Armed with such knowledge, we might be able to predict the likely outcome if the teams met again, or whether the match would be worth watching, or whether the coach is likely to keep his job. Moreover, none of this is genuine understanding. Understanding might come from having played ice hockey, and having coached it, and having watched many matches.

We can use the info pyramid as a model for examining many situations, but here our only interest is in the phenomenon of free information and the impact of the internet.

In the nineteenth and twentieth centuries, the distribution of information was heavily subsidized by government in its provision of universal education, educational broadcasting, libraries, and museums. At the beginning of the twenty-first century, the distribution of information is being heavily subsidized on the web by the same kind of people and organizations, but they are being joined—for the moment—by many commercial organizations who currently view a website as a shop window and are filling their shop windows with free information. The truth is that there are many apparently free things happening on the internet that are not free at all—they are just inexpensive or are paid for indirectly.

The net itself has reduced the cost of information. It is not expensive to access the internet: there is an access cost and you need a computer and electricity. There is lots of data out there available at no charge, and miraculously it is all information, because the existence of search engines (to identify useful links) and the links themselves form an organizing force. Some of it may be low-grade information, but it is information nevertheless.

The very existence of the internet has thus destroyed many information businesses that did little more than organize data in an accessible fashion, either turning data into information or turning low-grade information into higher-grade information. The cost of accessing information has fallen very steeply for those who are connected. Although some would claim that the information out there is free, it is not. We have already paid for it by paying taxes. Our taxes support education, whose role it has always been to distribute knowledge and information. They are now distributing it on the net. As for the commercial organizations that are apparently giving away free information—they are not. It is simply a loss leader.

If we now look at the situation in respect of knowledge, we can see that exactly the same process is taking place. The open software movement is a creation of the educational systems of the world. They are giving away knowledge for free. Doing so will undoubtedly destroy many software businesses. The companies that have sprung up to help distribute the free software products have actually simply climbed up the info pyramid. They will sell software support. They will market their *understanding* of the software that they provide for free.

3

The Flight of the Roast Chicken

When I first visited California in 1991, I was shown around by a friend who had lived in Palo Alto for five years. We spent a few days at a database show in the valley, meeting software vendors she knew and talking to journalists. She also spent a day introducing me to some of the tourist attractions of San Francisco: the Golden Gate Bridge, Fisherman's Wharf, the trams, and the quaint boathouses of Sausalito. And in the evening we visited a restaurant that she knew well, called MacArthur Park, in Palo Alto.

The restaurant was very large and it gave the impression of being more like a canteen than a restaurant. It had an odd but enjoyable ambiance, a jazz pianist tinkling lazily on the piano, and the tables were populated by casually dressed business folk in their thirties. This restaurant, she explained, had once been an informal meeting place for the young entrepreneurs of the valley.

"Imagine what it was like in the early eighties," she said. "All those college kids falling out of Berkeley and Stanford writing software or designing circuits, building new devices, inventing the future. This is where many of them used to dine. The restaurant provided paper placemats that techies could draw diagrams or write code on. Some of these dining tables are historic. People came in here to be headhunted or make partnerships or talk to VCs. This is where it happened."

The restaurant did its best to preserve the spirit of those heady days. Stock-market prices were displayed in moving lights across the top of one wall—an innovation that some of the customers had requested. The paper placemats still existed and the waiters had handheld electronic notepads for taking orders, which transmitted directly to the kitchens. It was an enjoyable venue for a meal that exuded the spirit of Silicon Valley, and for some strange reason it had me thinking of the coffee houses of eighteenth-century London, where other entrepreneurs had gathered to chew the fat and make their fortunes.

In my final year before graduating from Nottingham University, I was warned by my careers adviser that "there is no point in standing around with your mouth open, hoping that a roast chicken will fly into it." Such luck is rare, but it is not impossible. At some points in history some individuals get to be in the right place at the right time and they prosper accordingly, just as every day of the week someone somewhere is made very rich by the purchase of a lottery ticket. The youthful entrepreneurs of Silicon Valley were just standing around when a whole flock of roast chickens appeared over the horizon and began flapping their wings towards them. Of course they were going to open their mouths—what would you have done?

In the 1980s, Silicon Valley was a place where fortunes were being made. In the spring of 1999, I was sitting in a different restaurant in Palo Alto, talking to an executive from a software start-up. He related to me the sad fate of those early Californian entrepreneurs, the 1980s millionaires.

"They are in their forties and they are worth maybe forty or fifty million. And they sit at their tables in restaurants like this, eating their *foie gras*, and they feel like failures, because over there in the corner sitting at some other table is some fresh-faced kid in his twenties and he is worth four hundred to five hundred million."

All down the West Coast of the US, from Seattle to Santa Cruz, flocks of roast chicken have been seen in flight again, and they are 10 times bigger than they were 20 years ago.

JOLLY HOCKEY STICKS

The first of our four hinges is the hockey stick curve. This is a model of market behavior that helps to explain the remarkable growth that some internet companies have experienced, as well as that of some companies in the PC market.

A normal distribution—or "bell curve"—of the take-up of technology products is illustrated in Figure 3. The buyers are classified as pioneers (or

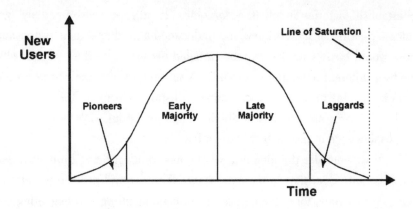

Figure 3 The take-up of technology products

early adopters), the early majority, the late majority, and laggards. In *Crossing the Chasm*, the popular book by Geoffrey A Moore dealing specifically with the sale of computer technology, the pioneers are further divided up into enthusiasts (early pioneers) and early adopters (later pioneers). Most such schemes apply motivations to the various groups of buyers and seek to provide marketers with some insight into the behavior of customers.

This model of the behavior of the technology market is widely accepted. However, it is only a rough approximation at best, and in respect of internet companies it is misleadingly wrong. A market is a very complex set of interactions between a finite number of buyers and sellers. In theory, there is undoubtedly a point of saturation when all the possible buyers have bought and there is no one left to buy. In practice, this rarely occurs because a market is not a static pool of buyers and sellers. New buyers do enter. In the automobile market, for example, teenagers become adults and buy cars. The simple curve also ignores the phenomenon of price. At a price of $1,000 the market for a product may consist of 10 million people, whereas it may become 25 million if the price falls to, say, $500, with new buyers, the "economic buyers," entering the market just because of price. Indeed, this is the primary message of the supply and demand curves of economics—at lower prices, higher demand materializes.

There are also many imperfections in any market. For example, it may be constrained by geography because of product transport costs, but this constraint may diminish if price falls or some vendors become wealthy enough to establish factories in other geographies. It may be constrained by igno-rance—if more consumers knew and understood a product's value proposition, more would buy. A market may be curtailed because a product is made obso-lete by a different but superior product. Also, vendors alter their behavior once a market begins to approach saturation and start to focus on the replacement market—improving products or altering them in various ways in order to cre-ate obsolescence in products that are a few years old.

If we consider the idea of a wholly new product being brought to mar-ket, it is quite clear that in the early stages the price will need to be relatively high. At that time, there are non-recurring manufacturing and marketing costs that need to be carried and that are only supported by thin revenues. If the product is successful and the "early majority" emerges, then profitability sud-denly increases through economies of scale and it may be possible to reduce the price and increase market size. There may be no need to do this—and it may even be a bad idea—but it usually happens in practice.

If the price mechanism is used a different curve emerges, as illustrated in Figure 4. The "early majority" increases in size. However, once the early majority phase is over and the peak is passed, then you are dealing with the law of diminishing returns. Every dollar invested in manufacturing and selling the product is suddenly providing a lower return. Once this happens, the manu-facturer is fighting a rearguard action.

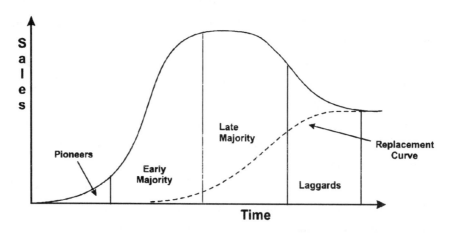

Figure 4 A more accurate curve of product adoption

This pattern illustrates the fact that sales never fall to zero unless a genuinely superior replacement product emerges. Instead a replacement market comes into existence, leading to a roughly constant level of sales from then on. The actual size of the replacement market will vary. Manufacturers usually build some obsolescence into their products in an attempt to maximize the size of the replacement market, but they have to be careful not to offend the consumer's perception of value. The graph shows the laggards simply blending in with the replacement market. This graph applies to many products, from cars through televisions to refrigerators, and it can also apply to computer technology.

We should note that for manufacturers this curve is fraught with problems, because it dictates that manufacturing capacity may have to be reduced and that margins will fall as the market matures and the economies of scale decline. For this reason, manufacturing companies are forever attempting to introduce new products and establish new revenue streams to offset the diseconomies of a mature market.

A further detail that the typical bell-shaped curve fails to take into account is the simple fact of the economic buyer. The psychological profile implied by the classification into pioneers, early majority, late majority, and laggards has clear validity. Some buyers are pioneers and hence trendsetters. Some, like the early majority, want to see proven value and wait to perceive this before buying. Some, like the late majority, are trend followers and need to see an established trend before buying. Finally, there is a deeply conservative group who are hard to convince, and they are the last ones to buy in.

This may all be true, but it ignores the fact that all purchases involve a value proposition. The economic buyer is the buyer who wants to buy, but simply cannot meet the prevailing price—either because the perceived benefits do not justify it, or because the money is simply not available. Psychologically, the economic buyer may be in any one of the classifications, but they do not appear until the price is right and for that reason they are unlikely to buy along with the pioneers.

For example, I am an economic buyer for a helicopter. I cannot afford one and even if I could, the price is too high for me to feel happy purchasing one—the value proposition is wrong. However, if the price ever does come down, I'll be there.

THE HOCKEY STICK CURVE

More than a few business writers have proposed the idea that the law of diminishing returns is being defied in some way by low-cost (PC) software products. They have noticed that the cost of software is strongly front loaded and that supply is very inexpensive, i.e., manufacturing costs are very low. Thus the ongoing costs of supply per unit (including sales and marketing costs) reduce dramatically as the numbers escalate. The economies of scale appear to continue and continue indefinitely as the market expands.

In reality, this is just an illusion—all that is happening is that the point of saturation is still far off. The situation is further confused by the fact that a replacement market for PC software emerged many years before any kind of saturation could be seen. Thus the usual conditions that accompany market growth were not present, and the increasing returns that come when a market expands were well beyond everyone's expectations. The phenomenon could be described as one of *extended* increasing returns. The action of the law of diminishing returns was deferred, not defied. The law of diminishing returns is like the law of gravity, it never gets repealed.

The phenomenon of extended increasing returns is represented by a hockey stick-shaped curve, which appears to refuse to hit saturation point and fold over into the expected normal distribution. The curve is characterized by its steep slope and its point of inflection, where suddenly the curve turns upward and accelerates toward the sky. This is illustrated in Figure 5.

The evolution of the market for a new technology usually follows a standard pattern. First the technology is introduced at a high price, normally as a technology for business use. The price gradually falls, generating greater demand until the business market is fairly well saturated. Then, if the technology is applicable, it gets introduced into the consumer market where even higher numbers of units can sell and the price continues to fall until eventually the consumer market becomes saturated.

PC software and component vendors found themselves in a delightful business situation. Actual demand for their products was constrained by the size of the PC market, but they never came close to saturating demand because

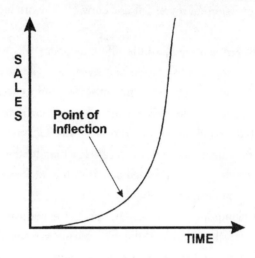

Figure 5 The hockey stick curve

the market itself was growing at a dramatic speed. In most years growth was over 25 percent, and hence the market more than doubled in size about every three years. If you sold any kind of necessary or popular component to the PC, then your revenues would increase at the same 25 percent rate if you simply managed to hold market share. You were on a hockey stick curve with increasing returns, year after year.

The PC software vendors leveraged the situation cleverly by building in very fast obsolescence cycles to their products. They regularly created new versions of their spreadsheets and wordprocessors, altering file formats to destroy compatibility with the previous version and adding new features. Thus with each new product version, the market renewed itself because the existing customer would buy again and new customers entering the market would buy for the first time. This extended the hockey stick even further.

For the PC software vendors, there was a further minor extension to the curve delivered by the phenomenon of software theft. As far as anyone can tell, the majority of business applications (wordprocessors, spreadsheets, databases) on home PCs are stolen software. Also, depending on the country, a fair amount of PC software used in businesses is also stolen. This is especially the case in Eastern Europe, South America, and some areas of the Far East, of which it has been said that if you sell one copy of your product you saturate the market.

Many governments make little effort to police this area of criminality, and in some areas copyright violation may even be covert government policy. If the situation remained static, then the software vendors would complain bitterly. However, a country can only pursue a *laissez faire* policy toward software theft for a limited period before pressure from the US government and international trade organizations comes to bear. Eventually, the offending country steps into line for fear of being denied access to the intellectual property that is required to run a modern economy.

When a clampdown on piracy happens, the software vendors, particularly Microsoft which dominates the PC business software market, see an immediate and significant increase in demand. Although Microsoft is active in trying to pull offending governments into line, it also keeps a close watch on its share of the stolen software market—with good reason. Its revenues in Italy quadrupled within weeks of that government taking action against software theft and it has enjoyed similar increases elsewhere. To such companies, stolen software represents an uncollected harvest that will one day be reaped.

Thus, the PC software market was blessed with an unprecedented hockey stick curve that was extended further by software obsolescence, and further still by an illicit free software market that is gradually being brought under control. To compound the commercial joy, the cost of distributing software products declined as the market expanded. Given this situation, it is possible to understand how Microsoft, the company that took the lion's share of the hockey stick curve for PC software, became the most valuable company in the world, worth over half a trillion dollars (as at July 1999).

What is the driving force that created this curve?

Cobra response time

If a cobra is within biting range and it decides to bite you, you can't stop it. It takes a cobra one-tenth of a second to strike, but the human reaction time from receiving an impulse through the nervous system (image, noise, or whatever) and reacting is just greater than one-tenth of a second. Because human response operates at this speed, a computer user will think that a computer is slow if it has a response lag of one-tenth of a second—for instance, if the pointer on the screen moves more than one-tenth of a second after you move the mouse.

This "cobra response time" is very important, because it established the need for personal computers. Two of the early and most useful PC applications, spreadsheets and wordprocessors, were strongly interactive. Every time you hit a key, the application would do something on the screen, even if it was only to display a character. The nature of these two types of application is that they don't work well on a computer that is shared between several users—the response time is not fast enough.

This technological reality walked hand in hand with the desire of many users for a devoted computing resource and laid the foundations of the PC market. From that point onward, the PC market exploded because of the rapid growth in CPU power that was accurately foreseen by Gordon E Moore of Intel. In 1965, he predicted that CPU power would henceforth double every year, but he later adjusted the figure to 18 months once it became an observable phenomenon. This doubling of power started to be a reality in 1970 and has been a reality ever since. As the CPU is the motor of a computer, we have experienced a remarkable exponential growth in computer power for nearly 30 years.

In reality, this amounts to an increase in power by a factor of about 32,000, but it dates back to before the PC era. The PC market, which properly established itself with the launch of the IBM PC in 1980, has seen an increase in power by a factor of over a thousand. Of course it is not just the CPU that has seen such dramatic improvement, but also memory, disk space, and communications capability.

Given this background of escalating capability, it was not difficult for software vendors to build obsolescence into their applications; in fact, it was hard for them not to do so. By about 1990, the PC had been transformed with the introduction of the graphical user interface (GUI)—an innovation borrowed from Apple, which had in turn borrowed it from Xerox PARC. Together with the mouse, the GUI transformed existing applications and introduced a whole new set of applications, including drawing programs, painting programs, desktop publishing, and even PC CAD. This just reinforced the demand for a devoted CPU. Measurements of PC CPU activity carried out in the early 1990s showed that on graphical PCs and workstations, 70 percent of the executed instructions were for mouse activity.

So as greater CPU power was being delivered, more and more of it was being consumed simply by the interface. Once the new mouse-based applications were catered for, PCs appeared with a higher screen resolution and a greater color capability, which meant that they consumed more computer power working out how to display the screen. Since then, we have had the addition of sound capability and the introduction of video. For a period, the growth of the PC market seemed remorseless, but this time is now coming to an end.

The final hurrah of the PC market was and is the rapid growth of the internet. As the PC—in the main—is the device that provides internet access, growth in the PC market has been fostered, but the price of the PC has had to be forced down to consumer-friendly levels.

Repealing Moore's law

Although Moore's law insists that CPU power will double every 18 months, neither Moore nor anyone else stated how long this would go on for. From a technological perspective, there is no reason that Moore's law should not continue to operate for the next 20 years. Several years ago, IBM's R&D labs discovered a way to "move an atom" when experimenting with an electron microscope. The ability to move an atom creates a foundation for digital circuits that are thousands of times smaller and hence faster than current silicon chips. If this can be implemented economically, then Moore's law can continue to apply.

However, it currently faces a series of challenges that may stop it in its tracks. The first challenge arises from diminishing need. As discussed above, computer power has been devoted to improving the user interface. This is clearly something that the market is willing to pay for, but not much more power is required at the interface. One further cycle of Moore's law should see voice recognition improve to a point where it becomes as fast as quick typing. It may be possible to increase screen definition with the extra CPU power, but the human eye is generally content with 300 dots per inch and current screens can already provide about 100 dpi or better. Video and animation are very demanding, but current CPUs just about cater for it. Unless there is a need for tens of millions of faster CPU chips each year, there is little point in developing the technology.

This brings us to the second factor involved: the cost of manufacture. Almost all the increase in power of a new generation of CPU chips comes from miniaturization, but the cost of building the fabrication plants that make the chips has escalated with each new generation of chips. It started in the tens of millions of dollars and it is now above the $1 billion level and still growing. The cost increases anywhere between 25 and 35 percent for each doubling.

This escalation in cost has led to companies that were once competitors—IBM, Siemens, and Toyota—cooperating to build a single plant. The costs have risen to a point where only one or two companies can afford the risk of building a fabrication plant on their own.

Historically, fabrication costs per unit and hence prices per CPU chip have fallen roughly 30 percent as volume doubles, balancing the market nicely. When demand for faster chips tails off, the economic equations will no longer work. Moore's law will be curtailed by the senior law of diminishing returns.

Metcalfe's magic

Mao Zedong initiated the "Great Leap Forward" in 1958 in an attempt to modernize China rapidly. His aim was to mobilize the immense amount of manpower that the country had at its disposal. Increasing the production of iron and steel was a priority, and his policy mandated the building of small backyard furnaces in every village in China. The idea was simply to create millions of steelworkers and ramp up the production of steel so that China could be industrialized very quickly.

The whole initiative turned out to be a great leap backward. The endeavor was a fiasco: mountains of unusable iron and steel were created and then iron and steel production started to grind to a halt.

The iron and steel policy within the Great Leap Forward sounds naïve, and it was. In making steel, economies of scale come from large, centralized operations where standardization of process, distribution, and quality control are all far less expensive to implement. This is almost so obvious that it is hard to understand how Mao Zedong could have believed otherwise. The policy was complete folly and was quickly reversed.

The inexorable rise of the PC foisted a similar folly on the organization of computers within businesses. Computer power was distributed and thus the responsibility for managing that power was distributed. The reality of "distributed computing" was significantly different to that of distributed steel manufacture, as it brought genuine business benefits—but it suffered from the same defect: centralized operation provides vast economies of scale and distributed computing forgoes these economies. At some point between 1980 and 1996, the incremental benefit line crossed the incremental cost line—the extra cost of deploying the newest generation of PCs exceeded the extra business benefit that was delivered. By 1997, the emphasis had moved to server-based computing, which was centralized computing by another name, and organizations began to consolidate their computing resource.

It seems strange in retrospect, but the right conditions were needed for the PC market to form in the first place. The technology had to have reached the right level of sophistication and the right price point had to be discovered. IBM failed twice to bring successful products to market, with the SCAMP in the late 1960s and the Datamaster in the 1970s. Start-up companies Commodore and Apple began to have some success in the late 1970s, and the explosive rise of the PC began in earnest with IBM's third attempt, the IBM PC, which came to market in 1980. Because IBM had had technical problems with the Datamaster and because it saw that the market was moving fast, it chose to subcontract much of the work. In particular, it gave the CPU chip to Intel and it gave the operating system to Microsoft. By 1983, IBM had captured about a 75 percent share of the whole PC market, which was riding a hockey stick curve that Intel and Microsoft would dominate.

As we now enter the declining years of the PC market, two distinct trends are visible: the PC itself is fragmenting, and the network is becoming the dominant force.

First, fragmentation. As a device, the PC was very versatile: it was a typewriter, an adding machine, an accounting machine, a graphical arts tool, an engineering tool, an educational device, an interface to the web, and so on. With the rise of the laptop computer it was all of these things, and portable too. Its versatility did much to extend its extraordinary hockey stick curve. However, it is not versatile enough. The PC is not the best device to use as a television or a walkman or a webphone or a web-browsing machine or a PDA (personal digital assistant) or a mobile telephone or a kid's games machine. In each case, either the weight is wrong or the price point is wrong or it is simply not built to purpose. So the market for personal computers is fragmenting as new devices come to market that will gradually marginalize their usage.

The second trend is the rise of the network. It could be said that the internet is now such a visible fact that it doesn't warrant much comment. However, as with the PC, the right conditions were needed for the internet to appear. After all, ARPANET existed for many years, and eventually became an educational network without anyone seeing its commercial possibilities. Various EDI (electronic data interchange) initiatives came and went without provoking commercial proliferation. Private commercial networks such as CompuServe and Prodigy grew and were commercially successful, with millions of customers using email and bulletin boards, but they didn't launch the internet. Even the "great idea" that Tim Berners Lee had of linking documents together directly over the world's networks did not, on its own, do that. A piece of mathematical magic called Metcalfe's law launched the internet and the same magic is what makes it grow.

In the 1980s, Bob Metcalfe, the inventor of the Ethernet communications standard, formulated a law in an attempt to put a value on computer networks and computer integration. He had an axe to grind—he could perceive the value of networks better than most people, and he wanted Ethernet to be used. Metcalfe's law states that:

> The "value" of a network is proportional to the square of the number of users.

What Metcalfe meant by value was the benefit to the user population as a whole. The law is actually a restatement of a mathematical truth about the number of connections that can be made in a graph with n nodes, but this does not make it any less important. In fact, we can represent Metcalfe's law in pseudo-mathematical style, as follows:

$$\text{Total network benefit} = KU^2$$

where K is a constant, and U is the size of the user population.

A simple example of the application of this law is provided by the telephone network. One telephone is useless: whom do you call? Two telephones are better, but not much—only two people can make calls and then only to each other. But once there are 100 users, 100 people can make calls and just under 5,000 different connections are possible. When most of the population has a telephone, then the network reaches its full potential and, as history illustrates, has a dramatic influence on business and society.

Another point worth mentioning is that in parallel with the benefits increasing, the unit cost of the technology falls as the numbers increase. In the past decade we have witnessed the remarkable effect of fax technology getting less and less expensive as the usefulness of the fax increased to the point where it became possible to fax almost any organization and many individuals. eMail has seen a similar transformation. Originally it existed within companies and then within networks such as CompuServe that gave a reasonable person-to-person coverage. With the internet it is a much more useful capability.

The importance of Metcalfe's law is threefold. First, the computer industry has been driven by Moore's law until recently and that influence is beginning to wane. As the world's economies move on to the internet, it will be Metcalfe's law that calls the shots. Second, Metcalfe's law does not just apply to networks but to groups of users. Thus 10,000 enthusiastic golfers linked to the internet will not necessarily support a website that sells golfing merchandise. Maybe 12,000 will. There will be a point of inflection where critical mass is reached and a website idea becomes viable. Finally, Metcalfe's law dictates that internet-based businesses will move along a hockey stick curve.

The abnormal distribution

The business market usually acts as the pioneer buyer for the consumer market and it does so at a much higher price point. There have been very few technologically based products that were not used and proven first in the business market before moving to the consumer market. The reason for this is that a business can usually garner greater benefit from the use of a product than can a single individual. Most labor-saving devices such as vacuum cleaners, washing machines, and refrigerators, as well as devices such as tape recorders and videos, were first established as commercial business products. There are very few exceptions—the Sony Walkman is one.

In most circumstances, businesses and consumers are best treated as separate markets. They have their own pioneers, early majority, late majority, laggards, and economic buyers. They have distinctly different channels to market and distinctively different marketing campaigns are required. However, on the internet the distinction is no longer as great and observing the business-to-business market is suddenly important, because it helps you accurately predict behavior in the consumer market.

Having said this, let us now consider the hockey stick curve from a slightly different perspective, since it is not driven by accepted psychological classifications. Consider the diagram from the perspective of the PC market (Figure 6 overleaf). The spectrum of pioneers through to laggards was played out quite a long time ago with only the pioneers contributing to its shape—as they determine the point of inflection.

The curve for the PC market is driven both by economic buyers and by the replacement market, each of which starts to manifest after the point of inflection. Thus for any given item of PC software, the psychological buying spectrum might apply, but the situation is interfered with by the existence of economic buyers and the replacement market. Also we have the added phenomenon of software theft, with the thieves boosting the hockey stick curve as they turn honest.

It is reasonable to argue that the whole hockey stick is created and supported by Moore's law, which makes further PC benefits available on a regular basis, creating a platform for a wonderfully active replacement market and

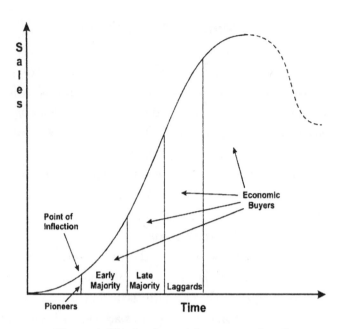

Figure 6 The hockey stick curve in detail

also dragging economic buyers in on a regular basis. As Moore's law wanes in its influence, this curve will collapse down to a thin replacement market. It is difficult to know how big this replacement market will be, but it is clear that the internet itself, rather than the PC, is becoming the *de facto* platform for running software applications. Those vendors that currently reap massive revenues from the PC market will see those revenues dissolve like snow in the sunlight.

A similar hockey stick curve also applies to the internet, except that it has only just begun and this time it is driven by Metcalfe's law. In terms of the numbers connected, the internet has already passed its point of inflection. The US, Canada, and Finland could be regarded as pioneers, with Australia, Japan, Hong Kong, Singapore, and most of Europe forming the early majority. However, on an individual basis, it is clear that the world is already awash with economic buyers (of internet connectivity). Many people in many nations would be connected if they could afford the cost, or would use the internet far more if the bandwidth were adequate.

If we look at the situation from a business usage perspective, it is clear that business take-up (in terms of connectivity) is very high—perhaps in the area of the late majority—but consumer take-up is significantly lower. Similarly, if we look at individual business areas, we see that some, like stockbroking, have moved beyond the point of inflection, whereas others, such as car sales, have not yet reached this point.

We are entitled to ask whether the internet hockey stick curve will be as long and extended as that for the PC market. After all, where is the mechanism that, like Moore's law, continually brings new capability to the network? There is no specific mechanism, but there is a major trend in action that has a very similar effect. This is the general on-going integration (or networking) of technology. In the coming years this will add integrated telephony as a capability, and integrated video, and integrated intelligent devices, and so on. Most of all, there will be the new electronic artifacts of the electronic economy. These will drive a hockey stick curve, the like of which has never been seen before. They will drive a curve that will transform the whole of the world economy.

A PERIOD OF INFLECTION

It would not be accurate to represent the growth of the electronic economy as a simple curve with a single point of inflection. In reality, it is the aggregation of a whole series of curves. Some hockey stick curves are off and running, and some are not. In respect of the electronic economy itself, rather than a single point of inflection, it is better to think in terms of a *period* of inflection. This began when the online retail market took off and it will probably end when the use of electronic money becomes pervasive. It covers a period that will be measured in years and its duration will depend to some extent on how intelligently the governments of the major economies behave—both individually and collectively.

The online retail market undoubtedly took off in the US in 1998. By the end of 1998, nearly 75 million Americans were accessing the internet and according to an Arbitron survey, 26 percent of them, about 19 million, were doing some shopping online. Less than half of these were shopping regularly, but consumer ecommerce was observably growing at around 8 percent per month—which means that it was doubling in volume every nine months.

The beginning of the beginning

In 1997, InterNIC—a website run by the US Department of Commerce that provides public information on internet domain name registration services—reported that new domain names were being sold at the rate of one per minute, or about half a million per year. By the end of 1998, InterNIC was showing that over four million had been issued—although there were probably no more than a million active sites. A US-based survey of medium to large organizations carried out by IBM in the second half of 1997 indicated that 90 percent had a website and an email presence, but most were using the web only as a marketing channel. Only 10 percent were using it to enhance customer support and only 5 percent were involved in ecommerce. Corporate America was dipping its toe in the water, but wasn't ready to dive in.

In 1998, Iconocast started reporting exponential growth in the eretailing market, in excess of 200 percent per year. At the end of 1998, the top 10 publicly traded online retailers had collectively reported year-on-year revenue growth in excess of 160 percent and revenue per order was increasing. North American-based eretailers posted figures of $4.4 billion for the first six months of 1998, but the full-year figures were above $13 billion. The online retailers had captured 1 percent of the retail market in the first half of the year, but by the end of the year it was 2 percent.

A survey in early 1998 by J.D. Power and Associates revealed that 16 percent of US new car buyers were using the internet to help make purchasing decisions, but no significant new car buying was occurring over the web. By September, the company was reporting that 25 percent of all new vehicle buyers were using the internet to assist in the shopping process and that internet shoppers often knew more about the vehicle they wanted to purchase than did dealership salespeople. Additionally, web-based car auctions were beginning to show volume activity.

Throughout 1998, market research companies were raising their estimates. Forrester Research began 1998 with a consumer ecommerce forecast of $4.8 billion, which it upped to $7.8 billion by November, only to discover when actual 1998 figures were available that this was a clear underestimate. For the business-to-business market it forecast $43 billion, but the WEFA

Group reported an actual figure of $77 billion for 1998. Of course, Forrester was not alone in having to revise its figures; everyone was doing it. Attention-getting forecasts that were predicting a $1 trillion ecommerce market by the end of 2001 began to look plausible and might even turn out to be conservative.

At the end of 1998, the second *Annual Ernst & Young Internet Shopping Study* reported that 10 percent of US households were shopping online and that these shoppers were primarily male heads of household (49 percent) and 40 years old or above (68 percent). However, this situation was also in flux. A study by CommerceNet and Nielsen Media Research showed that the population of female online shoppers almost doubled between June 1998 and April 1999, from 5.8 million to 10.6 million, while the figure for males increased by less than 23 percent to 17.4 million. According to the survey, the number of online shoppers had risen by 10 million in less than a year. The picture was clear—the act of shopping online had passed the point of inflection, from the pioneers to the early majority.

The big picture

The web is far more mature in the US than elsewhere, but other places will probably catch up quite quickly. In 1998, the IDC/World Times Information Society Index, which attempts to measure the difference between countries in their exploitation and acceptance of information technology, put the US about 35 percent ahead of the closest other country, Finland. Scandinavian countries all ranked highly, as did the UK and Germany. Behind them followed the advanced economies of Europe and Asia. The CIA comes up with similar figures. With the exception of Germany and Japan, all the leading countries have English as a first language or a very strong second language, providing them with a greater incentive to use the web, where English is massively dominant for the moment.

While eretail was taking off in the US in 1998, internet populations were rising dramatically across all of these economies, indicating that eretail would follow quickly. Dataquest has predicted that the number of computers connected to the internet in Europe will grow from 13 million in 1997 to 69 million by 2002, but this is likely to prove an underestimate, because the advantages of connection to the internet are growing daily.

I have been unable to find any US-based price studies or any extensive studies done elsewhere. However, a shopping comparison done in June 1999 by *the net*, the UK's biggest-selling internet magazine, indicated that there are already strong shopping incentives for internet connection. (It should be noted that the UK is less mature than the US in internet shopping.

Item	Internet price (£)	Street price (£)	£ diff.	% diff.	Internet shop time	Street shop time	Delivery penalty
US holiday home	90,000	113,000	23,000	20	15	60	
Classic car	2,850	3,500	650	19	20	30	
Portable minidisc player	208	249.99	42	17	2	25	Yes
DVD player	490	850	360	42	45	60	
Lingerie	29.59	37	7	20	15	30	Yes
Refrigerator	186.99	254.99	68	27	15	40	
Rare CD	10.99	16.99	6	35	7	40	
Expensive gents' watch	89.5	139.99	50	36	10	25	Yes
PC	544.85	632	87	14	20	90	Yes
Bed	229	329	100	30	25	75	Yes
Designer clothes	67.52	89.98	22	25	5	40	Yes
Airflight to Australia	4,920	6,300	1,380	22	15	75	
Wine	51	65.94	15	23	30	20	Yes
Novelty item	10.24	11.98	2	15	15	60	Yes
Toy	57	65.97	9	14	30	30	Yes

The picture this presents is that in the UK there is a general price advantage that averages about 24 percent for this fairly random selection of items. Also interesting is the fact that the shopping time is uniformly less on the web, although in most instances there is also a delivery penalty, with the consumer having either to wait or to wait longer for delivery of the item purchased. The indications here are that those who are not connected to the internet are already paying a premium on some of the goods they buy. As internet shopping mushrooms, the world will gradually separate between the economically privileged "connected" citizens and the PONA (persons of no account)—the economically and electronically unconnected.

If we look at what is selling over the web, the following list, derived from figures provided by Forrester in November 1998, ranks products by value.

Rank by value	Product category
1	Stocks and shares
2	Leisure travel
3	Computer hardware
4	Clothes
5	Books
6	Software
7	Gifts and flowers
8	Health and beauty products
9	Consumer electronics
10	Music
11	Videos
12	Toys

As can be seen from the figures, stocks, travel, PCs, software, clothes, and books were the first vertical markets to flower. There are no real surprises here. The items being sold are primarily small-ticket items that are easy to transport or may not involve transport at all, such as travel and software. The only exception on the list is computer hardware, but this was already sold extensively by telephone and delivery capabilities were well established.

To complete this overview of the web, the table overleaf gives the leaders in four important sectors: search sites, shopping, news, and directories. It is derived from figures provided by Media Metrix for February 2000 and popularity is measured in terms of the numbers of unique visitors per month, measured in thousands. (Unique visitor means that each visitor is counted only once, no matter how many visits they make.)

The reader is recommended to visit the site at www.iconocast.com for a comprehensive and up-to-date picture of the economic state of the internet. Iconocast aggregates figures from a multitude of sources and publishes the latest situation on a monthly basis.

Rank	Search sites Unique visitors, 000s	Shopping Unique visitors, 000s	News/entertainment Unique visitors, 000s	Directories Unique visitors, 000s
1	Yahoo.com* (44,698)	BlueMountainArts.com (16,554)	AOL New Channel (14,303)	Infospace.com (8,064)
2	Lycos.com* (27,121)	Amazon.com (13,609)	AOL Entertainment Channel (11,385)	Switchboard.com (2,586)
3	Go.com (19,487)	eBay.com (11,791)	ZDNet* (9,535)	Classmates.com (2,461)
4	Excite* (15,552)	AOL Shopping (10,738)	About.com (9,339)	GTE Superpages* (1,992)
5	AltaVista Search Services* (11,969)	AmericanGreetings.com (7,033)	AOL Sports Channel (9,256)	Anywho.com (1,863)
6	Snap.com Search & Services (10,923)	CDNow.com (5,690)	AOL Computing Channel (8,874)	1800USSearch.com (1,618)
7	Looksmart.com (8,812)	BarnesandNoble.com (5,176)	MSNBC.com (8,570)	Zip2.com (1,067)
8	AskJeeves.com (7,631)	MyPoints.com (4,875)	CNET.com (8,280)	Knowx.com (917)
9	Goto.com (7,208)	eGreetings.com (4,161)	Weather.com (7,552)	BigFoot.com (891)
10	Iwon.com (6,480)	CoolSavings.com (4,038)	Disney Online* (6,016)	YellowPages.net (858)

*Indicates multiple sites

THE BONFIRE OF THE BRANDS

An observable fact of the web is that established brands have not been very successful. If, for example, you look at a list of the top websites for February 2000 given above, you quickly realize that it contains very few established brands. The only bricks-and-mortar brand under the top 10 shopping sites is BarnesandNoble. Under news and entertainment, we find three established brands: ZDNet, MSNBC, and Disney. However, Disney has since consolidated under the Go brand, and MSNBC is a hybrid brand. No established brands are represented among the search engines or directories. We would find a similar situation if we looked at the leader board for most vertical segments of the electronic economy.

This has led some commentators to suggest that established brands do not work on the web—that the internet has created a bonfire of the brands. Established brands *can* work on the web—and the web brands are not yet as valuable as they might seem.

First of all, there have been hundreds of internet start-ups, most of them with ideas of running established businesses in distinctly new ways. In the early days of the internet, they were unopposed by established companies and got a head start that will be very difficult to catch. A whole new set of brands was bound to emerge.

Secondly the "dot-com" effect has transferred an almost instant validity to start-ups with unrecognized names. It is unlikely that any marketing consultancy would ever have argued that Monster.com or eBay.com or Yahoo.com were excellent choices of brand name, but on the web they work. There is also a big spoiling factor—most possible English dot-com domain names have been taken in one way or another. Many good branding ideas cannot be used because you cannot register the domain name and you cannot afford not to have the domain name of your brand.

To this, we can add the fact that many companies have deliberately rebranded for the web in sympathy with the trend to dot-com brands so that they are not automatically classified as "old hat" by web users. There is also the reality that if you are surfing the web for a site that specializes in, say, chess, then you may just type in www.chess.com to see what is there. If you find something, then you are likely to remember the domain name. If it comes up in a list provided by a search engine, you are more likely to click on it that on other, more obscure domain names.

A web-based brand is best if it is immediately associated with the object of the search or the content of the site. Thus Ticketmaster, CDNOW, MovieCritic, eToys, and E*Trade are good brands because the domain name is easy to remember and explicit. Established brands need to make a greater effort to prove themselves on the web, but they can be successful, as Barnes & Noble and Charles Schwab have amply demonstrated. Nevertheless, such names would be poor choices as domain names if they did not already have a very valuable brand.

All bricks-and-mortar brands have some amount of brand equity. Consumers are familiar with the brand and attach a level of quality or an expectation of service to it. If the brand equity is strong then it can transfer to the net, but it does not automatically do so. The evidence seems to suggest that the consumer treats the net as a completely new context and thus does not necessarily transfer the brand expectation to the web context. The situation is compounded by the fact that many bricks-and-mortar businesses have no clear idea of how to establish and run a website and often set up a poor website, which only serves to damage a perfectly good brand.

The new net start-ups have no brand equity, but if the website attracts many visitors then it can quickly establish very high brand recognition. High brand recognition is not high brand equity, but it will eventually lead to it if customer service is good. Thus, although Yahoo! sits among the 10 most recognized brands, its brand equity can only be a small fraction of Coca-Cola's. The success of companies that are riding hockey stick curves can be deceptive in this respect. The reason that they are successful is that the curve is helping them. If they have the largest market share, then the curve gives them an exceptional advantage over all their competitors and thus they are often complimented on having talent that they don't really have. Leading companies are often credited with being excellent at marketing when really it is the hockey stick curve that is excellent at marketing.

Franchises and communities of interest

If we wish to understand branding, then we need also to understand the concepts of a franchise and a community of interest. Products can carry brands, in which case the value of the brand matches the value of the product in the market. However, a brand is far more powerful if it is attached to a community of interest. Both Microsoft and Apple have brands that are attached to communities of interest, the users of their technology.

The need to address a customer community goes some way to explaining Intel's bizarre "Intel Inside" campaign. It was not run for the consumer—consumers never care much about the components of a product. It was run to convince the manufacturers and the whole supply chain that consumers would care about the processor—and naturally, some consumers did ask about the processor because of the advertising campaign. The supply chain was the community of interest that Intel was targeting with its brand. Microsoft had no need to target this community, as it had no clone competitors such as AMD and Cyrix to fight off.

The power of the Virgin and Nike brands lies in the fact that they are lifestyle brands representing whole age groups with significant disposable incomes. These are very large communities of interest. Vertical markets also have communities of interest. Book readers represent a community and there are even very identifiable segments of that community represented by categories of books: business books, children's books, thrillers, science fiction, and so on.

Very few internet brands could yet be described as solid brands—most websites, no matter how much traffic they are getting, don't represent any specific community of interest. Even clear attempts to represent a community, such as Women.com, have not yet achieved the status of a solid brand. WebMD appears to be doing so. Probably the most powerful brand on the web at the moment is The Motley Fool. The branding work done on the website is brilliant and it genuinely represents a community of interest.

Amazon is, by contrast, a weak brand, even if it is an unquestionably successful business. If you ask most people about Amazon they think "books," because the brand was built around book retailing. Amazon has moved into distinctly different markets representing distinctly different communities of interest, so far without any overt effort to reposition the brand. To see this more clearly we need to consider the idea of a franchise.

A franchise is a business process, which can be outsourced. A franchise itself cannot normally be branded, because customers very rarely buy the business process, they buy the product or service it produces. Amazon is a franchise by any reasonable definition. It retails and it franchises the logistics of delivery. It is pursuing a business model based on its ability to build and manage the retail process for small items that can be delivered easily and cheaply, and it is gradually expanding its portfolio. The Amazon brand at the moment is indistinct because Amazon is not a bookshop. The brand is being confused with the franchise.

Now consider Coca-Cola. Coca-Cola is a clear brand and it is also a bottling and canning franchise, but nobody associates the brand with the franchise because the brand is indisputably the product. The same applies to McDonald's—the brand is the fast-food experience, but the franchise is the ability to set up and supply strongly branded restaurants.

At auction site eBay we have an example of a web company where the service and the business process that creates it are very close to each other. Its franchise is the ability to run and manage internet auctions. The company has created one of the most loyal customer bases on the web and in doing so it has created a very powerful brand with genuine brand equity. The eBay brand represents the auction experience, it does not represent the franchise.

WILD IPOS

The IPOs (initial public offerings) of internet companies that took place in 1998 and 1999 are clear indications of the expectation of hockey stick behavior from investors. In the 1980s and the early years of the 1990s, Goldman Sachs used to demand that a company report five straight profitable years before it would handle an IPO, but the Netscape IPO in 1995 finished all of that. The stock market has since witnessed a series of IPOs valuing companies with no proven record and no profitability at absurd multiples of revenue and bizarre price/earnings ratios.

To provide a quantitative illustration, Geocities had its IPO in August 1998. Its 1997 sales were less than $5 million, achieving a loss of $8.6 million for the year, and its run rate for 1998 was expected to be below $15 million, given that its first quarter sales for 1998 were just over $2 million. Nonetheless, Geocities was the leading web community site with a membership that had grown from about 10,000 in October 1995 to over 2 million—its members having created 17 million web pages. It also regularly appeared among the top sites in terms of visitors per month (regularly over 10 million) and page views (usually over 900 million).

The traffic figures were excellent, but it had not proved that it could turn the traffic into solid revenues. Although Geocities was significantly ahead of search engine Infoseek in popularity, search engine revenues were more solid than web community revenues, which attract lower banner ad rates and run the risk of offending community users. For the March 1998 quarter, Infoseek had revenues of $6.2 million compared to Geocities' $2.17 million. At the time of the IPO, Infoseek's market value could be measured at about $61 per user, so perhaps one would think in terms of valuing Geocities at about $20 per user. This would have given it a value in the region of $300 million. However, the more optimistic analysts were suggesting that it might attain a value in the region of $1 billion after IPO.

Nothing of the sort. Geocities came to market on August 11, 1998 with 4.75 million shares, at an offer price of $17.00, valuing the company at around the $500 million mark; the stock opened on the first day at $33.00 and closed at $37.31, valuing the company at just under $1,150 million. Within three days the share value had risen to $50, giving the company a value of over $1.5 billion. In early 1999, Yahoo! acquired Geocities in a deal valued at around $3.5 billion. At the time Yahoo! was worth $19 billion, the same as CBS, which had revenues 37 times greater.

On the day of the takeover, Alan Greenspan of the US Federal Reserve was issuing dark warnings about the absurd valuations of many internet stocks and commentators were comparing internet mergers to Jewish marriages—internet companies could only merge with each other. Nevertheless, none of this dented investor confidence.

The wild IPOs continued into the summer of 1999. In July, the CEO and founder of MP3.com became a billionaire on the back of a hot domain name and an unproven business idea. MP3.com uses the internet as a channel for selling music. Its stated goal is "to empower the artist." Artists that sign up have to make sample tracks available on the site, and can sell CDs through it, but they do not sign away the rights to their music. Over 100,000 artists have signed up.

Prior to its IPO, MP3.com's revenues were small. For the first six months of 1999, revenues were $2.58 million, and it lost $6.34 million in its last quarter. Only 15 percent of its revenues were actually generated by CD sales, the other 85 percent coming from advertising. Nevertheless, the company gobbled up $344.4 million at IPO and at one point its share value took it to a market valuation of $7 billion, before it settled down at a conservative $2 billion or so. The only justification for such a valuation would be if MP3.com had some chance of dethroning Sony from its premier position in the music business.

It is galling for CEOs of organizations that have been built up over decades of careful management and prudent investment to see the net upstarts with miniscule revenues and inexperienced management achieving extraordinary valuations. It is even more galling for companies like American Airlines, which runs the extraordinarily successful Sabre system for the electronic sale of air tickets, not to be treated as a dot-com company—after all, it has been doing ecommerce for years.

It is clear that the investor community has made some very optimistic assumptions about net businesses. They are assuming that, as early web-based businesses, such companies will establish a lead over the competition that makes it very likely that they will become dominant in their chosen sector of ebusiness and be highly profitable in the long term. They are assuming that such businesses are riding a hockey stick curve—which they may be.

Ironically, a dramatic IPO can be self-fulfilling in the right circumstances. It provides the company with an influx of money and the on-going ability to raise money on the market very inexpensively by share issue. Any company that has gone through an IPO suddenly has finance for expansion or acquisition. But none of this alters the fact that the competition is only a click away.

The value of a share is determined entirely by supply and demand and thus its current price is, by definition, what the market thinks it is worth. But history demonstrates that when shares express values that do not reflect either an ability to pay dividends or rising asset values, then the price is unsustainable, because the only force sustaining the price is temporary and unsustainable demand.

The wild valuations of the last three years of the twentieth century put flocks of roast chicken into the sky, but the conditions for this kind of financial success never persist for long and may already have passed by the time you read these words. When the bubble bursts, it will destroy some of these new internet businesses.

However, the older net businesses (such as Amazon, eBay and Yahoo!) have built genuine foundations. They have revenue-generation models that can quickly be manipulated to generate profits, and I doubt if they will be greatly damaged. Amazon, for example, only needs to cut its marketing spend in order to go into profit. These companies are already riding a hockey stick curve and their value rises with each new individual who acquires access to the internet.

4

Leveling the Playing Fields

A 3,000-word document addressed to Pope Sylvester I and signed by the Roman Emperor Constantine did much to establish the power of the Church of Rome. According to legend, Constantine contracted leprosy, but the disease was cured miraculously when he embraced Christianity. He was deeply grateful and he rewarded the Church of Rome in an imperial manner, recording his gifts in an official document that later became known as the "Donation of Constantine." The Donation was very generous, giving unprecedented power to the Pope, including primacy over the universal church, and also conferring the provinces and cities of Italy, Lombardy, Venetia, and Istria on Rome. Naturally, the Donation quickly became an instrument of power, repeatedly cited by various popes as the origin of the church's secular authority and forming a legal precedent for medieval lawyers and theologians.

The document was a fake. It was not even a particularly good one, and it was exposed as such in 1435 by Lorenzo Valla, an expert in Latin. He examined the Donation and found that it was full of inconsistencies. The Latin language used was barbaric and clearly dated from a later period than Constantine's era. The Donation referred to Constantine's "golden diadem," something which no Roman Emperor would have worn, and it referred to Constantinople as a "patriarchal see" when it hadn't been established as such at the time.

The Donation of Constantine is only one of many forgeries that have been introduced for political reasons at various points in history. As another example, in October 1924 the British press published a letter signed by Grigorii Zinoviev, head of the Comintern, Arthur McManus, head of the British Communist Party, and Otto Kuusinen, head of the Finnish Communist Party, which urged British communists to work for the ratification of

Soviet/British trade treaties. The treaties had been signed in January 1924 but not ratified by the British parliament, as there had been a change of government. At the same time, the letter ordered British communists to infiltrate the armed forces and trade unions in preparation for a revolution.

The publication of the Zinoviev letter gave the newly elected Conservative government a good pretext not to ratify the treaties. The letter was also used to discredit the Labour Party of the day for its "treasonable" partiality to what was clearly a hostile foreign government. The letter was eventually proved to be a forgery, just as the Soviet government of the day claimed, but by then it had served its political purpose.

On a regular basis, politicians and political activists forge, invent, or distort information, convinced that their dishonest acts are justified by their "worthy" goals. On almost as regular a basis, they are rewarded for their dishonesty. As Mark Twain said, "A lie travels half way round the world while the truth is still putting its shoes on." The examples discussed here produced the desired result, even though the deceptions were eventually exposed.

In *The Prince*, Machiavelli observed astutely that "power shared is power lost." He could also have added that information controlled is power seized. Despots control the information channels with an iron hand. The right to free speech, enshrined in the First Amendment to the American Constitution, is a declared defense against this—the first-line defense of democracy. The right to free speech is, in practice, the right to distribute information, and it is a consequence of paper-based information technology.

The second hinge is all about new mechanisms for the distribution of information, the publish–subscribe mechanisms. These have both political and economic implications. Print technology did much to level the playing field between the rulers and the ruled. The publish–subscribe mechanisms will do more.

SIGNAL AND NOISE

The days of broadcasting are numbered. Broadcasting is a dictatorial means of communication where a central authority sends a single, identical stream of messages to a whole population of receivers that has no ability to respond. For most of the twentieth century, the broadcasting function was in some way an instrument of government control. It is a cliché that when a coup takes place, the primary military targets are the presidential palace and the radio and TV broadcasting center. In a dictatorship, the broadcasting network is the main instrument of power. In democracies, the sitting government cannot be seen to manipulate the broadcast media, so various subtle and not so subtle news management techniques are employed by government to influence the news.

From a communications perspective, the "truth" constitutes a pure communications signal and anything that distorts that signal is simply "noise on the line." Direct lies are noise of the most destructive kind, but many other kinds of noise are deliberately introduced into the information channels of society. Consider, for example, the terms "rapid oxydation," "energetic disassembly," and "abnormal evolution."

What do they mean? They are terms that the US nuclear power industry introduced after the nuclear disaster at Three Mile Island in 1979. They are supposed to describe "fire," "explosion," and "accident" in a way that does not excite public hysteria. One can only presume that the PR adviser who suggested these words was supremely optimistic.

Such attempts to shape the tone of the news are common, and often emerge from supposedly professional quarters where spinning the news has achieved the status of a profession. US President Carter's description of the failed attempt to rescue the US embassy hostages that were held in Iran as an "incomplete success" is another good example.

News manipulation is a necessary part of any policy implementation plan in a democracy. Take the government of President Woodrow Wilson, elected in 1916 on a peace platform. Once elected, Woodrow Wilson quickly changed his ideas about joining the war that was raging in Europe, but he needed to convince the public that his *volte face* was sensible and he needed to suppress the antiwar sentiment that his own electioneering had helped create. So he created a propaganda group called the Creel Commission and, via media manipulation, the government gradually convinced the public that it was worth fighting the Germans.

Woodrow Wilson may always have been in favor of joining the war, but could have believed that he could only get elected on a peace platform. This highlights the fundamental paradox of democracy—the majority opinion can be a fairly dumb one. So democratic politicians regularly manipulate public opinion to bring it into line with their intentions. As the politicians in power command greater attention from the media than opposition politicians, they are better placed to spin the "news" in the direction of their agenda. It is not just politicians—a whole host of organizations use "spin doctors."

Chief Seattle of the Duwamish Indians, ruler of six tribes in the area of Puget Sound, wrote a letter to Franklin Pierce, the US President from 1853–57. In the letter, he declared that the earth was the mother of all and that he had seen a thousand rotting buffaloes on the prairies left by the white men who shot them from the passing trains. He pleaded with President Pierce to examine the consequences of his people's actions and asked what would happen when the buffalo had all been slaughtered and the wild horses tamed. What would happen when his view of the hills were blotted out by talking wires?

Chief Seattle couldn't write. His letter was composed by Ted Perry, a Texas screenwriter, for a 1971 film on ecology, and when written was not intended to deceive. Nevertheless, the letter was used for fundraising by the environmental movement and included in various passionate public speeches. Chief Seattle was a genuine Indian chief, but almost certainly never laid eyes on a bison or a locomotive, neither of which were to be found within hundreds of miles of him while he was alive.

In democracies, lobby groups naturally form to support some specific interest and they influence government via funding politicians and by their efforts at spinning the media. The most effective means of gathering popular support is through political gestures that resonate with the electorate. Benjamin Netanyahu's appearance on CNN with a gas mask when the Iraqis were firing Scud missiles at Israel was a very powerful and effective gesture. It boosted support for Israel and it helped to bring him to power. Similarly powerful to non-Germans was President John F Kennedy's speech in Berlin after the building of the Berlin wall and his declaration "Ich bin ein Berliner." (The Germans of the day knew what he meant, but were slightly bemused by his poor German. In fact, he had declared himself to be a doughnut. He should have said "Ich bin Berliner," which is the correct German for "I am a Berliner.")

Democracy is protected from subversion by freedom of speech and the independence of the broadcast media. Where either of these is compromised, so is democracy.

Most of the content delivered by the broadcast media (newspapers, radio and television) does not need to be delivered at a specific time. Some information is best broadcast—important news, live sports events, and other forms of live entertainment. There is an economic imperative in this, as the value of the information is higher because it is current. There are very few events where this applies. Thus there are very few events where broadcasting makes economic sense if there is another alternative.

The question is, how will the mass media function once the internet has become the dominant medium? The mass media constitute an information market for perishable information. The value of the information dies very quickly, rather like a butterfly, rarely living longer than a day. Television and radio are supported by advertising and must provide compelling viewing and listening in order to survive. The need to entertain and fascinate is clear—the most colorful news wins—and this creates opportunities for spin. As a medium, newspapers differ only in that their content is measured by the column inch rather than the minute. The dynamics of news are the same—after an earthquake, the headline with the largest number of casualties wins.

The internet will become the dominant news medium with time; indeed, it could be argued that it already is. Statistics suggest that when the US sent tomahawk missiles into Afghanistan and the Sudan in retaliation for the bombing of the US embassy in Kenya in 1998, the US population went to the web first for the news. The traffic on news sites was so heavy that most of them ground to a halt. The internet is video capable, sound capable, and written word capable. Newspapers suffer from a lack of video for dramatic events, and television suffers from an inability to represent and explain complex events. The internet can marry the two types of representation and it can also get the news to you faster than television. What is more, it is a medium with a memory.

The old pull and push

To get a view of the effect of all this, there are three ideas we need to discuss:

@ pull
@ push
@ publish–subscribe.

Some activities work on the basis of *pull*. With pull, if you want something, you have to go and get it—you pull, you are active. Going shopping or going out to a restaurant involves strong elements of pull. Voting in an election is pull. Going out and climbing a mountain is pull. With pure pull, the consumer is an active seeker of the product.

Similarly, some interactions are *push*. In most societies, you are pushed into the education system and you may be pushed into the army. With push you are passive. Most on-going media services involve a high level of push. Billboards are advertising push. Junk mail is push. Banner ads on the web are push. Radio and television, indeed all forms of broadcasting, are push. The stronger the level of push, the more passive or involuntary the receipt of the service is.

It is easy, on first thought, to conclude that pull is freedom and push is despotism. Dictatorship involves a very high level of push, and under this kind of rule pull activities, like expressing your opinion, are normally controlled. However, this view is too simplistic. Sometimes people need to be pushed for the common good. Societies and governments impose laws to control behavior, usually with beneficial effect, and these are pushed on to the population. There is also the helpful "alert" to consider. In many situations information is broadcast (pushed) as a warning, such as "Danger, accident ahead," or as a legitimate directive, such as "No parking" or "No smoking." Broadcasting is used because it is the most effective way to relay important information.

If we analyze human interactions, it quickly becomes obvious that one person's pull becomes another person's push. Pull and push behavior may also alternate, and usually do. The drug dealer (the pusher) pushes to create demand, but in the longer term it is the drug addict who pulls. A great deal of legal commerce also has this characteristic: advertise for attention and then let the consumer momentum build—push, then pull.

Clearly, pull and push are extremes and between them are different kinds of interaction. A conversation is a balanced pull and push interaction, whether it is in person, over the telephone, via email, or by snailmail. It is neither pull nor push—it is a publish–subscribe situation. One person publishes and the other chooses whether to subscribe or not. If the choice is to subscribe, then they publish back and the interaction continues. Publish–subscribe is a pull–push arrangement, where the fact that pull is taking place indicates consent.

All forms of monopoly are push and thus all forms of government are push. The virtue of democracy is that it embraces a useful publish–subscribe mechanism. Elections can be thought of as a publish–subscribe interaction. The politicians broadcast to the nation during an election campaign and the electorate votes in response, telling politicians what they think in terms of a "yes" or "no." It is a complex event, as the election campaigns usually have an element of interaction. Members of the electorate also end up telling each other what they think when they vote, albeit in an imprecise manner. The beauty of a publish–subscribe arrangement is that it involves the continuing consent of both parties.

In order to understand the concept of publish–subscribe better, it is worth identifying where the term comes from. It is a term used in computer networking, where many computers need to interact. With push, messages are broadcast from one computer to all the others in the network and the computers that are not interested ignore the messages that do not apply to them. The problem with this push arrangement is that in large networks it creates too much network traffic. Imagine a room where many conversations are taking place but everyone is shouting to be heard. Push arrangements can be used effectively in master–slave arrangements where one computer is the master and all the others follow its orders. In peer-to-peer arrangements, where no computer is master, they will result in all computers broadcasting to all the others whenever a message is passed.

The alternative pull arrangement goes by the name of polling. This involves all computers regularly asking other computers if they have any messages to send. This also clogs up computer networks, but with huge numbers of polling messages rather than broadcast messages, and it is also unusable in a peer-to-peer arrangement when the number of computers becomes large.

The publisher–subscriber procedure involves each computer registering subscribers for messages of various types so that when it sends messages, it routes them only to subscribers. Technically there are different mechanisms by which this is achieved, but the end result is the same. When networks get large, publish–subscribe becomes the dominant mechanism for interactions because it is the only one that works. The internet is a huge publisher–subscriber network and it is so because it has to be. It is a peer-to-peer arrangement between millions and millions of computers.

The publish–subscribe arrangement provides a greater degree of freedom between participants. It leads to more even peer-to-peer interactions, but it should be noted that it does not imply equality. From a communications perspective, equality occurs only in one-to-one interactions. Publish–subscribe interactions are one to many in most instances. The publisher leads and the subscribers follow, but the subscribers are not coerced in any direct manner. They may subscribe, but they are volunteers and if they do not like what is published they will cease to volunteer.

Publish–subscribe is not a completely new kind of interaction, it is just far easier to do and more powerful than it was with the technologies of the internet. Publish–subscribe mechanisms have always existed as part of the economy. For example, much of the black economy, embracing drug trafficking, prostitution, pornography, and the selling of stolen merchandise, works via publish–subscribe mechanisms. Such activity cannot be promoted through the broadcast media, so it is advertised very subtly. The buyers of these goods and services know that they are participating in crime and thus they are clearly volunteers who are willing to take the risk.

In the visible economy there also are many examples of the publish–subscribe mechanism in operation. A taxi is a publisher–subscriber business on wheels. It publishes via a sign and subscribers hail it. A shop publishes via its shop window and the passer-by chooses to subscribe or not. A cinema publishes movies and the audience subscribes. We could even argue that every market of any kind is a publish–subscribe mechanism, because the seller publishes the availability of product and the consumer chooses to subscribe or not.

This is true, but far too simplistic. The majority of markets are inefficient and the consumer is often poorly informed. The paper economy, even in its current mature state, often unwittingly prevents consumers from even knowing of the existence of some buying opportunities. The efficiency of the market mechanism is sometimes subverted completely by highly effective broadcast advertising or simply an irrational wave of fashion among consumers. It may also be subverted by the establishment of a monopoly or by the operation of cartels that fix prices in their own interest. The paper economy is a complex web of pull, push, and publish–subscribe.

Companies naturally try to establish monopoly positions because this allows price to be controlled and profit becomes an almost effortless certainty. The tactics for this are simple, even if they are not so easy to implement: create barriers to prevent new entrants to the market, grow market share, be ruthless with the competition. Minimize the number of publishers, maximize the number of subscribers. Democratic governments naturally try to discourage most monopolies and cartels, and they will usually break them up when they form. They are not in the interest of the consumer and ultimately they lead to commercial stagnation. This constitutes good economic management.

The program of privatizations that the British government pursued under Margaret Thatcher in the 1980s was based on this. Even though it was executed imperfectly, it freed up a number of significant markets, including the all-important telecoms market, and has been imitated by governments all over the world. However, it also exposed the fact that some features of an economy, particularly elements of infrastructure such as roads, railroads, power supply, water supply, electricity supply, and communications bandwidth, are very difficult to arrange in a free market publish–subscribe manner. It is simply impossible to establish a large number of publishers and it is probably not desirable either. Thus there are constraints.

THE GANG OF FOUR

There are four specific public–subscribe mechanisms used extensively on the internet—email, the website, the search, and the MUD or community. They are all relatively new, and they are fundamental to the electronic economy. Each can be the genuine basis of a business and, as you might expect, they all have analogous processes in the paper economy. But in each case, the capability provided in the electronic economy is far greater.

eMail

eMail is rapidly becoming the dominant form of non-interactive communication and it qualifies as a publish–subscribe mechanism because of the way it works. You can either send an email to an individual or you can send it to a list. Similarly you can, if you want, subscribe to email lists that distribute information you want. eMail is implemented extensively throughout organizations large and small, and it has become indispensable to most of them. Indeed, at a meeting for CEOs organized by Microsoft, the CEO of Boeing is reported to have said that "the availability of email is as important as the availability of dial-tone."

In 1998, the total number of emails sent in the US was about 618 billion, with over 80 million users sending and receiving. This is more than three times as much as the paper mail figure for the US Postal Service, which delivered 186 billion items in 1998. Moreover, the vast majority of items delivered by paper mail were either bills (over 50 percent) or junk mail (over 40 percent).

Paper mail has long been the basis of specific businesses, notably mail order and magazine or newsletter distribution, but email can give rise to businesses with a slightly different flavor. Take Craig's List. Craig Newmark moved from New Jersey to San Francisco in 1994 and in order to acquire and grow acquaintances in a new town, he began emailing the small group of people he knew in the area about upcoming events in San Francisco's arts scene. Within six months there were 200 people on his mailing list and he was running out of computer resource and time to devote to the activity. So he got a friend to create a far more automated electronic mailing capability, and that was the beginning of Craig's List.

Craig's List (www.listfoundation.org), officially known as the List Foundation and now merged with MetroVox.com, has thousands of subscribers and is a non-profit-making operation. It exists only because and precisely because Craig Newmark wished to be social. Although he originally intended to distribute information about fringe theater, jazz clubs, shows at art galleries, and so on, he responded to anything that came up. His subscribers began to ask for help in finding jobs or apartments or locating lost friends or finding homes for kittens. Because he enabled it, the content began to make itself, with the subscribers beginning to provide most of the information. This, incidentally, is a general pattern with all web businesses, which we will discuss in greater depth later. A business emerged and Craig decided that it should be non-profit, although if he had decided otherwise he could easily have made serious money.

There are many other email-related businesses based primarily on building up lists and supported by advertising revenues. Some are really very simple ideas, such as www.jokeaday.com, which has accumulated a list of over 350,000 internet users.

The website

Trying to identify the right analogy for a website is not simple, because websites can do many things. In reality, a website is a window into somebody else's computer network. It can have the nature of a marketing brochure, or a shop window, or a genuine shop, or a magazine, or a newspaper. However, it might also be a simple utility, such as a site that tells you the current exchange rates, and nothing more.

The whole purpose of a website is to attract visitors—not just any visitors, but visitors who are customers or have the potential to become customers. This is not such an easy task. Even though there are well over 200 million web users (as at March 2000), there are, according to Netcraft.com, over 10 million active websites and that figure is growing daily. As of March 2000, there were over 15 million domain names registered worldwide and of these, over 9 million were "dot-coms," according to DomainStats.com.

In order to attract visitors and keep customers, websites must offer inducements: news, entertainment, informed comment, and so on. They need to provide something that attracts attention and differentiates.

An interesting website that illustrates this principle is Moviecritic.com. The main business of the site is to sell videos. However, its main attraction is that it can tell you whether you are going to like a movie or not. The way this works is that you register for the site and you rate at least 12 movies you have seen according to one of twelve ratings, on a scale between "I hated it" and "I really loved it." Using a software product called LikeMinds from Andromedia, it then identifies people who have a similar taste profile to yourself. If you select a movie you have not seen, the program will consult the opinions of other "like minds" and tell you how it thinks you would rate it.

This proves to be surprisingly accurate (at least for me and others I know who have used the site) and, in my opinion, is a better way of identifying a movie you will like than referring to a real live movie critic. The real business of the site, selling videos, is a side effect of the main reason for customers coming to the site. Indeed, the site encourages the customer to rate or enquire about movies that are still in the theater and not yet available on video.

The search

The web is a massive collection of information, estimated to be above 250 million pages or 100 billion words (not all of them in English), and it grows daily, so the need for search mechanisms is obvious. The paper economy provided search mechanisms of its own in the form of indexes to books, complete reference works, card files in libraries, and directories, including communication directories such as the phone book and the *Yellow Pages*. Their utility is dwarfed by the comprehensive search capabilities that the internet offers. Here one of the huge benefits of the internet becomes clearly visible. Because websites link to each other in many ways and because of the integrating power of the search engines, the web can be regarded as a huge but complex single document. Rather than having a single index, this document has a whole series of indexes in the form of various search engines, some of which are general and some of which are specialist.

An internet search engine behaves as an information broker. On the one hand, it searches the web continuously using software agents (and also real people), finding things to index; and on the other it makes this index available to all its users whenever they seek information. Thus it publishes an index capability and its users subscribe. As a publish–subscribe mechanism it is extremely important, because it allows users to form relationships with multiple websites that they can store as "bookmarks" in their browsers.

There are many different search engines, perhaps more than one might expect. If we just consider those that allow you to search for a word or phrase, there are standard search engines such as AltaVista, Excite, GoTo, HotBot, Infoseek, Lycos, Thunderstone, Webcrawler, Yahoo!, and many more. There are also what are called meta search engines or parallel search engines, which don't carry out searches themselves, but present the words that are entered to several other search engines at once. These include Ask Jeeves, Inference Find, MetaCrawler, SiFM, and others. There are then some specialist engines that provide "intelligent searches." These include Direct Hit, which works by providing paths that previous web users most commonly took when searching for the same word or phrase, and Google, which applies intelligent rules to a search in an attempt to provide more accurate answers.

There are also geography-specific search engines such as SearchUK, and topic-specific search engines such as IT-Seek. There is even one site, About.com, which has "guides" that will do manual searches of the web on your behalf, and beyond that there are large numbers of sites that simply provide directories of links. All of these sites have revenue models that are based on advertising and some specialize in presenting adverts that are relevant to the word being searched for.

The MUD or community

The multi-user domain, as already mentioned, is an evolution of the bulletin board. It has the character of allowing a community of users to form and interact with each other. As such, it is a highly important and often underrated mechanism. Its commercial power can be seen in the following example.

WebMD (www.webmd.com) was originally known as the Sapient Health Network (www.shn.net), but changed its name to a more commercial brand name once its business model had begun to prosper. From the user's perspective, the primary purpose of WebMD is to provide an interactive health information service, and it has targeted 11 different "communities" defined by the type of health problem being encountered. Currently these comprise breast cancer, prostate cancer, asthma, depression, diabetes, women's health, obesity, heart disease, fibromyalgia, chronic fatigue syndrome, and Hepatitis C.

The site's objective is to provide information and support services beyond the boundaries of the "five minutes per patient" turnaround common to health systems throughout the world, but it makes no attempt to replace or undermine the advice provided by doctors or other health professionals. Detailed explanations as to the possible side effects of different forms of treatment, the typical progression of the disease (or condition), and alternative treatments are made available and provided in a personalized format.

Self-help communities are established to sustain mutual support, and topics that are difficult to handle, such as advice on how to discuss death with family and friends, are facilitated because individuals are only identified to each other by nicknames. In other words, a classic MUD is implemented. Sensitive information that has often been withheld by some health authorities is also made available, such as which parts of the country—or world—have the doctors best qualified to treat a particular condition.

To participate in one of these communities users must register a nickname and password and supply an email address. Other condition-dependent information is requested, and is needed if a personalized service is to be provided, but is not compulsory. Users may periodically be asked to take part in a survey appropriate to their area of interest. While this is optional, the fact that surveys are highly targeted and very infrequent assures a remarkably high response rate, 25 percent being typical. Equally, some highly targeted advertisements are carried on the website, but as they are appropriate to the declared needs of users, they do not attract negative comment, and in fact have a very high drill-through rate. The website receives a very high hit rate from the registered users accessing both the formally presented information and interacting with each other via chat groups (MUDs).

WebMD has a small but targeted shopping area offering books and alternative remedies for direct sale to the public, for which registration is not necessary. But this is not the main revenue stream for the organization, and neither is the income from the advertisements carried. Surprisingly, WebMD is in business to sell statistical information to companies in the healthcare sector. No personal information or any other information that might identify individuals is ever passed on, but WebMD is in a unique position to carry out statistical analysis on the largest and most widespread sample available anywhere. As an example, the Hepatitis C community was launched in October 1997, and in the following nine months grew to a membership approaching 10,000. The statistics and user responses from this group have already been the trigger for a major pharmaceutical organization to embark on a new line of clinical trials on combination treatments.

What makes this idea work is that it is obviously appreciated by its users—visit the website and look at the testimonials. The health organizations that pay for statistical information seem equally impressed. Essentially, WebMD is a broker of information; or, to be more precise, it has created an information market, where individual communities are trading information about themselves and are being rewarded with better knowledge about their condition and support.

The web is often said to "disintermediate intermediaries," but here and in the case of the search engine, it has *created* an intermediary rather than destroying one. The intermediary is more of a "market maker" than a broker. It is a trusted third party that is supporting the needs of the user community and the business community in a way that would be difficult or impossible to achieve through any other mechanism. WebMD collects highly personal data in order to satisfy both the statistical dimensioning and the personalized service, and yet most individuals would be reluctant to provide this kind of information in an identifiable form to a multinational drugs company. It is all done in a professional and gentle publish–subscribe manner.

Ultimately, the cost of this service is paid by the pharmaceutical manufacturers, but while the cost may be significant, it is a small fraction of the cost of bringing a new drug to market, and will have little or no bearing on the ultimate pricing of any such new product. From the end user perspective it seems like a very valuable and yet free service, but it is not really free to the user. In the electronic economy information is money and the users of WebMD are buying their free service with data.

Bringing all four together

While all of these publish–subscribe mechanisms are important and each can be the foundation of a business in its own right, they also reinforce each other, and many businesses (Yahoo! provides a very good example) bring the four mechanisms together in some way and use them all. In fact, the classic business model for a portal is to do exactly that.

PUBLISH–SUBSCRIBE MARKETING

People send more emails than they ever sent letters. The email has the virtue of speed, the ability to attach electronic objects, and the ability to send to lists, forward items, send blind carbon copies, and so on. By any reasonable measure, it is far superior to paper mail. There are the additional factors that if you use an internet mail service such as HotMail, Yahoo! Mail, and so on, then your mailbox travels with you. You can also be anonymous if you wish and the service is free, which is about as low cost as you can get.

The table below illustrates the importance of email in volume terms, compared to other forms of communication. However, it does not tell the whole story.

Average daily no. of messages	
Telephone	52
E-mail	30
Voicemail	22
Postal mail	18
Fax	15
Pager	4
Cell phone	3

Source: *Workplace Communications in the 21st Century*, Pitney Bowes, May 1998

First, email is becoming the backbone of all internet push activities that are not interactive (as banner ads are, for example). It has the virtue that it is possible to automate and, hence, send emails to millions of people at once. It is also a very benign form of push—to the extent that we classified it as a publish–

subscribe mechanism because you can easily "unsubscribe," via adding an email filter to your email or by requesting to be removed from a mailing list.

New email start-ups such as ZapZone, Critical Path and eGroups are continuing to push the electronic envelope. ZapZone provides a service that lets small sites add free email to their site and then manages it on the site's behalf. Critical Path offers a similar capability, but is targeting the large sites, offering to handle email for ISPs, web-hosting services, and businesses of any size. By contrast, eGroups provides list management software, for managing extremely large lists.

As email is the pushiest of the publish–subscribe mechanisms, it naturally leads us toward broadcasting. Traditional broadcast content is piped according to a schedule. As the deployment increases of broadband cable and ADSL—asymmetric digital subscriber loop, a permanent and very fast connection to the internet—the use of the internet for broadcasting, or rather narrowcasting, will expand dramatically. However, my expectation is that broadcasters will discover a smaller market than they expected and that their traditional market is dwindling as the ability of the web to carry video improves. Broadcasting on the web is expected to happen through portals, which is why Disney bought Infoseek and why Yahoo! paid nearly $6 billion to acquire Broadcast.com.

Trends in this area do indicate a level of take-up. Over slow data lines the quality is too poor to be tolerated, but most of the listening and viewing is done over T-1 lines in corporate offices. This is what gives life to sites like Spinner.com, which plays music, or Silicon.com, an IT news service as well as an online television site. Additionally, broadcasting over the internet is not yet regulated or taxed. There are already over 2,000 internet radio stations and 185 of these are exclusive to the net. Some video broadcasts over the web have also attracted large audiences. The highly publicised Victoria's Secret webcast attracted about 1.5 million viewers and the video of President Clinton's grand jury testimony over a million.

All of this indicates that the whole of the media—from newspapers through film, radio, and television—is going to converge on the web, although we may have to wait a while for the right consumer device that makes it accessible to the broad mass of TV users.

Advertising on the web

When this convergence takes place, it will cause a crisis in the whole media supply chain. Nowhere will this be more evident than in advertising. The effectiveness of advertising was once poorly measured, but on the web, with its "click-through" mechanism, you can know exactly how effective an advert has been—you can produce the number who saw the advert and compare it with the number whom it called to action. Pretty soon we'll have web radio and video accompanied by a button that allows you to buy what you just heard or saw a snippet of. Instant gratification.

Pulling potential buyers into a website becomes the objective of the web advertiser. To do this, companies use the web's banner advertising and also spread awareness of their domain name through every other channel. At the moment banner advertising is inexpensive—a top price for placement on a popular website is roughly $120 per thousand "clicks," and the average price in the area of $40 (1999 figures), depending on how well the web user has been "profiled" as a likely customer. Banner ads work best on search sites where they have some relevance to the searched-for item.

Web advertising is undoubtedly in its infancy, but already it is far better targeted than other forms of advertising, because of the profiling that some sites carry out. Intrusive advertising is resented, but well-targeted advertising is usually not. "Context is everything" will become the guiding idea for the web advertiser. The day will come when advertising ceases to be intrusive—when it is always publish–subscribe.

It is interesting to note that individuals will in some circumstances volunteer to be advertised at. This is certainly the case with advertising in the cinema, because the advertising and the trailers for other movies, which are also adverts of a kind, form the build-up to the main feature. By contrast, most people tend to fast forward over the trailers when watching a film on video. The context is different because it is more interactive and thus the push adverts are most often rejected.

Website design

Many websites are themselves advertisements, or perhaps we should say shop windows. Websites with genuine style will attract window shoppers. Most of those who shop will be visiting because they have some kind of interest. However, a website is different to paper, film, or any other known medium. There is very little genuine expertise or design knowledge anywhere in the world in relation to the web. Almost all sites have design faults—in basic graphic design, in navigation through the site, in information presentation, and in product presentation.

It is important for businesses to appreciate this, so that they develop some genuine expertise or at least recognize how to seek effective consultancy assistance. It is important to look for well-designed sites to emulate or copy ideas from. Unilever (www.unilever.com) provides a very good example of well-thought-out product presentations, with colorful graphics and catering for multiple languages. There is also a very useful site, www.webbies.com, which provides details of the Webby awards presented by The International Academy of Digital Arts and Sciences at a conference in March each year. The site also lists websites voted as best by the public. Most of the sites referred to are worth visiting.

Even organizations that are not using the web to any great extent, perhaps for marketing communications only, need to think very carefully about website design. Customers, suppliers, and business partners will visit the website and so will competitors and prospective employees. Even for companies that do not use the internet extensively, the website is a big part of company and product branding.

Permission marketing

A fairly recent web idea that exploits the publish–subscribe model comes from Seth Godin and is referred to as "permission marketing." The idea is that web users will allow you to market to them if you get their permission first. Seth Godin is the president and founder of Yoyodyne Entertainment, a company that uses game playing as a means of getting permission to market to the consumer; it was so successful in developing this idea that it was quickly acquired by Yahoo!. According to Godin:

> *Traditional advertising and ad banners are based on Interruption Marketing because they interrupt a television show or a visit to a web site, but we've created a paradigm where consumers eagerly give you permission to market to them—and they choose to pay attention.*

Yoyodyne Entertainment is a consultancy that plans and executes marketing campaigns for its customers, using email and web promotions built around games and contests. Its customers include Happy Puppy, Geocities, ESPN SportsZone, and H&R Block. An example of a Yoyodyne campaign was the sweepstake it ran to promote access to Bausch & Lomb's website. Registered players were emailed trivia questions and prizes were offered that ranged from PCs to a week at a health and beauty spa.

Yoyodyne's promotion for H&R Block was based on "We'll Pay Your Taxes," a game that ran for 10 weeks, generated 46,000 players, and caused 1.5 million website hits. Banners were distributed at popular points on the web saying: "Click here if you want H&R Block to pay your taxes." This brought web users to the H&R Block site at a page that requested their email address, which 85 percent of those who showed up provided. From then on, Yoyodyne used email and the web to conduct correspondence. It sent some trivia questions about the H&R Block Premium Tax service, and web users went to the site to search for answers and respond. The conversation slowly educated willing participants about H&R Block's service in exchange for one of them winning a fairly attractive prize. The whole campaign cost about $60,000 and clearly represented good value. According to Seth Godin, the cost was "less than the cost of a couple of ads in *Time* magazine."

Seth Godin's belief is that traditional push marketing is being superseded by a model where the consumer trades or volunteers their attention. He points out that the response rates his company gets are far greater than the 2 percent that a good direct mail campaign elicits. They often exceed 30 percent. He offers the following principles:

@   People are fundamentally selfish, and they don't care about you (the
     marketeer) at all.
@   The marketeer must never rent or sell permission once it has been won.
@   The consumer is in control and permission is revocable.
@   Permission is not static: when you interact with someone, you either
     move them up or down the permission ladder.

The average US consumer will see or hear a million pushed marketing messages in a year, and will reject most of them without even considering the content. Permission marketing eschews the blunderbuss approach of the television
advertisement and the billboard in favour of smaller numbers and higher-
quality responses.

Another interesting publish–subscribe marketing idea is offered by the
Firefly Network. Visitors to the Firefly website assign themselves aliases and
register their likes and dislikes. The site uses an "intelligent agent" developed
by the MIT Media Lab to build a profile, and this profile can then be matched
against the likes and dislikes of one's nearest "psychographic neighbors." It
provides the user with a "passport" that Firefly partners, such as Barnes &
Noble, Yahoo!, and many others, can use to determine product or service preference. If you reach their sites via the Firefly network, then they can offer you
a better service. Firefly has the right to revoke a license from its partners if it
detects any abuse of the information it provides, although the anonymity is itself
a strong safeguard. Firefly provides permission marketing married to a faith in
psychographic profiling.

The publish–subscribe approach to marketing is non-intrusive but it is
"involving." Websites that pursue this idea need to be structured to welcome
every individual who shows up and then seek permission to have a continuing
dialog with them, in the hope that they have or may develop an interest in the
products or services available. It is a movement in the direction of one-to-one
marketing.

Speculation by various commentators about how ebusiness will evolve
suggests that it will eventually lead to one-to-one marketing. Many products
will be supplied in a tailor-made fashion and the consumer will be far better
served. It is easy to identify a trend over recent decades from mass marketing,

which was based on broadcast media and fewer consumer options (any color you want so long as it's black) toward market segmentation and greater consumer choice.

However, the end destination is unlikely to be a genuine long-term, one-to-one relationship between vendor and consumer, except for quite expensive items, simply because of the transaction cost. One-to-one transaction costs are inevitably higher than those for publish–subscribe, and must therefore be marketed as added value. The more pervasive situation can be expected to be based on one-to-many relationships with small groups of subscribers.

JOKES, HOAXES, AND DISINFORMATION

In the nineteenth century there was a spider farm near Philadelphia run by an immigrant Frenchman called Pierre Grantaire. Only two species of spider, *Epeira vulgaris* and *Nephila plumipes*, were actually being bred, and they were bred for the excellence of the webs they span. The spiders were sold across the US, but primarily to wine merchants who used them to give new wine bottles the appearance of age. Mr. Grantaire had named his most magnificent queen spider Sarah Bernhardt and called her mate Emile Zola. These two specimens were related to the bird-hunting spiders of Surinam and were dangerous. The lesser spiders were not and were sold to the public at a cost of $10 per 100. Orders could be satisfied by post as the spiders could be sent out in paper boxes and would survive the carriage. Pierre Grantaire did a roaring trade.

That, anyway, was the gist of a story that appeared in the *Philadelphia Press* about 130 years ago. It was placed there by a young journalist called Ralph Delahaye Paine, who had noticed that journalism in Philadelphia involved a good deal of plagiarism, with journalists borrowing stories and information from other newspapers. He also noticed that very few journalists bothered to check the facts. So, in order to observe the effect in a more controlled manner, he invented the story about the spider farm, all the details of which are complete lies.

As Paine had expected, rival newspapers noticed the story and ran with it. Not that it stopped there. Newspapers across the US took up the story and it even made guest appearances in Europe. It could be seen in the science section of some very reputable papers and made it into a bulletin from the US Department of Agriculture, Division of Entomology, which simply mentioned the existence of a Philadelphia spider farm. Several of the scientific magazines of the day mentioned the story.

Paine received hundreds of letters from the public, many of whom wanted to invest in the spider farm industry, and he was obliged to disillusion them, one by one. Ten years after Paine's death in 1925, reports about the spider farm were still appearing in publications. Paine had more than proved a point, he had exposed an awful weakness in the media: it devotes very little time to the verification of fact.

The publish–subscribe nature of the web will do battle with the attempt by individuals to influence the news. We may have had free speech for centuries, but we have never had free speech like this. On the internet every individual has the right to speak, and the publish–subscribe mechanisms give them the chance of being heard.

The internet is a very good place to start a hoax. For example, in 1998 a story appeared claiming that the Alabama legislature had passed a bill to redefine the mathematical value of *pi*, changing it from approximately 3.1412 to 3. College professors and NASA engineers were said to be deeply upset about the change. The story eventually made its way on to a Huntsville radio station and prompted calls to *The Huntsville Times*. It began to die when the Alabama legislature received calls from a Chicago radio station and was able to make a denial, pointing out that many of the details in the story were wrong, including the name of the Governor. (The name Guy Hunt had been given in the original story and he had not been Governor since 1993.) Apparently, the story started life as an April Fool joke, and may have been based on the fact that in 1897, the Indiana House of Representatives actually did try to legislate the value of *pi*, although it never got into law as the Indiana Senate killed the bill.

Wherever the veracity of information is highly valued, it has become part of the methodology of information creation to include audit trails, so that it is a simple task to check up. Thus in the sphere of science, published papers clearly reference the origin of quoted facts, so that any proposed theory can be investigated in detail.

The web has begun to create its own mechanisms for audit. eMail is particularly powerful against various hoaxes. Take the computer virus hoax. This consists of an email reading something like this:

Attila the Hun Virus

In an announcement to the press yesterday 25th, Microsoft warned its customers about the circulation of a new malicious virus called Attila-the-hun which attacks Windows 95 and Windows 98 computers. The virus is spread as an attachment to email messages which arrive with the title "Win a holiday in the Bahamas." If you click on the attachment it runs a program which destroys the FAT table, making your disk unusable and then displays a window on the screen with the words "Attila's a bit of a killer, n'est ce pas." Please pass this information on.

Responsible net users tend not to like being hoaxed and so when such an email arrives, they recognize it for what it is and they inform the sender and other recipients that the email is a hoax. People don't like to be fooled, so this has the effect of stopping the hoax in its tracks.

Word of mouth sometimes becomes a mass medium, but only in respect of certain content: jokes, fascinating stories and, to some extent, gossip about famous people. These pass entirely because they are fascinating and are generally referred to as urban myths. They are rarely true and are often embellished as they journey from mouth to mouth. There is a usenet group and a website covering the subject of urban myths (alt.folklore.urban and www.snopes.com/info/whatsnew.htm), both of which are mainly devoted to debunking, or in the odd case establishing the truth, of the myth.

The internet acts equally well as a conduit for lies and a conduit for the truth. Because of its publish–subscribe nature, it provides a more solid audit trail than other mass media, so it is more possible to verify stories for those who are concerned with the truth, and again there are websites and MUDs that specialize in it.

In some areas of the push media, newspapers, radio and television, there is a prevailing ethos of honesty and dedication, but it is not dominant. Many newspapers and magazines treat news stories as items of entertainment rather than attempts to print the truth—and there is good reason. The first law of push media is simply this:

The content sells the advertising space.

Content is king. The reader, listener or viewer needs to be fascinated. Thus the best content is not the truest content, but the most fascinating content. On the internet the game changes, because on most good websites you can respond to news stories, and readers who recognize disinformation and lies will post their opinions accordingly. The interactive nature of the net levels the playing field.

5

Apples from Alaska

For existing businesses, survival and success in the electronic economy can depend critically on when they get the "internet wake-up call." Something has to happen to make them see that they face extreme commercial challenges and that time is short. They have to start to see the whole picture. They have to "get it."

For me, the wake-up call began in a bar on Fisherman's Wharf in San Francisco, in 1996. I was relaxing with a cool lager in my hand on a hot Saturday afternoon. The barman seemed to know the guy who was sitting a few yards down the bar very well and was telling him about his latest girlfriend. He said that he had got to know her first on the internet, then he had met her in person in a kind of "blind date" encounter at Los Angeles airport, and now he had been going steady for a few months and sent her email every day. The bar man was not particularly young and he was clearly not a computer geek. In fact, he could be described as an "average Joe." The man he was talking to was also an average Joe and, as far as I could deduce from the conversation, he too was internet savvy. I suddenly realized that for these people and presumably many others in California, the internet was as much a part of their existence as the telephone.

Soon after, on returning to the UK, a business acquaintance of mine announced to me that he was now buying his Apple computers from Alaska. He informed me in a matter-of-fact way that the web-based supplier he had found in Alaska provided him with Apple computers cheaper than those he could get in the UK, and also, more importantly, they were delivered faster. This stunned me. This completed my wake-up call.

The simple example of a web-based purchase of computers from Alaska combines three factors illustrating the economic power of the web:

@   *The shrinking of geography*. Because of the internet, the geographic bar-
    riers that separated markets are collapsing—a retail outlet in Alaska
    won business in direct competition with British suppliers, without the
    British suppliers even knowing. Events like this are now happening daily
    on the web.

@   *Consumer education*. Consumers can and do shop around electronically
    to find the best price—finding the best price for an Apple Mac involv-
    ing risk-free delivery had taken an hour on the web. There are now a
    whole multitude of sites aimed at informing the consumer.

@   *Speed of service*. Web traders can provide a better speed of service—this
    Apple Mac supplier had geared up for two-day delivery worldwide.
    There are now many examples of trading where the web-based service is
    an improvement over the normal retail service.

The Alaskan example is useful, because it is so bizarre. It is unlikely in the
extreme that Alaska will become the prime supply point in the world for Apple
computers. In fact, there is already a strong trend for computers to be supplied
direct from the factory, with the consumer specifying individual details of the
computer configuration and software to be ready loaded. Thus the wholesale
and retail chain for distributing computers could disappear altogether with time.

The example demonstrates the sudden impact that the third of our four
hinges, the force of automation, can have. Technologies and ideas for automation are being invented all the time, but every now and then a change occurs
that suddenly introduces a discontinuous change into the economy. At that
point, the force of automation suddenly hits like a sledgehammer. The building
of the railroads and the introduction of the automobile represent discontinuous
changes of this type, because they affected the whole economy and they reduced
costs significantly and they made some transactions possible that were not previously possible.

To take another example, in about 1800 it took 13 days to send a letter by express mail from London to Rome. As the decades rolled forward, the
time to send such a message diminished. The railways established a faster
postal mechanism and it became possible for a letter to take as little as seven
days. With the advent of air travel, the time reduced to three or four days.

Then came the fax, and the time reduced to minutes, or at least no worse than hours.

But the fax still involved some delay, as the recipient of "the letter" was not necessarily standing next to the fax machine. In any event, it is being superseded. eMail is faster still—it takes no more than a few minutes and goes directly to the recipient without the need for intervention in any way by anyone.

So is this the end of the story? Not the absolute end, because on the one hand the telecommunications channels over which email travels are themselves becoming faster, so the speed can still increase a little. Also, we are now getting mobile devices so that we can receive email (or indeed a fax) wherever we are. We can thus send to where the recipient is, not where we think he or she is.

ARBITRAGING THE PLANET

In July 1997, at its annual meeting, the London International Financial Futures Exchange (LIFFE) was taking stock. The LIFFE board announced its belief that its open outcry trading system was "the fairest and most efficient" and would remain the dominant trading platform for the foreseeable future. Open outcry trading is the system where a number of traders deal by shouting out prices and making deals on a managed trading floor. It has served the City of London well. The expertise of its traders has helped to preserve London's status as the financial center for Europe.

One year later in July 1998, the game was over. The days of open outcry trading at LIFFE and elsewhere across world were clearly numbered. In the summer of 1997, Frankfurt's Deutsche Terminbörse (DTB) introduced an electronic trading system, Eurex, and competed directly in the trade of LIFFE's flagship contract, 10-year German Bund futures. LIFFE's share of the market in this contract fell from 75 percent to 10 percent in 12 months, and it withdrew from that market.

The facts were simple. Open outcry trading cost three or four times as much as electronic trading. This fact was never a secret, but apparently LIFFE was in denial about it.

A new LIFFE chairman was appointed, Brian Williamson, and he is fighting a difficult rearguard action while the exchange tries to get its electronic trading system, LIFFE Connect, in place and functioning. In 1998, LIFFE lost about $100 million and it is expected to have shown significant losses in 1999 as well. Its shares have fallen to record lows and many of its floor traders, some of whom earned around $250,000 per annum, have found other work. It is possible that LIFFE will survive, but by no means certain.

The exchange is caught in the awkward position of having to make considerable losses in its trading pits until its electronic systems give it the ability to compete. The game is not over, because some of the contracts that LIFFE trades are complex and the German Eurex system cannot yet handle them effectively, but it has now become a race between computer systems and the Germans have a head start. If LIFFE were a normal business then it might already be dead. It is not. It is one of the flagship businesses for the City of London and neither the Bank of England nor the British government will be happy to see it fail.

If you want to know how long it takes for a business to be destroyed by a nimbler electronic competitor, then the answer is clear—it could take a whole year. LIFFE was not undermined by the internet—if it could rethink its business, then the internet might perhaps become its salvation. It was undermined by the inability of its executives to carry out simple arithmetic. They had a few years in which to do the sums but they never did them. Like the owners of the *Titanic*, they thought their ship was unsinkable.

We can examine the sledgehammer blow delivered by the internet under four headings, all of which alter the competitive position significantly: geography, information, time, and assets.

Trampling on geography

Some internet commentators have announced "the end of geography." This is an exaggeration, but has the merit of emphasizing how dramatic the change is. The internet allows you to sell to anyone in the world. It is possible to create a widely dispersed organization—a so-called virtual organization, whose computing and communications infrastructure is the internet. This releases an organization from many of the constraints of its geographic location.

Currently, most organizations can only recruit staff who live within a specific catchment area. They are constrained in their ability to market to potential customers outside their geographic and cultural area, and are similarly constrained in their choice of suppliers.

The reduction of these geographic constraints leads to five changes:

For some roles within an organization, it will be possible to recruit and employ staff in a vastly wider geographic area, reducing the cost of staff or improving the quality or both

This trend is already visible among computer technology companies, many of whom have placed some of their R&D activity in regions where talent is available at a low price. There is extensive intellectual talent in India, particularly in Bangalore, which is now becoming a recognized center of excellence, and also in China. Both countries have effective education systems and are producing a surplus of educated talent. The situation is similar in the Philippines and Pakistan, not to mention Eastern Europe. Fujitsu has developed software centers in Beijing and Fujian.

In a similar way, call-center technology has allowed companies to deploy call centers in areas where staff costs are low, although this has been more local, with call centers located in the Mid West in the US and in Scotland and Ireland in Europe. This is an active trend that will extend into other areas of employment and of the globe.

Establishing a presence in new markets will become less expensive and will be achieved far more quickly

There are many anecdotes of florists, delicatessens, and specialist shops of various kinds establishing a whole new customer base "accidentally" by doing nothing more than set up a website.

A more interesting and telling example is that of the "hernia holiday." In the UK, hernia operations are non-serious operations that do not require a stay in hospital. So the British Hernia Centre in North London and other clinics that offer the same operation are exploiting this fact by advertising hernia holidays to US citizens. One center offers a package deal for round $2,800, including flights, accommodation, and an evening of theater in London's West End. The equivalent operation in the US costs roughly twice as much as it does in the UK.

Establishment costs, office space, and associated infrastructure costs will reduce

Teleworking naturally reduces the requirement for office space. In a typical office where the workload permits teleworking, the occupancy of desks falls by half and hence the office space can be reduced and a regime of "hotdesking" implemented, with staff simply occupying any free desk when they come in. Most computer consultancies work in this manner and many other types of consultancy are moving toward this kind of arrangement.

Supply costs will reduce

Most organizations are already benefiting in some way simply by purchasing products and services over the web. There are some obvious transactions, such as the purchase of airplane tickets and the booking of hotels, where the web simply provides better value. The purchase of computer equipment and software is another area. Organizations are advised to review all their supply costs in the light of what is available over the web and to do so on an on-going basis.

The general level of competition will increase

All the opportunities described so far also work in reverse. Competitors will be able to hire in different geographies and reduce supplier costs. What is more, new competitors will be able to enter an established market from anywhere in the globe and they may offer tough competition.

The death of ignorance

In economic theory, a market is said to be efficient if there are a large number of buyers and sellers, and they are equally well informed. Furthermore, the product must be of a homogenous quality or at least gradable in an objective way. Such a situation gives rise to a pure market, as exemplified by commodity markets and financial markets. Consumer markets have never been pure markets, but they are being made purer by the internet.

Commercial decisions, whether taken by an individual in buying a car, or by an office manager in selecting office furniture, are nearly always made with an incomplete knowledge of the facts. Ignorance is a factor both for the buyer and the seller in most commercial transactions. Neither can know with much certainty whether they bought or sold at the most favorable price, nor can they know whether the most appropriate goods and/or services were agreed on. Commerce is carried out in partial ignorance.

In many areas of the economy, this problem is diminished by the presence of brokers or intermediaries who facilitate commercial transactions by providing knowledge or expertise in a specific area. Their value is that they "know" the market, but they may bring more than knowledge to the transaction. They may arrange finance or delivery, or carry out the import/export paperwork. In other words, they may also "know a process" or know how to involve all the necessary parties to a transaction.

In some areas of the economy there are no intermediaries and *caveat emptor* holds sway, but the cost of a transaction is very high. For example, the purchase of any expensive item such as a large metal-pressing machine, an industrial printer, a large computer, or a packaged software system requires a good deal of effort. It can involve a comparison of vendors and products, testing and proving, finance, planning and installation costs, and so forth. Even if no third party gets involved, much of the cost of the transaction comes from the need to understand aspects of the purchase.

Specific websites can and do take the place of the middleman or third party. As electronic commerce has expanded, this "disintermediation" has become common and it will continue to proliferate, rewriting the established rules of business as it does so.

The reduction of the constraint of ignorance leads to four changes:

The nature of broking alters—some brokers may become retailers, increasing competition in that area

The fundamental shift here is to automated broking. All of the search engines—AltaVista, Excite, Lycos, *et al.*—are automated brokers and they make the skills and information base of many established brokers in different fields far less relevant.

However, it is important to understand that the word "broker" is often applied to the company that owns and manages the relationship with the customer. This is particularly the case in the insurance market, where the insurance broker is actually the insurance retailer. Similarly, some businesses, for instance that of the wholesaler, are fundamentally broking businesses. If wholesalers choose to sell directly and circumvent the retailer, then the facilities they have—warehouses and delivery capability—may be better assets than those retailers have for a web-based business.

One of the things you notice when you surf the web is that most companies advertise job vacancies on their websites. The incremental cost for them to do this is very small. Consequently, it is quite possible that the current business of the job agency will change, because some of the "employment transactions" will go away. Job agencies will have to add much greater value than simply connecting the buyer to the seller; as indeed will lonely hearts clubs.

The consumer will be better educated and better informed and therefore more discriminating

Already there are websites that exist just to provide pricing information. Visit www.compare.net and see for yourself. This particular site provides pricing details for consumer goods in the US.

Also worth a visit is BottomDollar.com, which describes itself as a shopping search engine. BottomDollar is interesting because of its business model. It is a software-based broker. It pays websites for click-through traffic and banner ads, but it also provides the ability to launch its price comparison searches on your site. This means that your website will include a sophisticated piece of search technology at no cost. Your website becomes its website, or if you like its website becomes your website. BottomDollar claims, probably with justification, that adding this capability tends to lead to repeat visitors to your site.

There are also specialist comparison sites like SmartShip, which provides competitive shipping prices between the likes of UPS, DHL, and FedEx. It asks a user for the "to" and "from" zipcodes of their package and its weight. It then shows a chart of current prices to ship the package, listed in order by several shipping couriers. It also provides a tracking service once the package is sent. This is, of course, a broking operation.

In the health sector, the web-surfing patient is already far better informed than patients have ever been and is making greater demands on healthcare professionals. Doctors are already grumbling about "cyberchondriacs"—patients who surf the web for information about the symptoms of obscure medical conditions and then come to believe that they are sufferers. On the positive side, doctors and healthcare in general are now far more open to scrutiny than ever before, as the customer is able to query the doctor's opinion with reference to the mass of medical information available on the web. The same is true of veterinary services.

For those with a very specific and fairly rare complaint, the internet provides the welcome service of allowing you to discover who the experts in the field are very quickly, and also enables you to find out useful information in terms of treatment costs and effectiveness.

Businesses will become more responsive to their customers

In 1995, Professor Nicely posted a statement on the internet that there was a flaw in the Intel Pentium chip. The story was picked up by the computer press and CNN took the story from there. Intel eventually bowed to media pressure and offered to replace every flawed chip, necessitating a write-off of $475 million. It never knew whether the flaw was genuine or not and had concluded that even if it were, it was highly unlikely that any applications would be affected, but it had no option but to act.

Customers have always complained, but when their complaints are being published in usenet groups they quickly become common knowledge and responding to legitimate complaints is the only viable course of action. The positive side to this is that the internet allows the customer to become more involved in specification or even product design.

One example of this is Cerberus, a digital music retailer that allows customers to mix their own CD from recordings stored on a computer. The company pays royalties to the original publisher on a track-by-track basis. The CDs cost about $10 and generally cater to minority tastes. As is often the way with the web, Cerberus was not without competition for long. K-Tel International entered the same market in 1998 with a service called K-Tel Express, allowing users to choose from more than 250,000 songs and related artwork to be cus-

tom compiled into CDs. The announcement saw the company's stock surge by
70 percent.

Some businesses will become commodity businesses and the number of players in that particular market will reduce

Currently there are 43 stock, futures, and options exchanges in Europe and
every European country has its own exchange in the same way that each country has its own airline. It is an expression of national pride rather than an economic necessity and the situation is unsustainable. Small exchanges offer no
advantage to the buyer, seller, or issuer of shares and other paper instruments.
Consequently, there are mergers in progress.

In January 1997 the Amsterdam stock exchange merged with the Dutch
futures and options exchange, and in September 1997 the same kind of merger
happened in France. More recently, in early 2000 there have been moves
toward a merger between the Dutch, Belgian, and French bourses. Medium-
term expectations are that there will be six or seven regional bourses throughout Europe, but this will surely reduce further.

There is competition to create a pan-European stock index. Frankfurt's
DTB teamed up with the Paris Bourse and Dow Jones to develop the Dow
Jones Stoxx index, made up of the largest capitalized stocks in Europe.
Meanwhile, London's LIFFE teamed up with the Amsterdam exchanges to
offer pan-European futures and options in conjunctions with FTSE
International. The rationalization of markets will probably happen very
quickly. No pan-European system of financial markets can emerge until all
major European companies are included, but once this has occurred, investors
will be able to compare the performance of all these European companies in
the same terms, and commentators predict that the level of stock trading will
double within a few years.

They are dreaming—it will more than double. Whichever way you look at
it, a stock is a commodity and all that buyers and sellers care about are that the
transaction costs are as low as possible and that the trade is securely carried out.
In a commodity market, guaranteed quality and transaction costs are everything.

The European bourses may well see their existence completely undermined by the internet—a common stock index is the beginning of this. In the

US, broking costs have fallen dramatically on the net by a factor of 20 and this has prompted share traders to trade more frequently. The average internet stock trader trades four times as much as one who does not use the internet and business is moving to the web at a bewildering pace. The investor has no reason to finance national bourses for the sake of national pride and will not do so when given the choice.

The compression of time

An increase in the speed of a business process usually delivers competitive advantage. The classic illustration of this was provided years ago by the massive success of the Sabre system for American Airlines, which allowed customers to buy air tickets faster, rather than cheaper. There have been many other demonstrations of this in recent years, from just-in-time manufacturing to telephone banking. The customer prefers speed and will pay for it if necessary. Time is money.

On the internet, the same general pattern is visible, only with the added nuance that the cost actually falls. Until now, there has usually been some element of latency (delay) in nearly all the business processes in which computers have been involved. For example, while there may be some very large sales order systems, the business process usually involves a written, faxed, or telephoned order, and rarely involves the customer using the computer system directly. Someone comes between the customer and the computer in some way and injects an element of delay into the business process.

The side effects of this are not immediately obvious until you consider business on the web. Customer-facing systems on the net do not involve any immediate human buffer and thus transactions happen faster. Indeed, popular wisdom claims that internet years are dog years, passing seven times faster. This effect ricochets through the supply chain and end-to-end business processes happen faster.

The web changes the business constraints imposed by time in three ways:

Continuous, 24-hour operation, seven days a week

The web never sleeps. Charles Schwab, the largest US retail stockbroker, provides an interesting perspective on this, as it has invested heavily in its web-based system (www.schwab.com) and is the largest online broker, with over two million active online customer accounts and nearly $2 billion in trade taking place per day on its website. In its first nine months of trading, Schwab acquired more new clients than in the previous dozen years and it watched its online trading activity increase at a rate of more than 25 percent per month, for month after month after month, with transactions coming in at all hours. In the first quarter of 1999, it had 10 times the traffic of the same quarter in the previous year. Schwab moved on to the web because it was concerned that it would lose business to E*Trade, a discount stockbroker that had set up and operated only in cyberspace. E*Trade has been successful, but Schwab has been more successful.

Stock trading is a 24/7 business. As America goes to sleep, the Far East becomes active, and later Europe wakes up. Schwab and E*Trade and all the other ebrokers are now 24/7 operations because they have to be. When E*Trade's systems went out of action for three days in February 1999, because of a software upgrade that didn't work properly, its share price fell and it lost business. It was estimated that the direct cost of the downtime was about $50,000 per hour, but the damage to confidence was probably greater. E*Trade's embarrassment was shielded to some extent by the fact that nearly all of the top online brokers—including Charles Schwab and Ameritrade— have endured system problems. Most internet stock traders deal with more than one broker just to cover the possibility of downtime.

In reality, all internet businesses are 24/7; what varies is the cost of being out of action. Amazon.com lost some trade in mid-1999, when its site was unable to handle the traffic generated by an email promotion from Jeff Bezos himself, and the share price dipped accordingly. However, eBay, the leading auction site, seems to have set the record in this area. In June 1999 it lost a whole day and this severely disrupted trade for two days, infuriating thousands of online buyers and sellers. As a consequence, the company lost a remarkable $2 billion from its valuation. When technical problems persisted, it eventually resorted to recruitment, appointing Maynard Webb as president with a brief to sort out the engineering and technical operations. Webb has an appropriate background as chief information officer at Gateway and the market added a remarkable $1 billion to eBay's value.

The availability problems of eBay, Yahoo!, and a number of the other very popular sites suddenly became headline news again with the hacker raids in the early months of 2000. Hackers, allegedly from Germany, decided to overload many of the popular sites with traffic by installing viruses in a whole series of vulnerable computers with poor security and have them automatically access the chosen sites. This had the same effect as if you drove an extra million cars into any capital city: the traffic ground to a halt.

The victims of these hackers failed to find it amusing, realizing that their businesses could easily collapse under any concerted attack of this kind. However, the hackers melted away into cyberspace and have not since re-emerged. For internet businesses, the computer systems are the business and they have to be robust and available at all times.

Faster commercial processes involving data self-service and process sharing

The internet compresses supply chains and accelerates the movement of inventory. It may also allow an organization to outsource some of its activities to the customer or supplier. An organization's website is, or can be, an advertising medium, a marketing medium, a help and support mechanism, a sales order mechanism, a showroom, and in some instances (as in an online casino or an online magazine) a delivery mechanism. The internet is awash with examples of this. Nearly half of the Fortune 1000 give internet access to business partners and most smart ecommerce sites provide a wealth of supporting information and help links for the customer.

At the moment this is mostly evident in the speed of passing information. However, the sale of software from many sites, including both software retailers such as Dr Download or Egghead.com as well as from the authoring companies, now happens as a matter of course via download, and most sites offer special download versions that allow you to try before you buy. As a consequence, the speed at which software is purchased has increased. The speeding up is occurring with the sale of music and video with the same try-before-you-buy process coming into place.

A more interesting example of speed is provided by Rbuy Inc. (www.rbuy.com), an online real-estate auction site that is controlled by real-estate agents. While there are many sites that list details of properties, charging buyers and sellers for the privilege, Rbuy's customers are exclusively real-estate agents. Together, agents and sellers set the terms and conditions of the sale and the property is auctioned during a period of between three and ten days. Interested agents can view the property on the website or visit it if they wish. The evidence seems to indicate that the process yields a good price for the property and reduces both the cost and the time of a sale. The cost of doing business on Rbuy.com can be as low as 0.5 percent of the final sale price.

A trend toward soft products

In the electronic economy, a product either becomes more of a commodity or more of a customized item. Ultimately, companies that focus on responding to the customer eventually begin to involve the customer in the design process, or allow the customer to negotiate the nature of the final product. This moves the provider toward the idea of a soft product—one that is tailor made. There are already some examples of this. Andersen Windows, a large manufacturer in the US, now sells windows that the buyer specifies using design software.

Cars, clothes, and holidays can be customized, and will be more and more so with time, but more mundane products such as books, videos, and music CDs seem to offer little scope for added value. However, Amazon managed to add value to books by having customers rate them and even in some instances discuss the book with the author—and when the author participates in the discussions, the book sells better. The business model of MP3.com, with its thousands of musicians, is based on the same idea of adding value. If you like the music, get to know the musicians. Similarly, the stockbroker sites add value to commodity by providing free information to assist the trader: advice, discussion groups, charts, and so on.

Asset rain

The final major change that the internet introduces is a likely decline in the actual value of existing assets. The problem of assets turning into liabilities is one that accountancy has attempted to deal with over many years, and for all types of businesses there are accepted accounting mechanisms for dealing with the problem. However, there is no easy way for accounting to deal with what may amount to a financial earthquake.

Accountants are already finding it very difficult to assign value to the informational aspects of a business. It is not easy to value branding and goodwill and all forms of intellectual property, especially software. How, then, do you value a website? It costs money to create, anything from $50,000 to "the sky's the limit," but how do you put a realistic value on it, and do you depreciate it over time or not? Do you value it according to web traffic? If not, then what is the metric?

Another good question is: Do you need to reassess the value of other assets? The answer may well be yes. The internet raises these real issues:

Existing property or plant may be or may become a liability

There is a glaring structural dislocation between some internet businesses and their bricks-and-mortar counterparts. The effect first became apparent when it was noticed that teenagers in New York were going into Tower Records and HMV to listen to the latest CDs, and then going home to buy them over the web from CDNow or CDUniverse. The dilemma that this poses is far greater for retailers of larger items such as furniture and white goods.

These businesses can turn into showrooms for their internet-based competitors, and most will do so before they die out. The CD shops and bookshops at least have the advantage that they can deliver the goods speedily—a fact that may preserve their existence in the long term—but the furniture stores and white goods outlets may not even be able to promise faster delivery. As we shall see later, goods are already significantly less expensive on the internet and it has not by any means yet delivered its full potential.

Existing channels to market may be or may become a liability

The internet is a new channel to market and as such, it immediately creates channel conflicts for many companies. Two obvious examples of this are provided by Compaq and Barnes & Noble.

As a PC vendor, Compaq is challenged by other vendors, particularly

Dell and Gateway that have a direct selling model. Originally, their direct selling was carried out via magazine advertising and a call center. With the advent of the internet, both Dell and Gateway quickly exploited the new channel, cutting costs substantially. By the end of 1998, Dell had an internet run rate of $5 billion. Compaq was less able to exploit the internet because of its valued reseller channel, an undoubted asset that had suddenly also become a liability.

Barnes & Noble was caught by a different dilemma. Having launched its website, BarnesandNoble.com, it was suddenly in conflict with its own retail operation. It was offering discounts on its website that were not available in its bricks-and-mortar outlets. It resolved the dilemma by floating off the internet-based business.

Existing brands may be or may become a liability

For reasons discussed in Chapter 3, bricks-and-mortar brands rarely work well on the web. For Coca-Cola and Nescafé there is no real dilemma, but for insurance companies, retailers, and banks there is a genuine problem. The power of their brand is reduced by the "dot-com" effect. The new exciting brands are Yahoo!, Excite, eBay, E*Trade, Amazon, MP3, Monster.com, and so on. With most such brands, even if you have never heard of them, you can tell that they are internet-based brands because they are usually talked about with ".com" after their names.

Walt Disney dealt with this problem by buying into Infoseek. This was a shrewd move, given that it was done prior to the massive explosion in the value of internet stocks. It provided Disney with an alternative brand for distribution—and Disney clearly intends that Infoseek will eventually become a media channel, the equivalent of an internet television network.

A UK insurance company, the Prudential, whose ability to compete on the web was already challenged by the fact that its brand conflicted with a strong US insurance brand, set up Egg.com, a banking and financial services website targeted at the UK market. In terms of gathering customers this was an instant success, and the fact that a trusted bricks-and-mortar brand was behind it only helped it.

As the internet becomes more successful, the effect of the internet brand will become more pronounced. Older brands will begin to be associated with failure as their owners are outpaced by the nimbler new businesses of the net. A bricks-and-mortar brand may already be losing value, but in time it will be a liability.

THE FORCE OF AUTOMATION

It is not possible to predict where automation will strike next, but it is possible to view its impact when the automation applies to an element of information systems. Consider Figure 7.

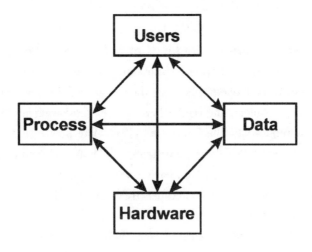

Figure 7 The system components map

This shows a simple model called the system components map. It illustrates the fact that computer systems consist of four distinct types of component:

@   users, who use the system;

@   the (software) processes that run the system;

@   the data that the system processes;

@   the computer or networking hardware on which the system runs.

Any individual computer system could be represented like this, as, indeed, can a communications system such as the telephone network. Although computer systems may be complicated, computer networks are even more complicated, as they involve many different users doing different things, many different software processes, many different types of data, and with many different computers involved (and/or other components such as printers, disks, networking hubs, communication links, and so on).

As the diagram indicates via the arrowed lines, a system involves multiple relationships. Users employ different software processes to process various groups of data utilizing various hardware. If you change the components of any one of these groupings, then you may find it necessary to alter some of the others. This is even the case with the grouping of users. With most computer systems, if you replace trained users with untrained users the systems will not work unless they have an extremely intuitive interface. (Ask the victims of any poorly planned merger or acquisition if you want any confirmation of this.)

The whole arrangement is actually very tightly knit. It behaves a little like an ecosystem, as a change in any part of it could affect everything else. This, incidentally, is why computer systems are so very difficult to design, build, implement, and maintain. They are awash with complicated relationships.

If we now introduce a new technology—a better way of managing data, perhaps—then it will affect everything. It may require less hardware or different hardware. It may need processes to be built in a different way and it may provide users with greater capability. This suddenly becomes a chain reaction. Now the stage is set for a corresponding improvement in the automation of processing. The stage may also be set for new hardware devices and for wholly new business applications. The information ecosystem changes.

Now consider the sledgehammer change of the internet. Suddenly users could access other computers, other processes, and other data. And these were the data and processes of hundreds of thousands of other computers across the world. The world started to become a huge, single network. It was like an earthquake in the world economy, with aftershocks that are still occurring.

Russian dolls

Figure 7 actually has a wider area of application than simply computer systems. We can put different words on the same diagram to have it represent something else. For instance, we could use it to represent the components of a business. The four boxes would then have the words: Employees, Business processes, Business data (or information), and Plant (and machinery and various other kinds of infrastructure or tools). This is something that we should expect, as a business is a system, although it is more complex than a computer system and it involves far more than just computing components. Indeed, it does not necessarily have to include computer components. After all, business systems were in place long before computers came along.

If we become more general still, rising further up the scale, we could draw yet another diagram, but this time representing the whole of humanity and all of its activities.

In this third diagram, we could label the four boxes with the words: Citizens, Activity, Information, and Artifacts. We would then have a diagram that represented all overt human activity and we could, if we wanted, think of humanity and all of its activity in terms of a system of some kind, in the same way that entomologists think of a beehive or an anthill.

We could then have three diagrams that represent the computer, business, and world viewpoints. However, these diagrams can be shown as nesting within each other like traditional Russian dolls, as shown in Figure 8. This provides us with a picture of the repeating theme—the force of automation.

Considering each of the four sets of boxes we can see the following:

@   Many people are involved in business activities of various sorts as employees, and many such employees are users of computer or communications technology.

@   Some human activity is business activity and the carrying out of business processes, and some of these processes take place on computers.

@   Some of the totality of human information is business information, and some of that resides on computers.

@   The sum total of human artifacts includes many that are utilized as

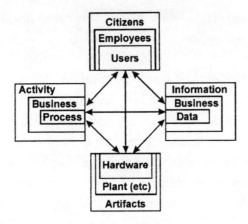

Figure 8 The repeating theme

business plant or machinery, and some of this is computer or communications hardware.

None of this is up for debate, these are facts. More interestingly, what is also a fact is that the innermost of the three diagrams is "growing" inside the second of the three. Computers are involving more employees and carrying out more business processes. This is partly why everything is speeding up. Computers are participating in more business processes and making them faster. To this, we can add the minor detail that the computers themselves are getting faster as each year passes and thus there is a secondary speed-up effect.

The second of the three diagrams is also expanding within the outermost diagram. In other words, businesses are becoming more and more involved in all human activity. We do not spend as much time growing our own food as we used to, or cooking our own food, or making our own entertainment, and so on. In whole or in part, we pay for it to be done for us, and as time passes we pay for more and more of it to be done for us. There are two effects in progress here:

@   businesspeople seeking out new and better goods and services to provide to people for commercial gain;

@   commercial products and services becoming more and more available to the whole population of the planet, rather than just the citizens of the developed economies.

This expansion does not just speed things up—it also integrates everything, making us more interdependent and less self-sufficient.

This, then, is the force of automation. With each passing year entrepreneurs seek to harness it, creating new enterprises that are more efficient and fleeter of foot than their established competitors. The force of automation in the paper economy initially revolved around the use of paper-based information systems and mechanical engineering, but gradually it has been migrating to electronic systems. Right now the force of automation is carving out a series of electronic highways across the world, an electronic communications and trading channel, an eroad.

Uncollected harvests

The early capitalistic era produced companies that owned whole towns and provided their workforce with housing, a company store, and even education for the children in some instances. Such organizations needed to manage tens of thousands, even hundreds of thousands, of staff effectively. We can contrast this with the new, small, energetic, networked organizations, where the "company store" is the disk farm attached to the company's UNIX server, and the ideal employment is not a job for life, but a job for five years with a good options deal ready to be cashed in after a successful IPO.

The modern economy consists of a whole population of interdependent organizations that outsource various functions to each other. Microsoft presents a good example of this. There is a very large market for consultancy in the use and implementation of Microsoft software products, which Microsoft makes no attempt to address. Large consulting operations, including IBM, EDS, CSC, and many others, make excellent revenue from this, as do many smaller operations. Microsoft even outsources the training for users of its products to business partners. It produces the curriculum and then certifies the trainers and they carry out the work, paying Microsoft a royalty for its curriculum.

There are many examples that illustrate the same effect. Many large organizations have outsourced significant parts of their IT departments to companies such as EDS, Andersen Consulting, and CAP Gemini. Perhaps the best examples are Nike and Benetton, both of which outsource the manufacture of the products that they market (and much else). There is also another trend hiding within this one—the younger a company is, the more likely it is to outsource many of its functions.

The force of automation has the effect of opening up new business opportunities. As it scythes its way through the economy pulling down the old guard, it also reveals new, uncollected harvests. It is worth discussing some examples.

Michael Denigan, "Mick" to his mates, is perhaps one of the best whip makers and whip crackers in Australia. Mick's whips are prized by many of Australia's best stockmen, and his whips are used regularly on some of the biggest cattle stations in the world. Mick even has a whip on permanent display in Parliament House, Darwin, having won an exhibition there in 1994.

So says his home page (http://www.ozemail.com.au/~whips/). Mick also has the distinction of having had one of his whips presented to Bill Gates, as a present from the Australian government. That was probably one of the best things that happened to Mick's operation, because word spread and it grew his web-based business dramatically. At last count, it was reported to be pulling in in excess of $10 million per annum.

There are other similar examples. A shop in Canterbury, UK, selling sports gear for cricketers, had only ever sold kit locally. It put up a website hoping that it would be able to sell its high-quality produce country wide, and immediately began to receive orders from across the cricket playing world—Australia, Pakistan, India, the West Indies, South Africa, and even some from the United States. It had never previously used a courier service to deliver goods and quickly found itself having to become familiar with serving a worldwide market.

With slightly more foresight, the US National Hockey League (www.NHL.com) set up a website aimed at promoting the growth of ice hockey worldwide and selling more merchandise. It was amazed at the response. It had been completely unaware of the extent of the popularity of ice hockey in Finland, where NHL matches are shown on television. Within a few months, 50 percent of the web-based market for NHL merchandise was coming from Finland.

All of these businesses—and there are many that we could point to—have done little more than put their catalog online and take orders, but it has been a surprisingly happy experience for them, because they have seen their market grow instantly. They provide one instance of the phenomenon of uncollected harvests.

There are many others. Auction sites bring together buyers and sellers who could never previously interact effectively. Job sites attract candidates who might never previously have known about a given vacancy. Travel sites sell airline tickets that would never previously have sold. What we are witnessing here is that the electronic economy is more efficient than the paper economy by virtue of velocity, coverage, and cost.

One particularly interesting example stands out, because it proves several points. This is the popular UK website, Lastminute.com, one of Europe's early internet successes, launched in November 1998. As the company name suggests, the business is about the online buying and selling of high-ticket last-minute items, from airline seats and hotel rooms to gifts. Within a year the site built up an email list of over 500,000 and became one of the top three travel sites in the UK. It is riding the curve.

In effect, Lastminute.com sells inventory that has a declining value as an unbranded item, allowing the vendor to maintain "official prices." However, it tends only to handle good-quality inventory and to sell to high-quality customers, people who have money but not time. This is obvious from the inventory on offer on any given day. The last-minute prices are not always cheap, but the items are usually interesting. There is a serious money section where you can buy an island or charter a Russian Mig. The site has also moved into auctions.

Lastminute.com has targeted a particularly lucrative section of the population, many of its customers being corporate executives or simply those rich enough to consider flying out from London to Milan on a whim, for a meal in a high-class restaurant and a trip to La Scala to watch *La Traviata*. Such packages were once unsaleable—but no longer.

Lastminute.com had a very high-profile UK IPO in March 2000, confirming, if any confirming were needed, that the wild IPOs were no longer just a US phenomenon. The statistics were typical of many US IPOs. Lastminute.com had miniscule revenues of £195,000 ($312,000) in the last full financial year prior to the IPO, recording a loss of about £4.5 million ($7.2 million) due almost entirely to very high PR and marketing spend. Naturally, on the first day of trading the company achieved a value of £768 million (over $1billion). However, within a few days share values had slipped back to below the float price following adverse press comment and access problems to the website.

THE GOAL POSTS IN MOTION

In July 1999, an internet start-up called Webvan announced that it had received a first round of funding of $100 million from several successful venture capital companies, including Knight-Ridder, Sequoia Capital, and Softbank. Like Peapod and NetGrocer, Webvan is a virtual supermarket, but one that intends to get big quickly. It plans to build 26 large, high-tech grocery warehouses, each with the capacity of 20 supermarkets, in the largest population areas in the US over the next two years. The cost of the construction work alone will be $1 billion, but hiring staff, buying inventory, and marketing will raise that figure considerably.

Webvan is already up and running. Its first warehouse opened in June 1999 in Oakland, California, and its second, in Atlanta, is expected to open in early 2000. Webvan expects to be price competitive. According to its calculations, the cost of operating efficient warehouses and a fleet of delivery vehicles is less then the cost of a self-service retail store. The US market for groceries is $650 billion per annum and Jupiter Communications has forecast that $6.4 billion of US grocery sales, a mere 1 percent, will be made via the internet in 2002.

Will the existing supermarkets be able to compete with this brash new start-up? The answer is probably no. The established businesses may well be better managed and they could also be more innovative and more efficient in their operation. These things will always count, but it is unlikely that they will compensate for the disadvantage that the established businesses suffer. The force of automation will have its say.

The huge advantage of the internet start-ups is that they have planted their foundations in the new electronic economy. Their business models are based entirely on the reality of the internet. When such a business decides to build, say, a warehouse, it is because its electronic business process requires a warehouse in the physical world. The location of the warehouse and its level of automation will be decided by the needs of the electronic economy. Established businesses cannot match this. Their businesses have been structured according to the dictates of the paper economy and unfortunately, the goal posts are in motion.

The mode of operation of some businesses will be completely destroyed by the web. They will be placed in the position of a pony express in competition with the railways. Not only will some of their assets quickly become liabilities, but the expertise that they have accumulated will have little relevance to the new way of doing business—just as managing a distributed horse-based transport system has little relevance to a delivery business based on the railway.

Businesses that are undermined by the web in this way are quickly faced with some very awkward choices. One company that saw the writing on the wall way ahead of time was Marshall Industries, a large US distributor of electronics components. Admittedly, it had the advantage of being close to the IT industry, and could see how fast the web was changing things. In any event, it opened a website that disintermediated its own salesforce and possibly the retailers it supplied, allowing anyone to order and also providing details of all its suppliers to anyone who cared to contact them. It even provided enough information to disintermediate itself, as customers could easily go directly to the manufacturer.

The outcome was positive. Marshall replaced its old business streams with new direct ones, created from the fact that it now addressed a worldwide market. Never having previously sold to the Far East, it quickly arrived at a point where 20 percent of sales were coming from there. New revenue streams appeared before old ones wasted away. Marshall had put its competitors at an extreme disadvantage. It was a wholesaler in a supply chain that would soon have no need of wholesalers, and it moved quickly forward in the supply chain to become a retailer.

Only one company in any given market gets to finance its rebirth by collecting worldwide revenues. For every company like Marshall Industries, there are 10 companies that will act too late.

Merciless mathematics

George Lucas may be initiating the demise of Hollywood, or at least Hollywood's control of the movie business. He is leading the drive to adopt digital projection technology, which will in time allow cinemas to download films directly from his company over the internet, rather than receiving the movie through the traditional channels. This cuts the cost of bringing a film to market by 95 percent, as none of the intermediaries in the traditional movie channel needs to be involved.

Traditionally, movie distribution works in the following way. The seven sisters of Hollywood—Buena Vista, Dreamworks, Metro-Goldwyn-Mayer, Paramount, 20th Century Fox, Universal, and Warner Brothers—distribute the celluloid prints, collecting over $1.5 billion worldwide for the privilege. This also ensures a reasonable chance of success for every movie they choose to promote, whether it be from their own stable or from an independent—so long as audiences turn up.

Digital projection changes the game; in fact, it probably brings it to an end. It means that cinemas can show anything, from live events through television programs to major movies. They are not obliged to select from within the relatively limited choice that the seven sisters offer them. On the other side of the business, film producers could go outside the traditional channel for every service they need, from finance to PR. Digital projection provides a better-quality picture and, at the time of writing, the digital projection kit only costs $100,000, a cost that will surely fall. The mathematics are merciless.

In early 1999, a Texas venture capitalist told me that he had been investigating the cost advantage that the internet delivers:

> *At the retail end of the chain, it works out at about 15 cents in the dollar, taking everything into account and that's where all the attention is. But up the chain they're getting 10 cents in the dollar and nobody is concentrating on that, and that's where opportunities are going begging.*

He is right and his figures offer a reasonable rule of thumb, although in some businesses the opportunities are far greater.

Let us consider some facts:

@   In terms of computer costs, the cost of presenting a web page to a customer is very small. It can be lower than 1 cent per page for a medium-sized website, and the larger the site the lower the cost. (Compare this to the cost of publishing brochures.)

@   The cost of placing an order via the web is likely to be one-third of the cost of ordering via a toll-free phone call (the cheapest alternative), and again, the larger the site, the lower the cost.

@   The cost of providing customer support and information via the web works out at only one-tenth of the cost of providing telephone support.

@   The cost of an email works out at about one-tenth of the cost of a fax and one-thousandth of the cost of paper mail.

In all of these things there are economies of scale, but consider the figures as reasonable guidelines. Now consider the fact that we have dealt with four of the most common business transactions: presenting information (marketing and many other things), placing an order, providing customer support, and communicating generally. This is the force of automation in action, moving the goal posts.

What have we missed?

Actually, we have missed two things, the invoice and actual payment. Here the situation is slightly more complex. Most invoices are sent by post. The switch to email has not taken place yet, even though it could have. The sticking points are that electronic information does not currently have the same legal validity as paper information, and that many recipients would like their invoices in a form that is recognizable by software so that they can process them automatically. These points will not stick for long and we shall be able to add invoicing to the above list. When we do, we will be able to claim that electronic invoicing is one-tenth or perhaps even one-hundredth of the cost of paper invoicing.

The same will happen with payments once electronic money becomes prevalent. Currently, credit card and charge card companies take a significant percentage of every transaction that they process from the vendor. This can be anything up to 5 percent, even higher in some areas of the world. This percentage will fall. The credit card companies themselves could cannibalize their own businesses by introducing electronic money—a scenario that is hard to envisage—but if not, they will be driven from the market by leaner and meaner competitors. In any event, the cost of making a payment and the speed with which it can happen will fall.

Just as it has proved valid to rethink businesses based on the use of the telephone, as has been done with telephone banking and telephone insurance where business costs have been cut considerably, so it is sensible to rethink business based on the use of the internet. Indeed, it is far more sensible. What the telephone banking revolution has taught is that we need to think in terms of *processes*, especially the customer's processes.

Nowadays, the value of a business is the value of its processes. This, more than the software or the website or the expertise of the staff, is where the true intellectual property lies. The company that can automate an important and expensive end-to-end process successfully, and owns the capability that automates this, can outsource every single aspect of the process. This is similar to Nike's outsourcing everything it does except the management of its brand. The company is then in a position to reapply the process to other areas of activity. Consider Amazon.com. Barnesandnoble.com is an online bookshop, but Amazon.com is something different—it is an online retail process.

It may have been the realization of this fact that prompted Jeff Bezos of Amazon to protect the company's one-click sales mechanism. The fact that this patent was upheld by legal action against Barnesandnoble.com is a bizarre legal result (possibly with damaging consequences for the electronic economy), but the desire of Amazon, and indeed other eretailers such as Priceline, to lodge business process patents indicates that they are not just retailers with websites.

NEW KIDS ON THE BLOCK

Those who have run internet businesses nearly always offer the same advice to those who are contemplating doing so: *just jump in the water and see what happens*. This is the best advice you will get.

I can illustrate this by an example from my own experience. In March 1999, Bloor Research launched a website based on a new business model. The idea was simply to provide IT executives with informed analytical comment on technology news for free and to sell IT analysis on the back of this. No other IT analyst was doing this. In the long run, it was hoped (and is still expected) to provide interactive IT research through the web. The business model involved building a revenue stream based on advertising and sponsorship, primarily from IT vendors.

The website created was IT-Director.com. It was not intended to be a large website but to cater for a select group of UK IT executives. We hired an editor and assigned one IT analyst to the site daily to comment on the news and manage what we hoped would become a select community. Our goal was to get the 1,000 top IT executives visiting the site on average once a week by the end of the year. This is a very valuable community with a collective buying power of over $20 billion, and thus it would definitely attract sponsors to our site.

A wonderful thing about the internet is that it is very measurable, and from the moment we set the site up, we could and did measure its usage. It attracted many IT executives, and we had 300 of our target group register with us within three months, moving us rapidly toward our initial target of 1,000. However, we quickly discovered that the number of IT executives was quickly dwarfed by the number of other visitors. Within three months, we were getting 5,000 visitors to the site per day, on weekdays, and the curve was upward. Only 1 percent of these were IT executives.

This put us in a quandary, because when we looked at where the traffic was coming from, only 20 percent was from the UK, another 20 percent came from elsewhere in Europe, and 10 percent or so from Asia, but 50 percent was from the US. Additionally, many people who were not part of our target audience were trying to register: software developers, project leaders, accountants, software sales people, marketing executives, and so on. The traffic caused technical problems. We had to upgrade our internet connection, and eventually we farmed out the whole site to an ISP.

We realized that the original business idea needed to be changed. We set up another website—IT-Analysis.com, aimed at catering for a wider audience—and began to try to split the traffic between the two sites. We also discovered that our content ideas had been wrong. Some of the articles we put up never interested the general population of site visitors. Humor and competitions worked well. Long articles don't work well, no matter what the content, as the typical internet user has a short attention span and prefers to read from paper than from the screen.

The community was far more active that we had ever expected, but rather than discuss technical matter with the analysts, site visitors wanted to give their comments on the news. Some news stories were attracting as many as 20 comments. We could see from user behavior which stories attracted attention and which did not. We realized that the site was rapidly turning into some kind of web-based magazine. But it is a different kind of magazine, because you know exactly which customers read which stories. Paper magazines have never known that. The magazine industry believes that roughly 10 percent of a magazine is read, but it only has a rough rather than a precise idea of which articles are popular.

We began to speculate about what a web magazine really is and whether it naturally involves interaction. If you are getting the impression from this that an internet business invents itself, then that is exactly right. That is why you have to "jump in the water and see what happens." The initial business plan you have for the web is probably wrong, but the correct one will start to emerge, if you manage to attract the traffic and relate to it.

And so the web has brought into existence some distinctly new kinds of business. While most of these can be depicted as electronic forms of an existing business, in reality they are not the same. You could look at some of them as distorted versions of bricks-and-mortar businesses, but the opposite view is equally valid. The older businesses are inefficient and distorted versions of the new reality, and some of these new kids on the block have no real parallel in the old world. We can classify the precocious new kids as follows:

@ portals;
@ commercial communities;
@ information subscription;
@ webcasting and narrowcasting;
@ software merchandising;
@ games and recreation;
@ pure advertising;
@ electronic market makers and information brokers;
@ supply chain enablers;
@ merchandisers;
@ pure ebusinesses.

Naturally, there is overlap within these categories. There are merely intended to present a spectrum of the new business models that currently exist on the web.

Portals

Rather like Chicago's O'Hare airport, a portal is a starting-off point for going somewhere else, or possibly an intermediate point in a journey. It gives you connections, but is also a reasonably good place to set up a shop to grab passing trade. The websites dubbed portals are really ISPs and search engines.

The main ISP portal is AOL. AOL customers log on to AOL rather than the web and may spend a great deal of time in AOL's network before venturing out on to the web. Consequently, they are likely to view the web from an AOL perspective, following links that AOL provides. Microsoft's MSN is similar. Subscribers are paying for the added value of the web experience as well as the internet connection.

Search engine sites are also jumping-off points, and most web users tend to remain loyal to a specific site simply through familiarity. Most of the search engine portals have pursued the line of adding more and more content to encourage users to return. Yahoo! was the first to encourage users to customize their access to a portal site by creating their own home page (MyYahoo!). It is the most popular search engine site, although Excite, Infoseek, Lycos, AltaVista, and others see massive traffic. New portal sites come on to the web all the time, but few achieve high volume. In 1999 we began to see the appearance of vertical portals (IT-Director.com is such a site), which attempt to act as a portal to a specific community or vertical market.

Initially, almost every type of business on the net wants to partner with the popular portals and the search sites have scooped up high volumes of advertising revenue. In fact, most of the advertising revenue for the whole of the internet is spread across a small number of sites. Figures from the Internet Advertising Board (IAB) indicate that about 75 percent of revenues go to the top 10 publishers, while the other 50 gather more than 90 percent of the total. These sites also provide sponsored links via high-priced annual deals. However, such linkages have not met the expectations of some of the sponsors. Charles Schwab and Fidelity, for example, decided not to renew their contracts with AOL for 1999. Most of the portals try to be "all things to all people," although they have special-interest channels that focus on niche interests. The revenue streams for ISPs include subscriptions, but all other portals make their money almost entirely from advertising.

The future commercial strategy of the portals is likely to involve providing the access device and offering more personalized capability (such as email, messaging software, and other applications). Their business goal is, of necessity, to retain users and grow the user base.

Commercial communities

Community sites can be portals of a kind. They are starting-off points or gathering points for small or large groups of web users who have something in common. Communities can arise around hobbies, professions, health problems, politics, and just about anything that might cause people to get together. They are driven by the dynamics of publish–subscribe and naturally grow in value geometrically according to Metcalfe's law.

The essence of community sites is normally the provision of some kind of MUD to allow the exchange of useful information, and possibly the provision of "experts" who participate in the MUD. Thus it is possible to set up virtual businesses based on a community: the travel community, the car-buying community, the PC-using community, and so on. Motley Fool is a popular electronic forum for stock investors. WebMD, already mentioned, is a specialist health portal. Warner Brothers has built an entertainment portal called Entertaindom, and *Rolling Stone* magazine has a site called Tunes.com, which is a music portal.

Any collection of web users with something in common could be said to form a community, so it is possible to think in the opposite direction and try to add a community to a website that is attracting visitors. Content-based web businesses such as AOL naturally acquire the nature of a community. The same can be said for some publishing sites, such as ZDNet.

The largest web community is Geocities, recently acquired by Yahoo!, which mimicked the form of a city. Geocities dates back to 1992 when founder David Bohnett put a web camera at the intersection of Hollywood and Vine and transmitted to a web page what the "eye on the street" saw. From there the site grew, almost spontaneously, into 40 different "neighborhoods," or interest areas, and acquired a membership of over two million "homesteaders." Geocities provides all subscribers with an email address and a home page, so in reality it is an ISP of a kind.

Another community site with a geographic twist is Planet Direct. Some of the pages it displays contain personalized information, created from the customer's zipcode. It customizes weather reports, provides driving directions and customized maps, and even provides local content.

A very recent community business idea comes from eCircles.com: allowing people to build communities around group calendars, gift lists, and photo albums. The eCircles.com site lets a community, probably a small group such as a family, share files and lists such as favorite movies, books, music, or whatever. These lists can then link to retail sites for buying gifts. The eCircles commercial idea is to get a commission on sales made through the links.

Information subscription

The idea of paying a subscription for access to a website has not been met with much enthusiasm, for reasons that will be discussed in Chapter 8. However, some successful sites do exist that charge users a subscription and some newspaper sites charge for access to their archives. The *Wall Street Journal* offers one of the few examples of a newspaper publisher providing a successful subscription-based service—but it is, after all, high quality and specialized.

Quote.com charges subscription fees for active investors wanting instant access to financial analysis, news, and research. The site offers time-delayed quotes for nothing. Auto-By-Tel provides car dealers with the names of web surfers who have checked in at www.autobytel.com and decided to buy at the "no-haggle" price it lists, for a monthly subscription fee of between $250 and $1,500.

At the moment most news services are free and there are many news sites, from television news services such as CNN and ABC to newspapers. There is also a wealth of sports news and comment sites, including the immensely successful ESPN Sportszone. All of this is supported by advertising revenue.

Webcasting and narrowcasting

Webcasting involves pushing information, possibly via email or via a bespoke delivery capability, rather than waiting for subscriber access. Thus tailored collections of web pages, news updates, advertisements, newsletters, images, sound, and video can be pushed to a particular audience or even a single person. TV and radio broadcasting is a one-size-fits-all approach to content, but the net can cater for much smaller groups than even a niche TV channel or magazine.

The process involves some kind of customer participation, either selecting content from a menu or filling out a profile and letting the provider decide. The webcaster's software monitors websites on your behalf, and sends information at the frequency you specify. One such service is InfoBeat, which will deliver a personalized version of the day's news to you via email. You provide a news profile and it customizes the news for you. Currently, the leading company in this market is PointCast, which has fairly sophisticated software for downloading content. The service is free for subscribers and paid for by advertising. Webcasting has the virtue that the provider does not necessarily need to create any of the content, it merely sends out the content that others create.

The main problems with webcasting are that it can appear intrusive and it presumes that the customer has the appropriate computer resources for the information sent, whether by email or by download. In its early days, PointCast was banned from a number of corporate computer networks simply because of the network traffic it created. Every webcasting company has to deal with the fact that it may also be barred by a corporate firewall.

Software merchandising

Probably the best-established web-based business is the sale of software. This started at about the same time as the internet was born and, because software is an electronic object like music and video, it provides a clue to the way in which these markets will also develop.

Software is the dream product for the web because the sales channel and the delivery mechanism are the same and they both significantly reduce the cost of sale for the vendor. Unless software products are very large indeed, it is possible to buy them directly over the web and it is often possible to try them out first for a limited period before committing to purchase. This is the way that Netscape originally established its browser customer base, and it is how Linux is now becoming popular.

There is a wild confusion of products out there with a far greater choice available than can be viewed by visiting a computer store or leafing through a computer magazine. This is made even more confusing by the existence of freeware, which costs nothing, and shareware, which is often very inexpensive, with the author only asking for a small financial contribution. Both types of product naturally create concerns about support, although all software except the very expensive products now seems to offer poor support.

There is no helpful classification system, as far as we are aware, to help resolve problems such as which software is compatible with other software and exactly what functionality software actually has. Thus there is a strong element of "suck it and see" in web software purchase. Increasing volumes of software are being sold via this route, not just direct from software vendors but also from specialist sites such as Software.net and Egghead.com. Customers are clearly happy to buy from an intermediary if the site provides ease of use and good classification of products. Such sites act a bit like insurance brokerages—they help you to determine what to buy. The top software sales site, Egghead.com, appears regularly among the top 10 shopping sites.

As the problems of music piracy and video piracy are addressed and bandwidth increases, the same channel will be used to sell music and videos. A similar industry structure is likely to emerge, with direct sales from producer sites and broker-assisted sales from specialist sites.

Games and recreation

According to a study by +Plan in 1998, about 13 percent of internet users between 54 and 65, and nearly a third of 18–24-year-olds, go online to play games. This is as we should expect and these figures would be much higher if they included gambling sites and the whole gamut of entertainment sites, from filmstar fan clubs through to porn sites. There is an extraordinary wealth of recreational activities, such as visits to the Red Dragon Inn where great fun can be had playing out a medieval fantasy, or the various fantasy sports sites where you can participate in fantasy sports team management.

The games software business is undergoing a slow transformation from individual "human versus machine" games to multiplayer network-based games involving "human versus human" or "team versus team." There are internet-based gaming sites, such as The Total Entertainment Network and Internet Gaming Zone, where you can stage multiplayer games such as Doom, and it has long been possible to play chess or bridge over the net. Yahoo! has a particularly active games zone for these types of game. There are also community games sites, such as GameSpot and Fastest Game News, which have the flavor of web magazines.

The popularity of "adult" sites on the internet is legendary, but it is difficult to know exactly how great that popularity is and how much revenue the adult sites are making. The problem is compounded by the fact that the whole subject of pornography on the web is a political hot potato and awash with misinformation. According to SearchTerms.com, "sex" is usually the most searched-for word in any given month and the top hundred most searched for words are littered with sex-related terms. There are also unconfirmed rumors that a housewife who provides a comprehensive list of all the adult entertainment sites on her home page is earning six figures in advertising dollars every month. Thus, it should follow that some of the most visited internet sites are of an adult nature. The published internet statistics do not show this, however— the highest rating for a porn site in June 1999 was Porncity.net, which ranked only 43rd in the Media Metrix monthly ratings with less than 8 percent of the traffic of AOL, the number one site in that month.

The possibility of community games, games where many thousands of players take part, has yet to be explored in depth and is an unprecedented capability that the web enables. There have, however, been experiments with crowd behavior. In 1990, Loren Carpenter had a crowd of 5,000 attendees at a computer graphics conference jointly operate a flight simulator. The experiment was carried out in an auditorium with each member of the crowd having a network-connected joystick and members of the crowd able to shout to each other. The 5,000 were almost able to behave "as one" once the crowd learned how to coordinate. Carpenter repeated the experiment five years later with a more sophisticated 3D submarine simulation. The outcome was the same.

The only attempt at a mass internet game was the game of chess organized by MSN in July 1999 between Gary Kasparov and the rest of the world. In theory, millions could have participated against the brilliant Russian, with the rest of the world's moves being orchestrated by a group of bright young chess players so that the collective intelligence of the crowd was raised. Chess is not ideal for this kind of environment and we can expect more sophisticated games to emerge once the commercial potential of this idea is recognized.

Pure advertising

Many of the business models for internet businesses depend on advertising and some sites exist purely as advertising sites. One that is very popular is

Mypoints.com. This site awards you points when you go on to the internet, which can be redeemed for merchandise or even exchanged for frequent-flyer miles. Naturally, the points awarded depend on your buying behavior in respect of the various MyPoints sponsors, of which there are many.

The site www.treeloot.com promises to reward you for subjecting yourself to adverts. What it actually does is present you with a game where you can win money by clicking on the right part of a "money tree." You improve your chances of winning by looking at the adverts and by providing personal details—in effect making yourself more available to adverts. Although I have only found a single site with this business model, the idea will undoubtedly be copied and improved on. These sites are analogous to the few magazines like *Exchange & Mart* in the UK that consist entirely of adverts.

Electronic market makers and information brokers

Websites that allow web users to compare prices could be classified as market-making sites or information brokers. This classification would apply to any site that connects buyers with sellers, however much they do to assist in the sales process. We have already mentioned Compare.net, BottomDollar, the shopping search engine, and SmartShip, which provides competitive shipping prices between courier companies. We can add to the list the Global Recycling Network (GRN), an electronic market aimed at helping businesses find possible trading partners for the sale of recyclable goods, and electronic auctions such as OnSale and eBay. At Jango.com or Shopfind.com, you can type in the product you want and robot shopping software searches the internet on your behalf for product reviews and low-price offers. More in the style of a brokerage, there is BizBuySell, which will assist in the sale of businesses anywhere in the US. The most comprehensive market-making operation is Buy IT OnLine, which allows customers to search over 30,000 online stores.

Job hunting is particularly active with information-broking activities. America's Job Bank shows details of about half a million jobs and is a partnership between the US Department of Labor and state-run employment services. Excite provides an impressive service partnering with Monster Board, a company that seek out jobs using a search agent and delivers details to the job hunter via email. Some sites such as Headhunter.net allow you to post resumés, while others such as Career Mosaic provide extensive information on salaries and the jobs market in general.

Software company Oracle is marketing software that enables a "buyer auction," which works by buyers specifying the goods or services they wish to purchase and soliciting bids from online suppliers. The software is part of an Oracle product, Oracle Exchange, that is aimed at the emerging software rental market, and levies a transaction charge. There is also a shopping engine from Inktomi that finds vendors for you and looks to referral fees for its revenue. As more sophisticated software emerges, the opportunities for information broking will increase.

Supply chain enablers

Just as physical supply chains include many companies that enable the movement of goods through the supply chain, so there are internet businesses based on the enablement of electronic commerce. This area is currently in its infancy since electronic watermarks, electronic money, and many other enablers for the electronic economy are not yet in common usage. However companies such 24/7 Media, Flycast, and others that distribute banner ads to websites can be counted in this category.

Also included here could be a whole series of software vendors that provide the infrastructure software of the electronic economy: companies that provide website design software, such as Net Objects and Altaire, companies that provide merchant software, such as Clear Commerce and Open Markets, and companies that provide the technology for secure internet transactions, such as Verisign and Certicom.

A company called Affinia offers an ecommerce-enabling service that can allow websites to look up, select, and sell products that match the interests of their audience. It has a large and growing database. Bigstep.com provides an enabling capability for small businesses that includes domain registration and the creation of an ecommerce capability. In the UK SCOOT, which also runs a directory, creates web pages for small businesses.

This category of businesses is set to explode, because it obviously grows at the same speed as ecommerce itself.

Merchandisers

Merchandising sites provide an opportunity to turn a merchandising opportunity, such as a sports team or a movie or a book, into an online shop, where it might not be feasible to open up a real shop, or even if it were, it would be impossible to address a worldwide audience with it. The extent to which merchandise can sell is often a surprise.

Apart from sports sites there are movie and television merchandising sites, which may not have as long a life as a sports-based site, but offer a greater amount of merchandise: toys, clothes, music, videos, and so on. Among many merchandising sites, there is *EON* magazine, which offers merchandise for various cult movies and shows such as *Star Wars*, *Star Trek*, and *The X Files*.

Many movies, especially the blockbusters, have individual websites. One of the best in the past few years has been Godzilla.com, which some have claimed to be a better production than the movie itself. It was a collaboration between Sony Interactive and Centropolis and offers video clips from the film, a fan club chat room, and a Shockwave game, but will also sell you T-shirts, toys, watches, and the usual marketing items. It is worth a visit before it is retired—if it ever is.

This raises an interesting point. Websites can persist forever and once they have been created, there is little point in removing them as the cost of maintaining a static website is very low. While at the moment there are websites for movies, in the future the movie will probably *be* the website, initially available only for a high fee, but with the price falling over time. The act of merchandising will become far more coherent and easier to control.

Pure ebusinesses

We can classify pure ebusinesses as being identical to pre-web businesses in terms of what is sold, but quite different in implementation. They are reinventions of non-online businesses. The most obvious examples are eretail websites like Amazon.com, CDNow, or Moviecritic.com, where the initial success has been for a specific niche. Webvan.com provides an interesting example because it carries a more varied set of products, even if they can all be classified as groceries.

Also interesting is the metamorphosis through which Amazon.com has passed. It began as an innovative bookseller with a distinct focus. It allowed the customer to browse through selections of books, look at reviews from other Amazon customers, and post reviews of books that they had read. Authors could also post reviews and customers were alerted to new books on their favorite subjects by email. Amazon is still best known for books and continues to invest heavily in that business, but it has also diversified.

Amazon made a foray into auctions, investing heavily in advertising in an attempt to challenge eBay's dominance. However, this initiative visibly failed against the sheer momentum of eBay, indicating, among other things, that there is a limit to how far Amazon can extent its operation and use its brand. Following this setback, Amazon extended its reach again, but with greater success. It invented a scheme called zShops, which allows other retailers or manufacturers to sell product through Amazon. The zShop partners are rated by customers for the service they provide and this helps to control its quality. It is worth nothing, however, that at the time of writing Amazon is only profitable in book sales.

In normal retail, the distinction between types of retail outlet is based on the buying experience and so bookshops do not carry many things other than books—CDs perhaps, and maybe some videos. This was the direction in which Amazon went initially, adding a CD and video retail capability, and it has since added toys, electronics, home improvements, and greetings cards. Amazon is now becoming more of a virtual general store, selling many items but offering a different buying experience for each. What all the items seem to have in common at the moment is that they are physically small and can be transported in the same way. In physical retail outlets the constraining factor is the physical nature of the goods, whereas on the web it is the logistics of delivery.

Stock trading has made the most rapid transformation of all to becoming an internet-based industry. While Charles Schwab has been very successful in moving on to the net, new virtual brokerages such as E*Trade and Datek have also grown rapidly. Their general business approach is to offer low commission rates and free add-on information services. One virtual broker, Suretrade, provides 100 free real-time quotes per day, an investor information service (called Digital Investor), five financial wires (from WiseWire), earnings estimates (from Zacks), stock, bond, FX, and sector analysis (from Briefing.com), breaking news (from Reuters), fundamental, technical, and earnings estimate analysis on over 7,500 stocks (from Baseline), free stock charts, and other information.

A similar approach in providing useful information to the customer has been taken by Microsoft with its HomeAdvisor real-estate site. HomeAdvisor pulls together information from many different sources: demographic information and crime statistics so you can check on the community, educational information so you can investigate the schools, and mortgage information so you can check out the rates. It also provides a good search capability so you can look for houses in a given price range or with specific numbers of bedrooms and so on. You also get what any customer would expect: descriptions and photographs of the houses that are for sale.

We could continue to provide examples from almost any sector. These are the easiest of the new internet businesses to understand because their business model is very similar to the equivalent businesses they threaten. In particular, the prices are generally lower and the value they add in informational terms is much higher.

THE VIRTUAL TAILORS

In the UK, the Social Services are responsible for looking after older people, and one of the services they provide is "Meals on Wheels." This is there to ensure that those who are too old to be able to shop have shopping done for them and those who have difficulty in cooking have regular hot meals. In Isleworth, on the western fringes of London, some of the local elderly population complained that social workers spent all the time shopping and no time chatting to them. Clearly, many of these older people were in need of more social contact.

The local office of the Social Services contacted Tesco, a large supermarket chain, to arrange a delivery service so that the wishes of the elderly could be met. Tesco decided to respond to this request and to do so via the web. The service now covers the whole London area and is spreading across the country. This, strangely enough, is how electronic shopping began with Tesco, not by a management-generated initiative to get on to the web, but by customer responsiveness.

Organizations seem to go through cycles of caring about their customers. They usually achieve success with a degree of customer focus, but growth creates a disconnection with the customer. This is re-established at a later time through a customer care campaign and then perhaps falls into disrepair. A simple economic imperative operates: Too little care and you lose business, but too much customer focus can be expensive. Most organizations are selfish and they care for customers only because they need to. Despite that, the primary rule of the electronic economy is that the customer is a subscriber. Customer loyalty will depend to some extent on the level of customization of products and services, and active managing of relationships.

Many commentators have suggested that the web will lead to mass customization of products and services, and some have even claimed that mass customization will supplant mass production as the base model for manufacturing. This may or may not happen, but the force of automation is certainly creating the possibility. It would not be a surprising development and there are many examples to support the supposed trend.

There is McGraw-Hill's Primis Publishing site, where academics can build their own textbooks, chapter by chapter, selecting from 12,000 different documents containing 150,000 pages spanning 20 disciplines. And both Hallmark and American Greetings are experiencing fast growth in the customized greetings card market. You can get electronic greetings cards to send by email or you can simply have them posted for you. There are also customized cars. Car manufacturers such as General Motors, with the Saturn, and BMW have web services that allow visitors to design their dream car, with custom colors, leathers, wood inlays, and even appliances such as refrigerators. The design is then forwarded to local dealers for ordering.

InterActive Custom Clothes offers made-to-measure jeans that give customers a choice of style, fit, and fabrics from the sublime to the ridiculous and all points in between. Customers can also choose the color of rivets and pocket labels to create a unique personalized product. Currently costs range from $65 for denim up to $250 for silk velvet jeans. ICC feeds the customer's 11 measurements into a computer program that generates the pattern and passes it to an industrial cutter that cuts the cloth. Similarly, Squash-Blossom provides a design studio for children's clothes that it will make to order, although the manufacturing is not automated.

Marshall Industries, silicon chip suppliers, probably offers the best example of customization. It allows customers to use an electronic design center to review technical specs, simulate chip designs by downloading and modifying code, and then testing it on a "virtual chip." Customers can analyze the performance and order a batch if they want.

Customized manufacture has some advantages over traditional mass production, although these are not so large that traditional manufacturing will be eclipsed. The main advantage is that manufacturing is only done for products that have already been ordered. Thus there is no need to attempt to forecast demand for finished product, you need only forecast demand for the earlier phases of the manufacturing processes where there is some uncertainty. There is an overhead in the fact that the customer has to be provided with the means of making a choice, which may be as simple as selecting from a limited range or as complex as providing genuine design software. Clearly, it is possible to conceive of providing customers with genuine CAD/CAM capabilities and have them simply rent the factory, but it is unlikely that consumers would wish to do that. It is much more likely to appeal to businesses at various points in the value chain.

Apart from customizing products and services, organizations can seek to manage the relationship with customers from the moment they gaze into the "shop window" that the website represents. Internet customer relationships evolve or die just like every other kind of customer relationship. The customer's first visit to a website needs to be met in a polite but welcoming way. Further visits may extend the relationship. Permission may be sought for email details and correspondence encouraged. The potential or actual customer may be sent special offers. They may be invited into a customer MUD and interact with other customers, and so on.

The main goal beyond selling products or services is to educate customers in relevant aspects of the business and get them to participate in the value chain in a satisfying and enjoyable way. The fact that customers enjoy the relationship is backed up by surveys such as one by Forrester Research in 1998, reporting that 66 percent of sites adding customer chat capability (i.e., a MUD) get an increase in traffic. Collectively, the whole process creates customer loyalty that is very difficult to break and produces the strongest possible differentiation.

6

Of Markets and B@zaars

There are a gazillion things going on out there in restless cyberspace. People are buying airline tickets and booking hotel rooms. Consumers are hunting for bargains at electronic auctions. Business are buying computers and routers and selling their wares to the never-ending stream of consumers who flow through the electronic b@zaar. The wires are singing and pulses of light are flashing through fiberoptic cable across the planet. The world's new nervous system is alive with information.

As night falls on one latitude the bustling activity of the net begins to tail off, while at the opposite side of the earth where a new day is just a few hours old, PCs fire up and messages start to fly. The many millions of net users beat to a 24-hour rhythm, moving like a tide across the earth that flows in the hours beyond the dawn and ebbs at the edge of night. The electronic b@zaar never sleeps—to it, night and day are invisible. The world's economy is in motion and the electronic b@zaar is singing with activity.

This is a vision of the future, but it is very close to becoming a reality. The time of the paper economy is almost over and the dawn of the electronic economy is here. And by a strange coincidence, the electronic economy dawned at the same time as the new millennium.

The key to understanding all this is the trading model, a simple diagram on which we can model the pattern of the buy/sell transaction that is at the foundation of every kind of commerce.

THE REVOLUTION IN THE MARKET

"I'd rather have a market than a mill" is a saying that has its origins in the North of England and almost certainly dates back to the time that the Lancashire cotton industry began to decline. Sayings and aphorisms get repeated because they encapsulate something more relevant than a historical observation and this one is no different.

Every industry, indeed every supply chain, can be looked at in terms of the market and the mill. The mill is located at the start, along with the raw materials that make up the product, while the market stands at the end of the supply chain with the customer.

For hundreds of years the market has remained relatively unchanged. Of course, there have been technologies that assisted in the operation of the market: cash registers, charge cards, barcode readers, and so on. There have also been structural changes in some areas: the grocery business gradually became a supermarket business and then a hypermarket business. But on the whole, retailing, broking, and the running of exchanges have been strictly human activities governed primarily by paper information technology. There has never been an outright technology revolution that swept through the market in the way that the forces of automation and mass production swept through the manufacturing sector in the nineteenth and twentieth centuries. There was an industrial revolution but no retailing revolution.

There is now.

More than anything else, businesspeople want to know how the internet will affect their business. The reality is that it affects all sales transactions and thus, within a company, it affects the whole of procurement and the whole of sales and marketing. Because of this, no company can afford to ignore the internet. However, the organizations that need to be most concerned are those whose business is retailing. As we say, the revolution is in the market, and not at the mill.

It is important not be too simplistic about this, since retailing is not just about shops and stores. The main business of many companies is to add value to the sales transaction and many agency businesses exist throughout the economy—insurance agents, mortgage agents, ticket agents, and travel agents. There are the retail banks. There are wholesalers in various parts of every supply chain who are really specialist retailers.

Many companies may have elements of manufacturing activity in their operation even though their fundamental activity is to make a market. Some car showrooms, for example, will make alterations to a new car prior to delivery, perhaps fitting a navigation system or a more advanced sound system. There are also businesses that straddle the divide between the market and the mill. For instance, are Dell and Gateway manufacturers or retailers? Clearly, they are both. So is Cisco, the company that makes most of the routers and hubs that run the internet. It went from zero web revenues to a run rate of $9 billion dollars in 18 months. Bizarre as it may seem, it has been selling 10 times as much product over the web as the leading eretailer. It is obvious that this market revolution is affecting a vast number of companies.

Rethinking the market

When a business sets up a website, it does not hire a new salesperson, open up another shop, or find another distributor—it does something quite rare. *It sets up a completely new channel to market.* Most companies will not remember the last time they did that and most have never gone so blindly into anything as they are obliged to with the web. There are very few experts who understand the new channel. There is no standard work on marketing on the web that has any credibility, because right now, even the designers of the most successful websites are not convinced that they fully understand this channel.

However, one thing they will probably all agree on—on the web, you don't know your customer.

Businesses become successful by understanding what they are doing and finding ways of doing it profitably while satisfying their customer base. Established businesses will tell you that they have a good understanding of their customer, but they are wrong. What they have is a good understanding of their customer *in the context in which they currently deal with them.* When a business opens up a web channel, the customer's context changes and they suddenly become unknown.

An excellent illustration of this is provided by Peapod, the web supermarket whose original business model was simply to do your shopping for you and deliver it. It started without any bricks-and-mortar outlet of its own, obtaining its goods by visits to large supermarkets. Because of the nature of its operation, Peapod discovered some unexpected facts. It cannot guarantee that you get exactly what you select, so it has customers identify first and second choices of brands. Interestingly, it found that shoppers got their first choice only 70 percent of the time, a fact that a supermarket would never capture. Supermarkets had believed that they satisfied customer preferences about 95 percent of the time, but they were wildly wrong.

The fact that you don't know your customer was something that we at Bloor Research took a long time to learn. Like many other companies we set up a website, Bloor-research.com, which was little more than a marketing brochure and an order form. We sold some of our research reports through the website and presumed that we were doing fine, as the web was not our main channel. Then in 1997, we embarked on a program of research aimed at understanding the business realities of the web. At the conclusion of this research we did what we would normally have done, we published an industry report, under the title *eRoad*, in 1998. However, we also had a meeting of executives to discuss how we were going to recreate the business, because our research plainly indicated that our business model would not work on the web.

When we implemented our web-based business model through the website IT-Director.com, we quickly discovered that visitors to the site were behaving in unexpected ways. IT executives did not have much interest in some of the articles we posted on the site, but had a surprising interest in others. The reality was simply this: we thought we knew our customers and we did not. Nevertheless, what was good was that now we could know them much better than before and we could also provide them with the information they needed. When someone visits a website they leave a trace. If they register, you can identify them and see what they do. You can then customize your offering.

If we consider the evolution of customer familiarity with a website, it proceeds like this:

Customer has never heard of the website

You may well be an established retail chain with a well-recognized brand and your regular customer may use the internet regularly. Nevertheless, this does not mean that they have any idea that your website exists. If no effort is made to publicise the website, then this situation can persist indefinitely. If you open up a new channel, you have to advertise the channel. Strangely enough, some retail organizations have set up websites and made little attempt to advertise them.

Customer knows of the existence of the website

You may have a well-respected and widely recognized brand, but that brand is not established in the web channel until it is respected and widely recognized on the web. The only way to move your bricks-and-mortar customers on to your website is to advertise. Use web advertising or have a general billboard/radio/television push media campaign that advertises your website. There are many tactics for getting people to know, but however you do it, getting people to know is a necessity.

Customer visits the website

One very obvious difference between the bricks-and-mortar shop and the website is that on a website you know how many people passed through; you can count them. You also know when a customer returns, since the computer can identify them (in most instances). If you have a large number of customers who visit only once, you need to understand why. You need to map out what they did and monitor the level of "stick"—the percentage who return. If you have a low level of stick, then the website is badly designed in some way. This is the truth. You are not satisfying the customer.

Customer visits the website regularly

The customer may visit the website regularly but never buy. It is a common phenomenon that customers are too timid to use your site because they are not sure what will happen when they place an order. This was something that happened on the British Airways website. They noticed that customers would fill in details and get all the way to the point of buying, but then leave the site.

They dealt with this intelligently. They didn't know what the problem was, so they deployed some software that opened up a window in the browser on the page where customers typically abandoned the transaction. The window contained a message saying that BA staff would assist in helping to complete the order via a chat capability. This was a neat human touch and it was successful.

Customer buys from the website

Once the customer buys from the website you are, at last, in a position that is far closer to the bricks-and-mortar business context. Now you can gather the same type of information that you are used to gathering and analyze much of it in the usual manner. However, the customer will not necessarily return. The logistics of satisfying the order via the web channel may well be different and you may discover that you have problems in this area.

Customer buys from the website regularly

In reality, you don't have a customer until the customer uses your website as a matter of habit. When they want whatever it is you provide and use the web to get it, and they visit your site for this at least some of the time, then habit exists. Even so, you need to be ever mindful that the web is a new channel. We do not yet fully understand how people get habitual on this channel—indeed, we don't know if they get habitual at all. On the web, the competition is one click away and the opportunities to visit the competition are great. The web is alive with links, and search engines, and information. *There are no guaranteed methods for making the customer stick.*

There are nevertheless a number of techniques that should encourage some "customer stickiness."

It is clear that the revolution that is occurring in the marketplace means it is necessary to rethink utterly the different forms of sales transaction that have characterized the market to date. Before discussing the effects of the internet on these, I should like to explore each in detail.

The five types of sales transaction

Stuart Feldman, the Director of IBM's Institute for Advanced Commerce (IAC), would probably tell you that in reality brokerage, retail sales, auctions, and all other types of sales transaction are, in a way, different names applied to almost the same process. IAC research papers contain mathematical models of these fundamental processes and they are indeed remarkably similar. In effect, they are all negotiations that involve movement from a "negotiable deal," via messages passing between parties that modify possible price and terms until there is a final deal. Different forms of negotiation are used to satisfy different business objectives such as best price, a guaranteed sale, minimal collusion between competing parties, and so on.

The five types of sales transaction are as follows:

@   the negotiated deal
@   the brokered deal
@   the auction sale
@   the retail sale
@   the pure market sale.

Actually there is a sixth, tax, but we shall discuss this later rather than here, because it does not conform to the same model as the others.

The *negotiated deal* is where two or more parties negotiate both the price and the goods and services to be provided. A good example is the sale of airplanes or weapons, where each individual deal is complex and different. With such deals there may be a very large number of parties to the transaction, including subcontractors, independent consultants, financial enablers, and so on. These deals are normally competitive and each party or consortium that is tendering for the business may be offering a distinctly different deal. In such situations, simple comparisons can't be made and the decision to buy from one party rather than another depends on a multitude of factors.

A *brokered deal* may also be complex. The broker earns his fee by acting as an agent for either the buyer or the seller to enable the purchase or sale. In effect, the broker makes a market. This may involve finding buyers who can be sold to or sellers who can provide a particular product or service. It may involve providing information and helping to structure and simplify the deal. The term "broker," however, can be misleading and is sometimes used where the word "retailer" would be more appropriate. Insurance brokers, for example, are often nothing more than insurance retailers. They become brokers only when the insurance cover required is genuinely complex and they contribute to making a market, rather than simply passing on a standard product to a customer.

The negotiated deal and the brokered deal are characterized by the fact that the transaction does not take place in a well-defined market. The other three types of sale transaction all involve a structured market.

Auctions take place according to a clear set of rules for bidding and they are held in a public environment. They are labor intensive because they require the presence of a significant number of bidders as well as the auction staff, but the mechanism was and is extensively used in specific markets, from the sale of farm produce to the sale of expensive works of art. Internet auctions are far more efficient but just as highly structured. A specific feature of auctions is that the goods usually sell—failing to do so only if the seller places a reserve price on the item that is never reached by the bidders.

Negotiated, auctioned, and brokered sales are the norm in the business world for trades of large monetary value. Logic therefore suggests that these are the appropriate methods of arriving at a price when the transaction is complex or there are a relatively small number of buyers.

The *retail sale* is the most common form of sales transaction and takes place in a retail outlet that is specifically designed by the retailer to provoke customers into buying. Goods are displayed. There are special inducements and staff to help the customer to come to a purchasing decision. The retailer is making a market for the goods that are sold and customers normally come to the retail outlet with some interest in the goods that are on sale. With retailing, there is usually a notion that the product or service being sold has a "retail" price. This is in fact a reference price and will often be specified by the manufacturer, but the retailer may discount this price directly or offer general discounts for bulk purchase, and may even be prepared to bargain with the customer.

Retailing uses fixed prices because this involves a low transaction cost, although it does not prevent the buyer from "shopping around" for the best deal.

The *pure market* is only appropriate to pure "commodities," such as shares or raw cocoa or gold. Until they began to become electronic, pure markets were characterized by a trading floor and sales made by open outcry. In such markets, the goods on sale are of a standard, identifiable quality. Here supply and demand determine the movement of the price and product always sells.

Most pure markets also deal in futures and option contracts. These are mechanisms that allow individual buyers or sellers to avoid price volatility. With such contracts, the buyer can for example fix a price for a certain quantity of product for delivery at a future date, hedging against a severe price change taking place before the product is required. It is worth noting that a pure market sets the reference price for a commodity, from which all other prices derive. Naturally, some commodities such as coffee vary in quality and different qualities are sold at different prices, but the price at any given time is derived from the reference price on the commodity market.

These five, then, are the only ways in which sale transactions take place, although there can be a great deal of variety in each of these mechanisms. The problem for businesspeople—and it is a problem for every businessperson—is that the internet changes the efficiency of all five mechanisms.

Pause for a moment and consider this:

Whatever business you are in runs by virtue of sales and purchases taking place. These are the most fundamental of all business processes. Indeed, it could be said that all a business does is string together a whole series of such transactions according to a scheme that is aimed at making a profit or at least breaking even. Thus it is accurate to say that the internet changes everything, because the internet interferes with the efficiency and even the rationale of each one of these types of sale transaction.

Pulling customers with push

Electronic consumers meander from site to site leaving traces as they move through the web. With every click of the mouse, some organization out there learns something about the consumers' preferences or intentions. Every search engine can target individual users by dynamically posting an "appropriate" banner advertisement that relates to the word being searched for. For example, a software company that sells bamboo furniture can buy the word "bamboo" from a search engine for a week, a month, or longer. When anyone uses the word bamboo in the search engine, a banner advertisement will appear on the screen with a click-through to "bestbamboochairs.com," or whatever the website is called.

Websites can also form alliances. A consortium of websites assembled either as a set of content channels by the likes of AOL or Disney, or as a collaborative group, can, by the intelligent use of links and banner advertisements, escort the web user from site to site within the group without the web user realizing that their behavior is being traced. It is far more useful for the vendor to know as much as possible about a customer. A consortium can gather preference data with every click of the mouse without the web user being the least bit aware of it and target banner advertisements quite precisely—even tailor web pages to suit the customer. In reality, parts of the electronic highway already have dynamic billboards that are different for every driver who passes and phantom side roads that appear and disappear.

This is driven by "server technology" of various sorts. Companies such as NetGravity provide the software that serves up the banner ads, while companies like Vignette provide the software that recognizes the customer and serves up different pages according to various profiles. There is a growing software industry that deals with such dynamic customization and it is only in its infancy. NetGravity was the market pioneer in serving up banner ads and has by far the largest installed base of corporate clients. In order to support the sale of its technology, it has assembled a set of channel partners to assist in managing the deployment of advertisements. A whole series of agencies now exist to provide a service similar to the placing of advertisements on television and NetGravity attempts to serve up the "banner ad presentations" that they sell on to appropriate web pages that target specific types of web user.

Although it is difficult to predict, consumers may simply adjust to trading their personal attention (the distraction of banner advertisements) for services such as entertainment, time saved, or simply help in navigating the web.

This depends to a certain extent on the excellence of targeting, as consumers object less to well-targeted advertisements than to poorly targeted ones. They much prefer signal to noise. However, the evidence so far suggests that the consumer's ability to ignore banner ads improves with familiarity; but even so, well-thought-out banner campaigns do generate high response rates.

There have been calls for new laws that grant each of us "ownership" of all the transactional information generated as we move around the web—our information traces. If such laws existed it would mean that any interaction with advertisers would have to be explicit, so that we contracted to agree to be a customer for their advertising content. Such an arrangement is entirely feasible and would allow a separation between those who do not want advertisements pushed at them (and therefore might prefer to pay ecash for information) and those who would prefer to experience the advertising (and pay with their attention).

Interestingly enough, if we know the advertising rate (say 4 cents per click) and the probability of a well-targeted advertisement banner being used (say 10 percent of the time), then we know the kind of price that the consumer should pay for an advertisement-free page (in this example, 0.4 cents). Once microcharging becomes a reality, we may see technology that allows the user a choice. Either you have dynamic billboards on the highway or no billboards, but you pay a toll.

FORGET BRICKS AND MORTAR: CHOOSE AUCTIONS

By 1997, it was clear that something unexpected was happening on the web. Several auction sites had started up and had quickly become popular. By March 1998, Media Metrix was reporting that the most popular of these sites, eBay, was among the five most popular of all websites in terms of the total time spent at the site. In terms of the number of different users Amazon was the most popular eretail site, but in terms of time spent shopping it was eBay.

At eBay and other auction sites such as OnSale, you can auction anything you want and there are hundreds of thousands of items on sale on any given day: from toys to PCs, including collectible items such as stamps and coins. Auction formats vary, but in general there are fast auctions where the bidding is restricted to one hour and more leisurely ones that are spread over days. The seller can choose to allow bids according to the process of either a standard or a Dutch auction—where the seller opens with a high price and lowers it until a buyer is found—and weblinks are provided to connect potential buyers to information provided by the seller.

A variation of the auction idea is provided by Priceline, which deals in airline tickets and used cars. The process is simple: you bid a price and sellers have the choice of offering you a deal or ignoring you. Sellers can use this site to offload used cars and airline tickets that they simply have to dispose of within a given time. The attempt is to provide a bargain site, where the buyer could possibly pick up a transatlantic ticket for $20.

At the moment, the most common items sold at electronic auction are PCs, PC software, collectibles, books, music, and consumer electronics. A demographic study of eBay users in April 1999 by Nielsen/NetRatings indicated that there is a roughly even split between male and female (53/47) auction users and that people of all age ranges use auctions, with 25 percent of the total in the 35–44 age range. Similarly, there is a clustering among professionals on middle to high incomes. There is also a general belief, which is difficult to substantiate but probably correct, that the reason for the popularity of electronic auctions is that they are fun to take part in.

They are also efficient means of selling products and services. Bricks-and-mortar auctions have a very high transaction cost. Only one item can be sold at a time and in order to create the market you need to assemble a crowd of interested bidders in a single place. Electronic auctions are automated and can involve millions of bidders. Not only is the transaction cost much lower, but the whole mechanism is very efficient in its ability to arrive at a price that balances supply with demand.

Make no mistake, electronic auctions have become big business. Market leader eBay has moved very quickly to try to outdistance the competition. In early 1999, it acquired the San Francisco-based Butterfield & Butterfield, an established traditional auction house, for $260 million in an attempt to go upmarket, into the area of high-value items. In July 1999, eBay launched its own purpose-built browser based on Microsoft's Internet Explorer. This browser includes an Auction Tracker that tracks the auctions in progress and keeps the customer informed of their status, and an Auction Archive that allows the user to store records of their auction activity. This constitutes one of the first moves by a web business to offer specialization on their website by providing users with a device (a soft device in this instance) in a way that locks out competition, and it will undoubtedly spawn imitations.

The success of internet auctions did not remain a secret for long. A whole host of auction sites have now emerged. Sites with different sales models, such as Amazon.com and Lastminute.com, added auctions to their offerings. Amazon demonstrated how serious it was about this when it entered into a joint venture with the world's most renowned auction house, Sotheby's, paying approximately $55 million for a stake. The value that Sotheby's brings, apart from an impressive brand, is its expertise in authenticating valuable items. The joint website, Sothebys.amazon.com, sells valuable memorabilia, toys, stamps, and other collectibles.

Specialist auction sites have emerged, such as Micro Exchange, Computershopper.com and C-NET, all of which specialize in the auctioning of computers and electronic equipment, and AdAuction.com, which auctions advertising space. This example provides a clue to the attraction of auctions as a selling mechanism. If the population of bidders is large enough, then an auction is a highly efficient way of arriving at a fair price for specific goods or services. However, if the goods or services for sale are perishable, then the auction mechanism is even more attractive because it avoids the situation where something remains unsold and valueless. Adverts, airline tickets, tickets to shows and other events are all very perishable items and it may well be that eventually all such items will be sold by auction, or at least put into an auction as their sell-by date draws close.

The auction market has three segments: consumer to consumer, business to consumer, and business to business. However, these are not well-defined segments. The consumer-to-consumer segment is the most popular, driven by the entertaining nature of the bidding experience. It is dominated by eBay, but includes OnSale and many other sites. These provide the consumer with the ability to dispose of goods that are no longer required, and for collectors of stamps, coins, comics, and other collectibles to make a market. This segment includes sites like Million Dollar Auctions, which only deals in highly expensive collectibles.

Even though these sites are structured to enable consumer-to-consumer transactions, businesses sell goods through them because they can, and because they get an acceptable price. In the business-to-consumer market there are sites such as Bid.com and uBid. Priceline also falls into this category, dealing in hotel reservations and financial products as well as the airline tickets and used cars already mentioned.

In the business-to-business area we have Manheim Auctions, which helps businesses to buy and sell cars, Leasend.com for industrial equipment, and specialist sites such as AdAuction.com.

The new informed buyer

Negotiated deals will still be appropriate for many transactions, but because of the internet the buyer will inevitably be better informed than previously. In many negotiated deals the buyer is at a disadvantage, because the seller carries out sale negotiations all the time and the buyer does not. The internet interferes with such situations by allowing the buyer to get all the information they need.

Goodbye to brokers

It is well recognized that many broking activities disappear once an industry moves to the internet, simply because many broking activities depend on information that is freely available on the web. This is particularly obvious with stockbrokers, who traditionally have been trusted providers of investment advice and managers of small share portfolios. The role has not disappeared yet, but it has clearly diminished.

If we consider retailing, then it is clear that this becomes distinctly different on the web. With price search engines such as BottomDollar, which not only searches retail sites but also auctions, and sites such as Buyers Zone, which provides consumer reports on a variety of business items for small businesses, the retailer's ability to be flexible with pricing is diminished and in some instances destroyed.

Finally, although this has not yet happened, it is easy to foresee some items eventually being sold in pure markets that were previously retailed. It is highly likely, for example, that this will happen with the sale of airline tickets and similar perishable items.

The natural conclusion here is that all the basic transactions of every business are now in flux. Everyone's business model changes. There are no exceptions.

REARRANGING THE LINKS IN THE SUPPLY CHAIN

The internet is also revolutionizing the way that supply chains *within* organizations are put together.

The integration of most organizations' supply chains through the web can be represented by Figure 9. Websites naturally become interface points between departments in an organization, between organizations, and between the organization and the customer.

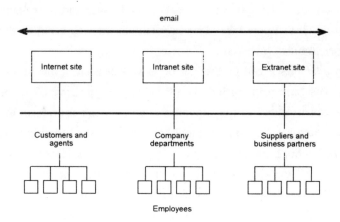

Figure 9 The supply chain, with websites

The computer world has different words for three different types of website:

@   Intranet site: a website that exists internally within the corporate computer network.

@   Extranet site: an external website set up to enable interactions between companies in the supply chain.

@ Internet site: the website as most people understand it. Usually presenting a capability directly to the customer.

Technologically there is little difference between the three, the words simply
describe different kinds of accessibility. An *intranet* site allows employees and
departments to provide access to, or "publish," useful information to smooth
the workings of the organization. Personnel information, departmental policies
and guidelines, and corporate procedures can all be usefully published.
Providing access to work-in-progress information is probably the best use of
such websites.

An *extranet* site allows customer/supplier/third party interaction. Such
links are often implemented as "closed user groups" so that only specific users
in specific organizations have access. Clearly, the publication of supply chain
information is what this is all about and this will usually consist of up-to-date
pricing, stock information, and work in progress. This kind of activity was previously described as EDI (electronic data interchange) and took place on private networks. It can now take place privately on the web using standard web
technologies at much lower cost.

An *internet* site can be thought of as an extension of an extranet site to
include the customer, with much of the site being generally available to the public.

If email is added to the capability a website can provide in any of the
above roles, then a flat communications capability is established not just within
an organization but throughout a whole supply chain. It is clear from looking at
Figure 9 that all the elements it shows, from customers through to suppliers,
form part of a loosely knit, networked organization. The intranet site shown is
clearly under the ownership of the company that is represented, but the internet
and extranet sites clearly *need* to be "cooperative sites," as they act as interfaces
between the company and the outside world. They are publish–subscribe hubs.

Looking at the supply chain in a different way, as illustrated in Figure
10, it is made up of set of employees who are involved in coordinating their
activities so that a product or service is made available to customers. Some of
the employees may be grouped into departments, such as sales, distribution,
manufacture, and so on, therefore if we assemble together a sensible collection
of departments and employees then we may have a viable company.

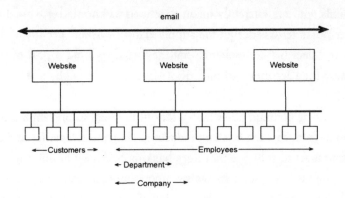

Figure 10 The supply chain compressed

The interesting question is: "If we could remake our supply chain, would we assemble it in the way that it is currently formed?" The answer is almost certainly no.

Why is the supply chain reforming?

Most organizations contain inefficient departments that are not economic, in the sense that the same function could be outsourced to the market and carried out by a specialist company that would provide better value. These departments are subsidised by the efforts of more efficient areas of the company. The publish–subscribe mechanisms gradually expose these departments to competition.

The general evolution of computer technology also makes it feasible to provide outsourced services via the web. This begins with price search engines and aggregators and comparison sites that guide you to the best prices for goods, but it may end with full outsourcing of the personnel function and accounting and software development, in a way that implies no loss of control. The level of outsourcing is set to increase, whether in the area of manufacture or distribution or software development.

Analysis of a supply chain from a functional point of view would find employees who worked alone, employees who worked in teams, and a number of natural shallow hierarchies that functioned as a unit. It would also reveal the fact that companies appear to have "condensed" around specialists—

individuals who are currently being described as knowledge workers. Thus it becomes possible to redesign the supply chain by asking groups of these individuals to select the components that they need to build a part of the supply chain and then let them go and do it. In fact, they might just go and do it anyway.

There is nothing, other than a lack of funding, to prevent a set of knowledge workers in, say, the banking industry from joining together and creating a bank from a set of software that does banking and a set of outsourced services that are already available. In reality, many internet start-ups are exactly like that. Middle managers with a knowledge of computing see the future, then go off and create it.

How the coming of the ASP takes us to another level

What does a specific examination of the supply chain of computer products, particularly software, reveal? After all, the computer industry foisted on us most of the technology that is reforming and rebuilding the supply chains of the world. Is it taking its own medicine?

Consider the business of the internet service provider (ISP). The ISP is really a "new age telco." Its customers access it directly through the telephone network or via a direct line, and it provides access to the internet. All large ISPs, whether in North America, Europe, or the Far East, have a direct connection to some point of the fast fiberoptic trunk circuits that are currently the physical foundation of the internet.

As a group, the ISPs and telcos (telecommunications companies) are waging a war to keep the internet functioning. There have been some high-profile glitches in the last few years as the internet sprinted past its own point of inflection. In 1997, AOL's network almost ground to a halt as a result of its drive for subscribers and the following year it spent $1 billion on network upgrades in an attempt to diminish the defection rate caused by its decline in service. In 1998, Californian telephone users began to have problems getting lines. In 1999, the volume of data on the world's telephone networks overtook the telephone traffic, having grown by a factor of 10 in a few years, and it will probably continue to grow at a similar rate for the next decade.

Even the best-constructed national telephone networks were only built to cater for one in fifteen of their customers being active at the same time, but the internet promotes much longer calls, so the ratios that were assumed in building the telephone networks are no longer valid. The only safe assumption now is that a permanent high-bandwidth connection will eventually be required for every user—all users will eventually have a line open all the time, as most well-connected organizations already do.

Most early ISPs were created in the first wave of the internet gold rush in the US. They were little more than local exchanges or networks of exchanges providing a specialized, fixed-fee service for internet access, also charging for storage capacity on the local server. Many of the consumer-oriented ones were squeezed out when the ISP giant AOL emerged and Microsoft also began to compete aggressively in this market. However, according to an estimate by ZD Market Intelligence in December 1998, there were then still more than 6,000 local ISPs serving 13 million consumers in the US. More recent figures from The List (thelist.internet.com) indicate a number in the region of 8,500 worldwide but a much reduced population in the US, with the site itself, which provides an ISP selection capability, listing fewer than 300 US ISPs.

In the UK the whole market suddenly took a bizarre turn in early 2000 as a price war broke out. The battle for customers had been primarily between AOL and Freeserve. Although Freeserve was ostensibly free, it was not so at all, as you still had to pay the phone bill and suffer the adverts. AOL had launched its counter punch complete with television ad campaign for internet access at £9.99 per month plus 1p per minute telephone charge, 24 hours a day (this is the UK off-peak tariff). Then AltaVista threw the cat in among the pigeons by announcing a scheme to charge users a one-off fee of £30–50 and an annual fee of £10–20 in return for unmetered internet access. This was not just an intelligent move, it was a PR coup as it got the company on to the television news, the best possible advert.

Competition was now very hot. Excite.co.uk announced plans to launch a similarly charged service before the end of the year. Freeserve immediately fell into line, saying that it would launch a "low-cost" unmetered service, but not announcing when or at what price—probably because it did not have time to invent a scheme, it just had to respond. Enter cable operator NTL, guns blazing, offering free and unmetered internet access, the only condition being that users switch to its cable TV/phone service and spend £9.25 per month. Cheap had suddenly got cheaper and Freeserve shares fell by nearly 20 percent.

That was only the beginning of a story that is continuing to unfold. Various ISPs have offered a whole series of inducements to attract custom, including free PCs and even shares (for the eventual IPO). It looks very strange, especially as different deals are being offered in different geographic areas, but all that is really happening is that vendors are bundling in an attempt to lock customers in. The sources of revenue are subscriptions, the sale of access devices, call charges, and web advertising. The marketing model is bundling, offering some elements for free while you make revenue on the rest.

New capabilities are soon to be available and this will undoubtedly confuse the situation even more. Internet telephony (also referred to as "voice over IP") will soon be here and when it arrives the telcos will have to watch helplessly while a huge revenue stream goes missing. It now looks as though this will take off in an unexpected way via chat software. Already, over 80 million people are registered through a chat software product (mostly via AOL's Instant Messenger or ICQ, a free software product that AOL acquired in 1998). This allows people to type messages and send them to each other in real time if they are logged on to the internet. Once telephony is added, the chat network transforms into a telephone network at local call rates, and the long-distance call becomes a thing of the past.

In addition to this, we are now watching the triumph of wireless technology over fixed lines, which began with the proliferation of mobile phones but has spilled over into the founding of wireless ISPs and the proliferation of wireless LANs (local area networks). Mobile phones are now available that offer primitive internet access via WAP (the Wireless Application Protocol), but we shall soon see this becoming more sophisticated and offering a further challenge to the established telco empires. Nokia has already announced that in 2001 it will no longer be selling mobile phones that don't support WAP. Ericsson and Motorola, the other two giants in the mobile market, will probably follow suit. As mobile phone users tend to buy new devices every two years at worst, we shall soon have a full population of mobile phones with internet access. The number of mobile phone users is actually greater than the number of internet users, and the two growth curves have the same shape. All of this indicates that the mobile phone will become the dominant internet access device. As a natural consequence, WAP devices will grow in sophistication and eventually decimate the PC market.

For many years, pundits predicted that remarkable things would happen when the communications industry and the computer industry converged. That is what we are witnessing. These are the days of miracle and wonder. The oft-repeated mantra of Sun Microsystems that "the network is the computer" is becoming a reality, except that it is the internet that is the computer. We have so far characterized ISPs as telcos, and indeed that is what they are for the most part, but they are soon to become major computing operations. The ISPs are about to become ASPs in a move that will begin to collapse the whole computer product supply chain.

An application service provider (ASP) is a company that runs software for you, similar in some ways to the computer bureau of the past, but the whole service is online. Outsourcing and facilities management companies like EDS and CSC could claim to be in the ASP business already, and so could most of the telcos that manage networks on behalf of large customers. However, there is a new set of start-ups that are targeting this business directly.

In mid-1999, Oracle began to promote a service called NetLedger, an ASP-based accounting solution for firms of 1 to 50 staff. The software rental price was quoted at less than $5 per month for up to 1,000 transactions—half a cent per transaction. For the small business, this could mean no need to install or maintain the application on a PC, concurrent access over the internet for as many users as needed, and an ability to access the application from any location.

Other companies with wider offerings include CORIO, Telecomputing, and USi. Such companies aim to enable organizations to outsource much more of the running of their software, possibly even to the point where an organization buys all its computer capability off the wire. There is even a company, PCTVnet, that provides set-top boxes under the HomePilot brand and makes Windows-based applications available to the home. HomePilot also offers home automation, alarm services, and remote metering via the TV, and is available across Europe and North America.

At the time of writing this market is just approaching its point of inflection and is set to take off. When it does the ISPs will quickly join the fray. ISPs are already ASPs, in the sense that many of them allow you to put up websites that they run on your behalf. But they could do much more and in the near future they will. They will start to run most of the applications on which the electronic economy depends.

THE TRADING MODEL

The trading model, the last of the four hinges, is a simple model of the buy–sell transaction and the supply chain that this chapter has been analyzing (see Figure 11).

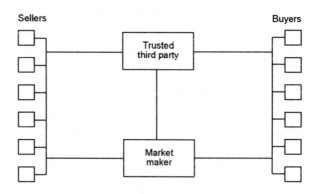

Figure 11 The trading model

The simple model in the diagram can be used to represent every one of the five types of sale transaction identified in this chapter, and more besides.

The model is an accurate depiction of a *pure market*. The lines simply represent information channels. In a pure market, all of the lines are fully open and carry information. The market maker is the organization that creates the market and enables buyers and sellers to trade. There are many such organizations trading pure commodities of different kinds including stocks and bonds: Chicago Mercantile Exchange, NYMEX, NYSE, London Stock Exchange, and so on. There are usually a number of trusted third parties involved in any pure market. These are the organizations that facilitate the market but have no bias in favor of buyers or sellers. In futures markets they are brokers and financial organizations. In physical commodity markets they are organizations that test the quality of commodities, or brokers that arrange for chartering or insurance, or indeed the insurers themselves. Such organizations are parties to the sale. The buyers and sellers are, as Figure 11 suggests, able to be well informed. They can freely pass information to each other through the market.

If we now consider an *auction*, it is really an open market and the same realities apply. There are well-informed buyers and sellers, there is a market maker, and there are trusted third parties. Under this heading we must also consider the reverse auction, where the seller bids rather than the buyer. The mechanism simply involves the buyer sending out requests for proposals, as an airline that is considering buying some new airplanes might do. However, in the case of a reverse auction, the request is well defined and the business goes to the lowest bidder from among the sellers. The reverse auction is likely to become a frequently used mechanism in the business-to-business market as a quick and efficient mode of procurement.

The operation of auctions on the internet has not yet matured and there have been a number of complaints, particularly by buyers who were dissatisfied with the goods they received. It is the function of trusted third parties to ensure confidence by preventing such outcomes. In a pure market, this can be done by testing for product quality where appropriate, or by holding financial deposits. Similar mechanisms are clearly required for internet auctions. At the moment, it is possible for buyers to protect themselves to some extent by taking out insurance. A tailor-made policy, BidSafe, is available from Auction Universe for $19.95 and offers protection of up to $3,000 against auction scams. It is worth noting that attempts to rig auctions usually involve attempts to distort the flow of information, but the web makes this more difficult.

When we consider the *brokered deal*, it becomes clear that the broker occupies the position of market maker, trying to bring buyers and sellers together. The broker usually also involves other parties (trusted third parties) to enable the deal. Problems with partiality often occur in brokered deals, as in many instances the seller pays the broker, who may then be inclined to act in the interests of the seller and deny useful information to the buyer. The web diminishes the likelihood of this and often completely automates the broking activity.

Search engines, particularly price search engines, are market-making brokers. An interesting example of this is the facility on the BottomDollar site to search through auction sites.

Let us now consider *retailing*. This is a form of market making, but the retailer usually limits the number of sellers because of the cost of stock. Additionally, retail outlets are geographically fixed and thus can only attract a particular subset of the actual number of potential buyers. Nevertheless, we see the same structure emerge of multiple buyers, multiple sellers, the market maker, and trusted third parties (credit card companies, insurers, couriers, etc.), all enabling the sale. With retailing we tend to move away from "commodity product" toward differentiated product. Retailers provide a service by offering choice and service, and manufacturers of goods cooperate by differentiating by design, functionality, and price.

When we represent the *negotiated deal* on the diagram of the trading model, many of the lines of communication are cut. The buyer normally tries to slip into the position of market maker by entering into multiple negotiations and passing information between these discussions. However, the seller also tries to take this central position and control the information available to the buyer. There are many variants of what can happen and, as with other types of sale transaction, there can be one or more third parties to the deal—financiers, distributors, consultants, and so forth.

Publish–subscribe in the electronic b@zaar

Every market is, fundamentally, a publish–subscribe operation. No matter what practical structure it takes, the sellers publish and the buyers choose whether or not to subscribe. How do publish–subscribe mechanisms affect the trading model?

eMail

The email mechanism enables every participant in the market to send information quickly to every other participant. It is a particularly useful mechanism for establishing informal links and it enables cheap and efficient one-to-many communications. It is already extensively used to encourage individuals into specific markets.

The website

A website, or possibly several websites together, forms the structure of the market where the sales occur. The information that trusted third parties provide or the services they provide can be provided through other websites.

The search

Because of its wide coverage of the universe of information, the search mechanism, more than any other, ensures that all the players in a market can be well informed. This has the effect of destroying all business models that depend on the relative ignorance of the buyer.

The MUD or community

The MUD reinforces the effect of the search, as it enables new and useful relationships to be formed between individuals with a common interest. This in turn leads to a more efficient and faster flow of information.

If all of these mechanisms are taken together, we can see the effect of the hockey stick curve, namely that the four phases of market saturation—pioneers, early majority, late majority, and laggards—compressed together at the start of the curve. On the internet, the publish–subscribe mechanisms massively increase the "word-of-mouth" effect. If there is a good deal available, it gets noticed.

Once the pioneers have had their day and a market begins to take off, the early and late majorities are quickly pulled in, followed by the deeply conservative laggards. But the decline in costs supported by market expansion then starts to pull in economic buyers—and all the time the population of the web is itself expanding.

This is, of course, why Jeff Bezos of Amazon does not care about profits at all (at the time of writing this book, but perhaps not for much longer). He only cares about bringing as many people into the Amazon market as possible, and he has relentlessly pursued the model of expanding the number of buyers and sellers as fast as possible with a huge investment in marketing—currently running at $200 million per annum. It is hard to argue with this strategy.

Before moving on, let us apply the market model to an economy as a whole. The buyers and sellers are made up of all organizations and citizens of a nation. The market consists of the aggregation of all the markets within the national economy. It is immediately clear that the trusted third parties consist of all those organizations that fall within the category of government and government institutions. This includes the central banks, but also the institutions of law that play a role in determining what behavior is and is not permitted within the economy.

If we tried to represent the global economy, then we could draw a trading diagram for each nation and represent in some way the movement of products between each national market. However, it is immediately evident that the publish–subscribe mechanisms are not at all confined within a national zone, but spread themselves freely between all the citizens and organizations that are connected together in cyberspace. Consider what this means: It means that in the electronic b@zaar, the trusted third parties of the national economies have a limited mandate.

The game of software leapfrog

According to received wisdom, the internet "disintermediates intermediaries." It doesn't. It automates the activity of intermediaries, and thus it will destroy many intermediaries whose business depends on the bricks-and-mortar-based business processes of the paper economy. At the same time, the internet also creates completely new intermediaries, most of whom are market makers. Such intermediaries spot opportunities that have newly come into existence due to the force of automation. In many instances, the opportunity is created simply because of the number of potential buyers and sellers connected to the internet.

A good example is provided by the National Transportation Exchange in the US, which helps road haulage firms with unsold capacity on a particular route to find a shipper who needs to send something along the same route. The haulage firm and the shipper could not easily have connected with each other prior to such a web-based service, because the logistics would have been impossible or they simply would not have known of each other. NTE finds appropriate loads, ensures that the loads are compatible, and helps to resolves other issues such as scheduling. It claims that unused transport capacity adds up to about $31 billion in lost revenue for the trucking industry. This kind of operation does not disintermediate anyone: what it does is make a market where one previously did not exist. What it also does is make some business processes economic that were not previously viable.

Another example is NextMonet, which launched a web art gallery in 1999, offering original contemporary art by lesser-known artists. The site targets affluent couples and individuals who are buying and furnishing a new home. The website features the works of 200 artists and is supported by art news and information. It intended to have works from 750 artists worldwide by the end of that year and, of course, it will sell to a global audience. NextMonet is establishing a "second-tier market"—an international market for relatively low-priced contemporary art.

Another form of intermediary is the arbitrageur. Arbitrageurs find inefficiencies in specific markets and even them out. For example, there is a distinct relationship between the price of shares in goldmining companies and the price of gold. If the price of gold falls, then the shares lose value because the goldmines inevitably make less profit. However, sometimes share prices rise or fall under the general impulse of the market, and goldmining shares may move with the market rather than with the price of gold. If this happens, then arbitrageurs take advantage of the disparity by selling gold and buying gold shares, or vice versa.

This is a very strange way to make a living, because arbitrage opportunities never persist for long. The first time that a price disparity is noticed an arbitrageur may make a killing, but simply by the act of buying and selling he or she may alert other players in the market to the opportunity that has been discovered. The next time the same situation arises, it is the first player to place a transaction who gets the profit. After a while, the market automatically compensates and the arbitrage opportunities never resurface.

One example of this kind of activity is provided by a website called Accompany. What it does is seek out bulk discount opportunities and attempt to assemble enough customers to make up the numbers that earn the discount. It then places a bulk order and arranges for delivery of the goods. Accompany is arbitraging between the single-unit price and the discount price. The differences can be surprisingly high. With electronic goods such as new computers and digital cameras, Accompany has achieved discounts of up to 50 percent.

Search engines such as BottomDollar that try to seek out the lowest prices are also performing an arbitrage function. By directing buyers toward the lowest prices, they are naturally forcing other prices down. Clearly, it is possible to automate arbitrage activity using software, and many large banks and financial institutions have software that seeks out opportunities in the financial markets and capitalizes on them. Nice work if you can get it.

What is clear from the trading model is that retailing situations on the internet will suddenly be transformed into informal electronic markets, and then organizations will begin to write arbitrage software to utilize the markets more efficiently. General-purpose software that performs shopping functions has already been produced by Inktomi, the company whose software runs the search engines for a number of sites, including Yahoo!. Inktomi's Shopping Engine works by providing a local software agent to analyze the products offered for sale on various websites and store information in a central database. Once sufficient information has been gathered, customers can state the products they are seeking and the features they require, and search the database for possible matches. They can then extend the comparison by looking at additional features and prices. The Shopping Engine will also integrate with the Inktomi Search Engine to provide a seamless search-and-shop service.

Inktomi also has a Directory Engine, which uses artificial intelligence techniques to categorize web documents. It employs neural algorithms that can be trained to identify relevant documents and web pages and categorize them according to a classification scheme, which could be customized to a specific set of requirements—such as to seek out specific types of arbitrage opportunities. This Directory Engine also integrates with the Search Engine and Shopping Engine.

Inktomi is by no means the only player in this game, it is simply one of the most visible, and its business model is to build useful software rather than trying to sniff out arbitrage opportunities to exploit. Naturally, other players will have quite different agendas and objectives and are destined to play a game of software leapfrog, as a whole business area emerges that tugs retail websites in the direction of pure markets. For instance, the retail strategy of loss leading—selling a specific product at a loss-making price to attract customers who may buy other products—may not be viable soon, because the outcome of such a strategy may simply be that price robots bring thousands of customers who buy that product from you, but nothing else! The problem of setting a price may become too complicated to be done by anything other than software that surveys the state of other prices on the web.

It is not difficult to imagine companies employing R&D teams whose sole target is the creation of mathematical pricing algorithms, or deploying data-mining software to analyze vast amounts of pricing information in a dynamic manner, or buying the fastest and most powerful machines and communication capabilities to ensure that their orders are placed ahead of anyone else. You could no longer think in terms of customer–retailer. In the electronic b@zaar, you would have to think in terms of customer–arbitrageur–speculator–retailer.

7

eConstructing the Enterprise

There will always be sunrise industries, just as there will always be industries disappearing with the sunset. As we transformed agriculture, so we transformed mining, drilling for oil, manufacturing, transportation, distribution, and so on. History provides many examples of how the economy has shifted. Strange as it may seem, in the 1950s two of the 10 biggest companies in America were meat packers, utilizing the railroad and refrigeration technology to build healthy revenues. Their time has passed and the economy has moved on.

The internet is introducing a massive wave of automation that is going to destroy jobs and destroy businesses. At the same time, it is going to create jobs and businesses at a rapid rate. In all probability it will be an "even sum game." What it takes away with one hand it will give back with the other. However, this can be of no comfort to the businessperson who sees the efforts of a lifetime vanish in a few short years.

If you are in business, let me summarize the situation for you. Your fixed assets, your computer systems, the skills of your staff, the value of your brand, your channels to market, and your competitive position are all in a state of flux. In reality, all of your assets are probably declining in value, possibly at a frightening rate. Also, unless you are in an extraordinarily lucky minority, the barriers to entry into your market are falling. If it has not already happened, then you are soon going to be facing competition that does not suffer from some of the handicaps that the emergence of the electronic economy has placed on you.

There is great danger—but there is also great opportunity. In this chapter we explore what can be done. Much of the advice we will be offering derives directly from the experience of the management team at Bloor Research, who pushed the company through the kind of transformation that is being discussed here.

PICKING UP THE GAUNTLET

The gauntlet thrown down to the CEO and the entrepreneur is the challenge to survive and thrive in the new business environment. In our travels down the eroad we have, as promised in the first chapter, repeatedly encountered a number of factors. Let us now revisit these factors with the benefit of the four hinges and, hopefully, a deeper knowledge of the internet.

Information freedom and globalization increase

Ignorance has died and been laid to rest. The publish–subscribe mechanisms are responsible. As a simple fact, the customer can now know just about everything it is possible to know about a particular product or service. Any business strategy based on keeping information from the customer is now fraught with danger. The opposite strategy is probably a better choice—to behave in a completely transparent manner and enable the customer to be as informed as possible. Information circulation has also become worldwide, which is leading to greater globalization.

Customers for most goods and services can now be considered to exist globally—if not, this is only because the delivery of goods or services to some areas of the world causes insuperable logistic problems. With global customers you are subject to global pricing. You are also subject to laws of which you may not even be aware. Consumer laws vary significantly from one country to another and so do customer expectations. This naturally suggests the need to partner across geographic boundaries or to establish in foreign territories in order to exploit those markets.

The challenge is to transform your business so that it is truly open, in terms of information flow, and is also truly global.

The internet creates more efficient markets

The trading model provides a template for the information flows in a market. The four publish–subscribe mechanisms create or repair information channels in the market, and hence they have the power to change the buy/sell transaction. In many cases, they will mitigate in favor of an auction operation or a pure market operation. The electronic economy turns inefficient markets into efficient markets by this means. Normal retailing is thus undermined for many products and services, particularly those that can be accurately graded for quality. Arbitrage will become a fact of life in the electronic economy. Nowhere will artificially high prices be sustainable.

In order to try to combat the action of the publish–subscribe mechanisms, some websites have chosen to bar access to the robots that obtain comparison prices. This is foolish, as it amounts to turning customers away. You cannot make the world conform to the way that you'd like to do business. For some manufacturers the route to market, the channels themselves, will be rebuilt. For some retail chains, the bricks-and-mortar retail stores will suddenly become a wasting asset that is destined to turn into a liability. This can only be deeply disconcerting for a business that once had to build new stores in order to grow.

The challenge is to re-evaluate the buy/sell transactions of your business, determine how they will alter, and remake your business around the realities of the new economy. This may involve very significant change.

Possibilities for customization increase

Any study of the pure market reveals very quickly that it can be brutal. Auctions are the same. Farm produce, for example, is mostly sold in pure markets or at auction. As we have already mentioned, our poor farmer may have a good harvest and find the price falls to a point where he loses money. The next year he may have a poor harvest and also lose money, even though the price is high. Therefore, most producers avoid such markets and do so by differentiating their product. They may manufacture a mass product, but their particular one has distinct features and the consumer cannot buy another product quite like it. This naturally leads toward customization as the obvious counter to efficient markets.

The first and most obvious strategy is to customize the price according to some mechanism acceptable to the customer. Loyalty schemes of various sorts will flourish on the internet because of this need. However, customization must and will go much further than that. The best defense against a pure market or auction-driven market is a hugely collaborative relationship with the customer.

The challenge is to remake the relationship with the customer, which in turn will almost certainly involve redesigning the product or service provided.

Transaction costs fall

The internet is bringing lower transaction costs and this will have a wide-ranging effect. In order to get a complete picture, we need to think of the whole supply chain. As we saw in Chapter 6, a supply chain is a "value chain" consisting of an aggregation of transactions, each of which adds value to the end product or service. While the price of the end product may be falling, in reality what is falling is the cost of each subtransaction that ultimately leads to the whole transaction.

The cost of most fundamental business transactions is falling and the cost of two more (invoicing and payment) are set to fall in the near future. This is the force of automation in action, having an effect at the foundations of a business.

The fall in transaction costs can deliver great economies to a business, although inevitably most of them will have to be passed on along the value chain. However, these cost reductions can also suddenly open up new markets or generate new product possibilities. One of the remarkable consequences of the popularity of auctions is that secondhand items are being sold that would never otherwise be on sale. A new market has been created.

The challenge is to take advantage of lower transaction costs as fast as possible and to think creatively about the new business opportunities this opens up.

New entrants appear in established markets

The web is creating new entrants to many established markets, and no company, no matter how entrenched, is safe from this effect. Even Coca-Cola has to be concerned. Companies with available capital are likely to follow one of two quite valid strategies in the face of new competition. Either:

@ wait until a successful ebusiness develops in the same business sector and buy into it; or

@ set up a separate ebusiness to compete on equal terms with any competition that arises (as Barnes & Noble has done to compete with Amazon on books).

Both of these strategies presume a good level of IT capability and both are passive, in that they involve waiting for the competition to appear. In almost all markets where the technology of the web is able to make a difference, new entrants will emerge. In many instances they will be start-ups, but some may come from other sectors. In most cases they will be tough competition and a passive strategy may not be enough to combat them. It is entirely possible that a new competitor will ride a hockey stick curve that brings competition to your door faster than you would believe possible.

The challenge is to formulate a business strategy that cannot be outflanked by new entrants to the market.

The exploitation of information technology

Information technology is the main force of automation driving the electronic economy. There are many areas of its impact that are worthy of attention, but two very specific areas must be addressed: speed and the website.

Just as the cost of transactions is falling, so the speed of transactions is increasing. This alters customer expectations of speed of service on a continuing basis. In a world where "time is money," speed of service is a competitive advantage. Leveraging information technology to improve the speed of service is, of necessity, an on-going effort.

Now consider the website as an information artifact. A market always has a context. The competition in retailing, once it moved beyond price, used to be based on the layout and ambience of the retail outlet—the shopping experience, no matter whether it was a supermarket, a clothes shop, or a record store. Those areas of retail that move completely on to the web will now have to compete in the web shopping experience. Electronic retailing is driven completely by web design and software capability. If you travel the net and visit the websites that are successful and those that are not, you quickly realize that it is all about website design and marketing, and both have to be good.

The challenge is to become knowledgeable about the possibilities of information technology and find ways to leverage them.

Mergers and acquisitions proliferate

The final factor to consider is the inevitability of mergers and acquisitions. Sad though it is, many businesses will simply not survive. As they start to fail they will be acquired for asset stripping, if for no other reason. However, it is worth noting that the internet is a huge community and that doing business effectively on the internet usually involves partnerships.

The publish–subscribe mechanisms encourage close business-to-business relationships. Although many mergers and acquisitions will come about because of businesses failing, there will also be many that are strategic and based on collective asset value, in that "the whole is greater than the sum of the parts."

Taken together, the emergence of more efficient markets, the lowering of transaction costs, the higher level of automation, and the global market that the internet is bringing are going to increase the maximum "efficient size" of an organization. In other words, information technology will make it possible for an organization to be much larger in terms of number of customers or volume of product sold. Consider AOL or Yahoo!. Both have more visitors to their websites in a month than most countries have citizens. There will be many mergers and acquisitions that aim simply to achieve the "right mass" in order to be able to operate globally. All such mergers will demand a genuinely flexible IT capability.

The challenge is to take advantage of the nature of the internet by partnership and possibly by merger and acquisition.

It is possible for an old, established bricks-and-mortar business to have early and quick success on the internet. Whether it was meticulously planned or not, the UK's Prudential (an insurance and financial services company) did just about everything right in the launch of its ebusiness. Its choice of its new brand, Egg.com, was brilliant, although it may also have been provoked into choosing a new brand because the Prudential.com domain was already taken by the unrelated, and also very large, US insurer.

Instead of launching straight into the insurance market, where there was no indication that the take-up of internet insurance would happen quickly and where it would be forced to cannibalize its main line of business, the Prudential sprinted niftily into the banking world. It had never previously run a bank, but initially offered checking accounts, then savings accounts and a credit card. This turned out to be the most successful launch of a financial services product in the UK for years. In the space of about one year, it attracted 550,000 customers and £7.4 billion in deposits. Since then it has been adding products and expanding toward a full range of services, with loans, mortgages, travel insurance, and so on. It has also, as a matter of policy, been running at a loss, by offering unsustainable interest rates (for a limited period) in order to attract new customers. It has ridden a hockey stick curve from day one.

Egg.com is almost a textbook lesson in how to get in to ebusiness and it is being driven by one of the oldest and most conservative bricks-and-mortar companies in the UK.

The internet invokes the Darwinian imperative: It calls for the survival of the fittest. So the question is: How can you be fit? Every bricks-and-mortar business that wishes to survive must work to satisfy three situations:

@ It must be able to prosper in the current bricks-and-mortar market.
@ It must be prepared for and be able to prosper in the period of migration, as its sector of the economy becomes increasingly web based.
@ It must have a strategy for operating effectively on the web.

In Darwinian evolution, the fittest are defined by characteristics that make them successful within their environment. It is no different for businesses in the new economy. Success calls for a combination of business talent, management talent, web savvy, design talent, IT skills, and vision. The need has increased dramatically for business leaders to understand the possibilities and limitations of the technology and the medium—for most, this will be the deciding factor in their success.

TACTICS FOR THE REARGUARD ACTION

It is said that only the best generals are good at fighting a rearguard action. Unfortunately, a rearguard action may be exactly what many businesses will have to fight. The word "rearguard" expresses the essence of what is required. An army is retreating in disorder and some of its troops must fight a stalling action while it reforms to choose a new battleground. In order to fight a rearguard action, you may need to divide your forces.

Two basic strategies can be pursued:

@   *Metamorphosis*: The company stays as it is and its operation is transformed directly so that it becomes an internet company.
@   *Death and rebirth*: The company divides into two. One part is the new internet company—a child that may grow rapidly. The second part is the old company that pursues a bricks-and-mortar channel strategy, trying to make the best of a declining bricks-and-mortar business sector. The second part has several possible destinies. It may dominate a business sector that never truly goes to the internet, it may be absorbed in a merger with the new company, or it may die.

Choosing which strategy to pursue is not necessarily simple, but it does need to done fairly quickly. The first strategy is best if the internet is not bringing about a severe restructuring of your business or business sector. However, the "death and rebirth" strategy becomes necessary if the internet team suddenly finds itself being constrained by bricks-and-mortar considerations. The easiest way to determine which strategy to pursue is to appoint an internet team that reports at the highest level and see whether its existence starts to give rise to conflicts in pricing or investment decisions or other areas of basic company policy. If it does, then split before it's too late.

Barnes & Noble provides the example that matters here. Its bricks-and-mortar business was unable to coexist with its internet business, so it went for "death and rebirth." Both halves have survived, and maybe both of them will thrive.

Whichever strategy is pursued there is a branding debate to conduct: Is the established brand suitable for the web? Inventing and establishing a new brand is not a simple matter, although it may be fun. The old brand should be discarded only if it is fatally wounded. Paradoxically, the stronger a bricks-and-mortar brand is, the more damaged it may be as a potential web brand—the consumer knows the brand and probably attaches bricks-and-mortar associations to it.

Technically, this is a matter of brand equity: What exactly does the brand denote? If the brand is strongly associated with abstract features, such as quality, dependability, or trendiness, then there is no reason that it should not transfer. Such abstract brand equity is an asset and in that case the web is just another medium. However, brands that are strongly tied to the physical nature of the service or specifically to a product have more difficulty in transferring. In the metamorphosis scenario the brand should probably remain the same, but in the "death and rebirth" scenario it probably has to change, if for no other reason than to avoid confusion between the two arms of the operation.

Either way, an investment is required to establish the internet brand, whether it is new or not. This is no small matter. Adopt the view that your brand currently has no value at all on the web, no matter how big it is elsewhere. You have to create that value.

JFDI directives

There are a number of things you need to do now whatever the circumstances, if you wish to go from bricks and mortar to the web.

The reason for doing them is that you will not understand the internet unless you quickly become part of it. You may already have done many of them, but I shall list them all anyway, for those who have not. The main purpose of these JFDI directives is to educate the whole of your business about the web. You could do worse than buy every manager a copy of this book :-)—but implementing the JFDI directives is better still.

The term JFDI directive was given to me directly by the CEO of a medium-sized UK company called Hawes that specializes in neon signs and branding materials for supermarkets and gas station chains in Europe. He told me he had built his company with a management style that was genuinely consultative. Normally this worked well, ensuring maximum contribution and a stream of intelligent ideas from his team. However, on some occasions it prevented him from making progress because someone would disagree and be obstructive, or a team would simply be unable to reach a consensus on something. Under those circumstances, he told me, he would send a JFDI directive to all relevant staff, a memo with "JFDI" written on the top issuing a simple, unambiguous command to resolve the situation.

"What does JFDI stand for?" I asked him.

"Just Do It," he replied.

Here are some JFDI directives, with explanatory commentary. Treat them as such. The only excuse for not doing these things is that they have already been done.

Make sure everyone in the company who has a computer terminal or PC has browser access to the web

If your staff don't have web access and exploit it for work tasks, they will never understand or be able to contribute. Some banks and defense establishments will excuse themselves from this on security grounds. Security is no excuse—it can be dealt with. If necessary, put in a separate network for internet access.

Implement rules of usage and a system of monitoring web-based activity to ensure that staff don't waste time. The actual cost per member of staff is likely to be relatively low, even if some of them don't currently have devices that can access the internet. However, it is also important to prepare for the time when every member of staff will be using the internet to carry out some of their work, so the investment cannot be avoided.

Order all executives to surf the web on a daily basis, if for nothing else then for industry news. Then ask each to produce a summary note on the ways the company can use the internet. Even if you are the CEO, you must participate too

This has the same justification as the above, the only difference being that it is even more important. Even if your executives regularly surf the internet at home, they don't necessarily know what resources are available on the web to help them carry out their work more effectively.

Another interesting fact is that almost everyone interacts with the internet in a slightly different way. They go to different news sites, use different search engines, and follow different links. Thus different staff will usually come up with different ideas. Our experience at Bloor Research bears this out and we have evolved a culture where, if someone finds something "neat" on the web, they email everyone to tell them.

Implement a company intranet

An intranet consists of one or more internal company websites. Set one up. Encourage staff to use it to exchange information informally between departments. Ensure that some community (bulletin board) software is used so that staff interactions are visible. Apart from anything else, this will give the company a sense of community.

An intranet normally pays for itself very quickly simply because it removes information barriers. When intranets were first introduced, companies reported a very fast return on investment—for some, an ROI of over 100 percent within nine months. Nevertheless, the actual benefits can be difficult to quantify and are sometimes difficult to envisage ahead of time.

What tends to happen is that communication lags between departments or even between people are reduced, because it becomes a habit for information to be made available for anyone who wants to use it. Thus cost savings may emanate from simple things like not having to fill in a form to make a certain process happen, or not having to call someone up to check something out, or find someone's home phone number, or whatever. The presence of an intranet has the effect of oiling the company's processes. They go faster.

Another consequence is that an intranet prepares a company's staff for task of building web pages and makes them more familiar with the technologies of the internet.

Encourage the use of email for all external communications and business transactions where possible

eMail saves money, but also the "inbox" quickly becomes a genuine "intray." In reality, email is the foundation for an informal workflow system that smoothes the flow of work between employees and assists relationships with suppliers and customers.

Two mechanisms are required to smooth all these relationships, one "pull," the other "push"—the website/intranet and email. Staff need to become familiar with these because they are fundamental tools of the new economy. If relationships are complex enough, then setting up a MUD to help information flow within them may also be desirable.

Insist that the marketing department regularly monitors the web to find out about competition

You need to know where the internet-based competition is coming from and you need to be able to respond to it quickly. In addition, some excellent competitive information is available for almost every industry. For publicly quoted companies, websites such as Yahoo!, Stockmaster, and Company Sleuth can provide you with an instant view of any competitor and a reliable supply of news about them. Search engines can also trawl up useful information.

However, there is a more important point beyond this. You need to closely watch your competitors' websites and the leading sites on the web to keep abreast of ideas that you may wish to use in your business. Consider this: For most businesses the web will become the main channel for all external relationships and particularly for sales. You need to become familiar with how it can enable processes and with what works. Even greater is the need to understand what is working for your competitors.

Insist that all staff whose jobs involve procurement use the web for that task, or at least regularly check the prices of web-based goods and services

This is going to save you money. As we have already noted prices are lower on the web, and this is as true in the business-to-business market as it is in the consumer market. The job of procurement can also be significantly helped by the wealth of information the web provides. It may throw up new suppliers you previously had never known of or thought to use.

If you have no website, set one up now and use it as a marketing channel and, if appropriate, establish an order-taking facility. Now implement software that monitors site usage

It is the last point here that is important. You need to understand the difference that being able to monitor a website makes to your understanding of the business you are in.

At Bloor Research, for example, the initial idea behind IT-Director.com was that it would be a "magazine site." We posted news stories and added analyst comment to them. By monitoring the usage of the site, we quickly discovered which news stories attracted most attention. (For example, we discovered that stories with the word "sex" in the headline and those using "internet tax" were equally popular, but neither was as popular as a story with the word "Linux" in it.) Such knowledge is highly valuable. It helps in framing editorial policy and can be used to attract visitors to the site. More detailed analysis can help to identify the type of visitor and allow for better targeting of advertising. You can only understand the power of being able to monitor web behavior by doing it.

JFDI...

The above set of steps don't constitute a web strategy. They are simple steps that everybody should take and that the company should enforce in order to bathe itself in the web. The odds are that they will pay for themselves very quickly, so they are not likely to constitute a significant cost. If you don't have the home-grown expertise to make them happen fast, then hire a consultancy that does.

THE VISION THING

Every company needs to be trying to implement a vision for its internet project. A clear long-term goal is required to support the short-term activity.

It can be difficult to set your vision in the right direction and there have been some significant blunders. For instance, in the early days of the web a number of companies, including MCI, IBM, and Barclays Bank, set up electronic shopping malls. This was an idea that occurred to many people and it was tried many times. The problem is that it does not work. Electronic malls have never succeeded in drawing large amounts of traffic, although they do attract some business.

Clearly the electronic mall is a wrong idea—but who would have known this ahead of time? Now we do know this, we can invent theories as to why it does not work very well, even though there is no denying that it sounds like a sensible idea.

It is fair to say that nobody understands the web and the collective behavior of the millions of individuals who use it. The only practical approach to finding out if a business idea works on the web is a scientific one: experiment. I know that doesn't sound very helpful and it would be good to be able to provide you with a simple formula—but there is none. However, the need for experimentation warns you against grandiose schemes.

The internet project is possibly the most important project that a company has participated in. It cannot be without a goal, but as the electronic mall experience shows, neither must it have too solid an objective—because that objective may well be quite wrong.

We know of several projects currently in progress where companies are investing millions of dollars to launch websites that we are convinced will not work. Of course we may be wrong, but nevertheless they are making the same mistake that destroys most unsuccessful computer projects: They are moving forward without first having prototyped. In this case, they have not prototyped the business idea and so are proceeding without any proof of concept.

It will usually be best to put the website up for a minimal investment to test the idea. Admittedly, there are some projects where this cannot be done, including Webvan's setting up of a US-wide supermarket chain. But even here, you start small with one automated warehouse and a web ordering system, and you change it as you learn. The entry ticket to that web idea just happens to cost a lot.

Thomson & Thomson provides a useful example of a company that was obliged to change its business plan quickly. It originally set up Namestake, a service that helped internet users research trademarks and domain names. It offered the basic information for free, charging a fee for more detailed reports. Namestake was well thought out. It provided information on close matches, domain names with slight variations in spelling or punctuation, as well as exact matches. It also offered visitors a variety of useful and free advice.

It was a very popular website, attracting large amounts of traffic, and web commentators recommended it. But the business idea never worked. Thomson & Thomson had two sites. Namestake was for free, but Saegis, its other site, offered a far more sophisticated subscription service aimed at intellectual-property lawyers willing to pay well for such valuable information. The idea was that Namestake would attract traffic to Saegis, but the opposite happened it: it attracted traffic away from Saegis. As a result, Thomson & Thomson shut down Namestake in early 1999.

Here is what I suggest for a vision.

Formulate a plan, and in it identify the following:

@ Your target community or communities. (Think of your customers as a community.)

@ Precisely what goods and/or services they are going to buy.

@ Your differentiators: a list of reasons the community will buy from you rather than the competition.

@ Your handicaps: reasons the competition may beat you.

@ Models: a list of websites to imitate.

The details of your plan have to include how you are going to test whether your differentiators work. However, the plan should still be a rough overview. If it occupies more than six pages of A4 it is probably too long. Now use the evaluative tools I have provided: the four hinges.

The hockey stick curve

Find out if any of your competition is on a hockey stick curve that has gone beyond the point of inflection. Avoid them as a matter of policy, unless you think you have enough funds to catch them (which means a lot of funds) or you have no option but to compete.

A hockey stick competitor has to be analyzed to pieces. To beat such a company head on, you have to innovate at an alarming rate. They have the audience and they will be watching you watching them. Every good idea you come up with they will copy quickly if they think it works. It is better to differentiate if you can so that you are not in their market but may be able to draw their audience away.

If you think you can own the hockey stick, then the reverse applies. Compete head on with all challengers.

The publish–subscribe mechanisms

The questions here relate to how you can leverage these mechanisms.

@   The website: list reasons for anyone in the target community to visit your site, invent new reasons, and develop the design of the site accordingly.

@   The email mechanism: formulate a strategy for maintaining an email relationship with members of the target community.

@   The search: formulate a strategy for appearing on relevant searches, probably by banner ads. Also provide your site with a search capability that works.

@   The community: formulate how to use a community bulletin board capability—allow complaints to be posted, perhaps?

The force of automation

There are a number of technical innovations that are going to hit the internet in time: integrated telephony, video, music on websites, and so on. Find out which ones, if any, might alter the way a web business in your market might function. Also consider the uncollected harvests, areas of your market where the business is not carried out because it is too expensive, but where the transaction cost is too high. What are the opportunities that nobody takes right now?

The trading model

Like it or not, you are making a market. Draw a diagram of the trading model and identify the true nature of your market. Identify how information flows. Imagine it operating as a pure market. Who would know more if that happened, and what would they know that would make a difference?

Assume that the information flows will happen and design your website to encourage them (restrictive strategies almost always fail on the web), even providing the information yourself. Now work out ways to differentiate yourself from your competition and plan to implement them. See how this affects the flow of information.

THE GROUNDPLAN OF THE STORE

A website is a shop or a market. If visitors are not buying something, they are simply costing money. If the site is advertising driven, then if the adverts are not working the visitors are costing you money. You may think your website is a whole environment of which visitors have a clear conception. It isn't and they don't.

Many passing visitors will not remember your website at all, never mind have any idea about how it is structured. Visitors may come and they may be exactly the kind you want and they may actually want to buy what you sell right now at the price you are selling it, but simply never get to the page that sells it. This may happen because of design faults or simply because when they came your site was busy and they got sick of waiting.

Visitors don't see a website, they see just another web page in their browser. They come, move around a bit, and go. Only after repeated visits do they ever think to explore your site. Most of your website is not a shop, it is a shop window. The shop is where they buy, the window draws them in.

When people design websites they don't think in these terms. They have got hold of some website software, they have visited a few sites they like, and they copy ideas. They build a home page and an "about us" series of pages, and a press releases page—and then they build the shop.

The largest multinational and the smallest retail outlet are exactly the same size on the web: the size of a browser window.

Success on the web is simple to describe:

@   People come to your site.

@   Your shop window attracts them into your shop.

@   The shopping experience is positive and they return.

Bringing people to your site is discussed in the next section. The other two steps are about web design. It is tempting to say that web design is everything, but it is not. The value you provide is what is most important—but web design is everything else.

Here are some general rules for web design:

Branding must be strong

Every page of the website must reflect your brand. Branding is not easy. A good URL helps. For example, Bloor Research's IT-Director.com works because it describes the target community. Good artistic design helps, but only by not putting people off.

One trend is the use of a graphic to brand the site. Some newspapers have traditionally had a graphic "trademark" next to the title, but most other companies have never used a detailed graphic for branding, preferring some kind of abstract design to go on the letterhead. But letterheads were for many years constrained by the cost of color printing, so an abstract design was a compromise that became a habit.

Websites worth visiting to look at the branding include TheRegister.co.uk, TheFool.com, and CompanySleuth.com. When we built IT-Director.com, we deliberately copied the style of The Motley Fool for the very reason that the branding was so strong.

Design for navigation

Imagine the customer entering your site and walking through it page by page as if walking up and down the aisles of a supermarket. Supermarkets are designed so you are given the best chance of buying everything you might need or want, but you can also just come in, get a few items, and leave. It is the same for websites that are well designed. Navigating through the site is easy to understand and easy to do. Most of the portal sites, Yahoo! in particular, are well designed for navigation.

Design for regular change

There is a balancing act to be pulled off. The web surfer is a creature of habit, but likes to be entertained or visually stimulated. You need to satisfy and leverage habitual behavior, but you also need to delight.

As a rule navigation should be habitual, and the general look and feel of the site need to be predictable for the sake of branding, but within these parameters regular change should be designed in. The only sites I am aware of that do this well are news and magazine sites, such as ZDnet or ESPN Sportszone.

Register your users

You need to know as much as possible about your customers—so ask them to register. Apart from anything else, you need their email addresses and you need their permission to email them. You also need as much information as possible about them so you can better serve their needs.

You may be able to gather a good deal of this information when a customer makes a purchase, and you certainly have the opportunity to ask for it (politely!). However, you also need information about those who don't buy; and not all sites are shops.

Visitors to your site should be rewarded for registration in some way. There has to be an incentive: a competition, perhaps, or a one-off discount entitlement. Once you have the information, use it—analyze it. Lastminute.com, for example, ran a highly successful registration campaign offering the possibility of an airplane flight for $1.50.

Site analysis is your feedback

I have strongly recommended already that site analysis be carried out in depth to get an idea of how visitors use your site. This analysis is the main input to future design. It tells you which ideas have worked and which have not. Abandon ideas that don't work quickly. They may have sounded good, but they weren't. Go with the traffic flow.

Use entertainment if appropriate

Any site can add some features for the sake of entertainment. If these don't jar with site users, they will be popular even if they have no direct relevance to the site.

On IT-Director.com we run competitions that are simple but generate amusing contributions from site users. The prize is not startling: a bottle of champagne. But the idea worked; much to my surprise, as I had expected it to fail. For example, we asked site users to suggest a collective noun for IT directors, publishing all entries as they were added. We only got about 30 entries, but the competition pages were visited thousands of times (the winning entry was "a budget excess") because many of the suggestions were amusing. Entertainment brings visitors to the site. Some will become customers.

A final word

You may be a company executive who believes that web design has nothing to do with you—it isn't your field. This is the same as an executive of a supermarket chain saying they don't care what their establishments look like or the kind of shopping experience customers have. In order to play in this game, you have to become an expert in website design.

You care. Believe me, you care.

THE IMPORTANCE OF DIFFERENTIATING YOURSELF

If competition is reduced to the single dimension of lowest price then, as in a knockout competition, there can only be one winner among a multitude of players. If markets were that simple, open competition would naturally lead to monopoly. They are not. Companies differentiate in order to distinguish themselves from the competition and they also raise barriers to direct competition wherever they can.

The problem that the internet creates for many companies is that a large number of fundamental barriers to competition have fallen. International trading and geographic distance were once massive barriers, but this is no longer the case. It was once possible to exploit the consumer's lack of knowledge and sell at a higher price than a well-informed market would permit. It was once possible to pay salespeople high commissions to use their persuasive talents on customers and bring in a pipeline of sales at a reasonable profit, but now in many markets the cost of selling has to be low. Software replaces the silver-tongued salesperson. And to cap it all, on the internet the competition is only a click away.

In the internet portal market, for example, it is difficult at first to see how the barriers to entry can be raised. A website is a published entity and publishing is all about content, as is broadcasting. There is a cost to establishing a portal, but it is not a massive cost. It is small enough for many new companies to enter the market. You can actually buy all the software you need from software providers. But there are not going to be many new entrants (at least, not English-language portals). Excite, Lycos, Go, Yahoo!, AOL, Infoseek, and Microsoft have just about tied up the market between them. Other competitors may arise, but these portals have traffic and have become habitual for many users.

So if you are a web retail store, how do you differentiate yourself so that customers return again and again? Low prices are not the answer, because on the web only the lowest price counts. Sites that compare prices will arbitrage prices until they reach a common level (or, at the very worst, promote price wars that destroy some participants and damage all others).

There are four answers: content, speed of change, service, and branding.

Content

Ultimately, content belongs to the author (or authoring group), whether we are talking about software, games, music, text, images, or video. Consequently, content creators will probably prosper in the coming years. As well as content, there is an editorial factor, as the aggregation of content also involves design and contributes to the quality of an information product. Just as editorial talent can be decisive in other media, so it will be decisive on the web regardless of the kind of website. Genuine website design talent will eventually command high fees.

Speed of change

This is simply a matter of learning faster than the competition. Most web businesses are dynamic, as the companies involved learn which ideas work and which ones don't. For the leaders in any particular field, speed is of the essence—but they have to move so fast that although competitors can copy ideas, they are still not able to compete. The website that is attracting visitors is the leader's, not the copycat's.

Service

Quality of product and service will be decisive in many areas. While most people will be happy to buy through the web, poor quality—either of product or service—will not be tolerated for long and may quickly become common knowledge. This could be deadly to a business. The service imperative should be obvious to anyone involved in ecommerce, but apparently it is not. A survey of around 10,000 web users, including customers of American Express, Procter & Gamble, IBM, and Toyota, found that only 35 percent were satisfied with the customer service they received from websites. The survey was carried out by e-satisfy.com and published in March 2000. Its findings included the fact that the online customer has a number of core requirements and expectations. These include a swift response to inquiries—typically within 24 hours—electronic confirmation of dispatches, and even something as simple as a courtesy email thanking them for their custom. However, few of even these basic services were in place on the sites whose customers were polled.

So poor levels of ecommerce service are still dominating the headlines in much the same way as they were four years ago when ecommerce was only just starting. Yet an innovative approach to service can transform a product from a commodity into a unique item. As matters currently stand, offering reliable service is a very competitive act. At Amazon's zShops, for example, inviting the customer to rate the service received from the ultimate provider is a positive step. Running a customer community where genuine complaints are posted and dealt with is also a good move that many sites have taken. The addition of a telephone call button, which some sites provide and which initiates a call from sales staff to the customer, is normally well received.

Branding

Branding and the intelligent use of a brand can be genuine means of differentiation. Expertise in this area will develop in web businesses, just as it has developed in bricks-and-mortar commerce.

Successful sites' tactics in these four areas can be explored by examining different ways of pulling the crowds and having them come back repeatedly.

Pulling the crowds

You have to advertise. Users log on to the web and meander from page to page until they decide to do something else. They have different motives for being out there. They may be shopping, seeking information, looking for entertainment. The only way to get their attention while they are on the web is via links, search engines, and web adverts.

There are three other situations to consider: getting to them via their email, advertising to them through another medium, and word of mouth.

So what works? All of them.

Links

The more links there are leading to your website, the more roads there are to your door. Here is the full spectrum:

@   *Guerrilla marketing links*: You can run a guerrilla marketing campaign by entering discussion groups and mentioning your website, but this has to be done very subtly if it is going to be successful. Communities don't appreciate people dashing in and shouting "BUY!!" Nevertheless, there have been some famously successful guerrilla marketing campaigns on the web, including the hyping of the movie *The Blair Witch Project*, which is of course a website (blairwitch.com) as well as a movie.

@   *Partner links*: An obvious and usually sensible tactic is to exchange website links with business partners and interest groups that might wish to hold references to your site. Obviously, you need to select sensible partners whose customers will legitimately want to visit your site. The most sophisticated approach is a formal "affiliates program." Amazon runs the most successful of these, which boasts a remarkable 350,000 plus members. It provides a commission on books and other produce sold via links from other sites. Other examples of partnering are sites such as

Firefly.com, which has subscriber sites to which it feeds sales opportunities. There are also large concerns like AOL and Microsoft that naturally cross-link between the many sites they run.

@   *Portal and reference site links*: Portals will, of course, charge you for placing such links on their pages. However, there are many aggregator sites
that compile lists of links that could include your website, and you can
always contact them and submit your details. Beaucoup.com is an excellent resource site for identifying aggregator sites, and you can also use
search engines to find examples.

@   *Press release-generated links*: Press releases can generate news stories.
On the web, the news site will normally, as a service to its users, add
your website link to the news story. As is the case with all press releases,
only genuine news works. There is a whole gamut of sites that will circulate press releases on the web. Pressi.com will even translate the press
release into 12 different languages (if you wish) and circulate it to a multitude of countries.

Search engines

Almost everything you need to know about the nature of search engines can be
found out at Searchenginewatch.com. However, there is not a great deal to find
out. They will sell you search terms and display your banner ad along with the
results. So if you sell widgets and someone searches on "widget," then even if
your site does not come up in the search, your banner ad does. You webmaster
will, assuming he or she is competent, have inserted the word "widget" into the
home page of your site for search engines to discover, but this on its own is not
enough to ensure that you appear in the first 10 sites listed with the term "widget." Most searchers don't look at more than the first 20 or so sites listed by a
search.

The cost of purchasing a search term for a month varies. At the time of
writing, Yahoo! charges $1,000 and guarantees 10,000 page views (of the
advert), while Lycos simply charges 5 cents per page view with a minimum
charge of $500 per month.

There are also price search engines that may be applicable to your site.
If you don't allow them to your site, you simply exclude all the traffic that passes

through the engine. The reason for excluding them could be that you don't compete on price. Fine—in which case you are not interested in "economic buyers." However, if you sell commonly available merchandise you probably can't ignore these search engines. What you need is a strategy for dealing with them.

Banner adverts

Banner adverts appear on sites all over the internet. There are major distribution agencies for them, such as Flycast and 24/7 Media. Additionally, portal sites that have huge levels of traffic and specialist news sites such as the Financial Times (ft.com), which has a well-defined high-quality audience, handle their own advertising business and set their own rates. There are also operations like Link Exchange that enable participating companies to exchange banner ads among themselves.

A banner ad is a graphic image or animated series of images of a standard size (about 460 pixels long by 60 high) that clicks through to your website. It is a stranger on the page and usually a distraction. It does not necessarily blend in—it is probably better for the advertiser if it stands out. Most web users ignore banner ads as a matter of habit, but they still see them and will occasionally click through.

Prices for placing banner ads vary. Mostly they are in a range between 4 and 8 cents per view, with well-defined audiences costing more. The cost may also relate to the likely click-through rate, which varies. It can be below 1 percent on some sites and average as high as 13 percent on others, but this also depends very much on advert design.

The principles of good banner ad design are simple: give the viewer a reason to click. They follow the AIDA model: Attention, Interest, Desire, Action. Once they have clicked, visitors should arrive at a page that is designed to the same principles. Free offers, competitions, and teaser campaigns work well on banner ads. Animation is good for getting attention.

eMail

eMail is particularly important as a medium for gaining attention. The email user is normally connected to the internet when email is read, so active web links embedded in email will often cause the recipient to click though. Consequently, most websites send registered users email encouraging them to do just that, but not so frequently as to irritate.

As well as building your own list primarily aimed at promoting a relationship with established customers, it is possible to rent email lists, some of which are reasonably well targeted, and nearly all of which are voluntarily signed up to. The list website Liszt.com is a useful point of departure for discovering email lists.

If you are going to run an email campaign successfully, then it has to follow the same AIDA formula as banner ads and other forms of advertising, but there is a sophistication you can add that is usually classified under the heading of "viral marketing." This involves asking the recipient to forward the email to friends and associates. If the email contains a joke or a special offer, then it may be passed on. The power of viral marketing is demonstrated by Hotmail, a company that used the signature at the end of every email as an advert for its free service. This technique lifted its user base from 3 million to 30 million in the space of two years.

According to an April 1999 study by Forrester, websites use banner ads and email more than any other technique to pull in the crowds, but email is rated to be the more effective method. (In the study, affiliate programs were rated as highly as email, but they are far less frequently used because they are more difficult to set up.)

Bricks-and-mortar advertising

Most websites that pull large numbers of visitors use bricks-and-mortar advertising—it works. According to the Forrester study, the most widely used bricks-and-mortar media were television and billboards. The jobs site Monster.com, for example, tripled its traffic in a year due primarily to bricks-and-mortar advertising. Its 1999 television campaign drew most of this with its SuperBowl ad spot that provoked an additional 1.7 million job searches on the site. This has to be regarded as an excellent response even for SuperBowl advertising rates of above $1 million.

On average, an American adult is exposed to 245 adverts a day according to the Advertising Research Foundation. The weakness of bricks-and-mortar advertising is the time lag between being advertised to and getting on to the web, but it also has some strengths. For example, television is a more complete and embracing medium (at the moment) and thus a television advert can have greater impact than any other kind. Billboards are often viewed once or twice a day by mostly the same people, so they have the impact of repetition.

With the use of bricks-and-mortar advertising, the importance of a memorable URL becomes obvious. The domain name as well as the impulse to act on the advert has to remain in the head of the recipient for as long as it takes for them to go online again.

Word of mouth

Word of mouth is both the best and the worst form of marketing. It is the best because people are more likely to buy on a recommendation from someone they trust than from any other marketing mechanism. It is the worst because it is slow and difficult to provoke. You may have hundreds of customers who are delighted with your products but don't talk about it. Why should they?

On the web it is somewhat different. Word of mouth moves faster because people post their opinions on community sites. They help each other. One asks for advice and another provides it, but hundreds or even thousands of people may actually read the interchange. You can, if you want, pretend to be Joe Average and post a recommendation about your website to a community site, but sometimes the community moderators see through this and delete the posting. Even if they don't, the public usually smells a rat.

However, there is nothing to prevent you from making it easy for your satisfied customers to pass on recommendations. You can, as we did at IT-Director.com, put a simple facility on the home page allowing the customer to enter a friend's email address. When an address is entered you automatically send a polite email inviting the recipient to the site and giving the name of the recommending person. About 10 percent of the early registrations on IT-Director.com happened this way. The "tell a friend" campaign was far more successful than we had expected.

Making it stick

A report on the internet travel market by Nielsen/Netratings in mid-1999 indicated that consumer loyalty to travel websites was low. Apparently, a good proportion of online travel customers visit several of the main travel websites before coming to a decision about a travel product. The study found, for example, that 15 percent of the users of Travelocity.com also visited Previewtravel.com, while 23 percent visited Expedia.com, and 10 percent visited Lowestfare.com. A similar "disloyalty" pattern was found when the other sites were sampled.

Shopping around is not something that anyone is ever going to prevent, but for a commodity product like an airline ticket, it indicates either that consumers have not yet built up confidence in a single supplier (they are still forming their habits), or that price variances are significant enough to make the extra surfing worthwhile.

Some analysts have sought to justify the current absurdly high internet valuations by counting customers and calculating a "lifetime value" for a website's customer base, using discounted cashflow formulae. The technique achieves the goal of justifying a high share price. However, examples of customer disloyalty like the one above indicate that this is a blind alley. The concern among web companies about how to make customers stick is palpable. It may not be a problem that can be solved completely, but there are techniques that can make a difference. Most of them apply specifically to web retailing operations.

Provide a high-quality buying process

Visitors to websites are often mildly afraid of the consequences of any specific click of the mouse. The ratio of site visitors to buyers on retail sites, for example, is very high. Few are buying, but once they have been through the process of buying and have achieved a positive result, the fear vanishes. The fear comes from many causes, particularly:

@   unfamiliarity;
@   concern over payment security;

@   concern over delivery of goods;

@   concern that returning unsatisfactory goods may be a problem;

@   desire not to be inundated with junk mail;

@   preference for seeing the goods first.

It is possible to address all of these fears by declaring a customer-friendly company policy and implementing it. The only difficult one is the last, but even this can be mitigated by providing the option to phone in and speak to your sales staff.

The ideal buying process is one that delivers instant gratification, something that is difficult to achieve at the moment but will become possible with music and video. Amazon.com, for example, has struck an affiliate deal with OnRadio, which runs a network of internet radio stations. Music on the radio is really an advert of a kind and a far more powerful one if the customer can instantly buy with a few clicks of the mouse. Such contextual selling will eventually pervade movie sites and, indeed, many magazine sites and communities that discuss and compare products. It is currently only held back by the lack of bandwidth in most geographic areas, and this will soon be addressed.

Another interesting tactic is one that is used by Innovations, a site that sells gadgets. In its online catalog it simply labels the products that sell well as "bestsellers." What is interesting about this is that the idea works online, because it provokes enough curiosity for the site visitor to click on the item to seek more details.

Provide a high-quality customer experience

You may address all the above points and still irritate the customer with poor website design. Easy navigation, good site response, and a pleasant look and feel all contribute to a positive customer experience. However, the follow-through also needs to be considered: the whole of after-sales service. The web-based retail operation has no bricks-and-mortar contact point for the customer. Many of the advantages of web-based businesses are disadvantages when it comes to after-sales service.

The delivery of goods now has to target a much wider geography, possibly worldwide. The returns policy must be workable for this geography, and it is best if it works along the lines of no cost to the customer and a full refund. However, it needs to be understood that the customer cannot show you what is wrong with the delivered goods. Also, it is not easy to field customer complaints. eMail is not a satisfactory medium for complaint because dialog is too slow, although chat software can be used.

There is an opportunity to use a MUD that includes, and publicly deals with, customer complaints and suggestions. The point here is that potential buyers can visibly see how you deal with complaints. The web retailer will almost certainly subcontract most of its after-sales service to partners, from couriers through to repair services. If so, then the MUD complaints area must also involve these subcontractors.

If a web retailer actually has bricks-and-mortar outlets, then there is a further problem to consider: how to integrate the two businesses. It is particularly important that a web customer's information details can be accessed by staff at the physical outlets and that these know how to respond to that customer.

If the web retailer is also a manufacturer that supplies retail outlets, then channel conflict is almost inevitable, with some customers expecting to get service from retailers that were never involved in the sale. From a channel management and customer service point of view, that is a disaster and must be avoided. The way to prevent this is to use a different brand for the web products and/or to subcontract service to the retail channel. The fact that web prices usually need to be lower than retail prices makes the second of these tactics difficult to achieve.

Branding

Strong branding is another important comfort factor. To create a strong brand, retailers must satisfy the customer at all points of contact. So branding includes everything from website design through to fast and accurate fulfillment. Offline advertising may also be critical to building the online brand. As we have already noted, TV, radio, and print advertising can all be successful in driving traffic.

Some fundamentally offline businesses have put great effort into online branding. For example, Canadian brewing company Molson runs a successful website with chat rooms and games. It includes a section on responsible drinking and a detailed corporate overview. The purpose of the site is to gather statistics to understand more about customers and to extend the brand.

The Guinness Brewing Company of Ireland is similar, but more ambitious, with an artistically presented company history and extensive links to the events that it sponsors: the Guinness Blues Festival and the Guinness Hurling Championship. As might be expected, it provides many web links to Irish pubs across the world, thus helping to promote its outlets. The website runs competitions, one of which offered the possibility of winning your own pub in Ireland, and it also acts as an outlet for Guinness merchandise.

The use of a MUD can provide a very powerful boost to branding. Among the cosmetics sites, Beautynet.com has achieved extra traffic due to its MUD, and has also become a place where women post queries about skincare or the whereabouts of lipsticks of a particular colour. Becoming a source of knowledge is generally good for business.

Sharing data and applications

The supermarket was a phenomenon of the 1950s that increased in sophistication with the passage of time. It was an outsourcing arrangement: the retailer outsourced the picking of goods to the customer, and the economic benefit of this was shared by virtue of lower prices. Clearly, the customer liked the arrangement and did not feel exploited.

The supermarket principle can be applied to websites in terms of data and software applications. The key idea is information self-service. From an organization's point of view, it is best to think in terms of what data should or must be hidden, and to make all other data available for customer or supplier usage, if it is economic to do so.

A good example of this in the business-to-business market is the Avnet Marshall (Marshall Industries) website. The company is in the electronic components business and the site provides an "Engineer's Playground," a combination of a product search capability with news, engineering diagrams, free sample offers, and so on. This whole area of the website has the feel of self-service about it.

Perhaps the most visible of the data-sharing websites are those of the international distribution companies—Federal Express, UPS, and others.

This whole business is now driven by computing and the web. UPS, for example, handles more than 750,000 package-tracking enquiries daily and spends about $1 billion annually on technology.

Promotional incentives

Promotional incentives—volume incentives, special price promotions, membership programs, and competitions—are frequently seen on the web and some of these are likely to become more popular. Special price promotions may well fade away in time because arbitraging sites will make loss leading unsustainable and destroy the phenomenon of incidental sales. Volume incentives and membership programs confer advantage, because they distort product pricing and hence make arbitrage more complex.

Competitions have a life of their own. If well thought out, they attract site visitors and are likely to improve the rate of return visits. A survey by Forrester Research in July 1998 found that 70 percent of websites were running competitions of some kind to attract traffic. Competitions are often used to encourage registration and acquire more information about customers. This then creates an email base to which special promotions can be directed, helping the website avoid arbitrage.

Feedback and customization

There are two more techniques to mention, feedback and customization. Both are so important they deserve sections of their own.

Monitor your traffic

The importance of using web analysis tools has been mentioned already, but it is worth stressing it again:

> *If you are not going to monitor the traffic on your website, then there is no point in running the website. Give up and go home.*

There is more to the process of getting feedback than the canned analysis reports that various software providers can offer. The online retailer needs to understand how website customers behave when they shop. How and when do customers decide to buy? How many go through the process of placing an order but abandon before hitting the "place order" button? What do customers like about the website and how does that compare with what they say they like?

The online retailer can solicit customer feedback by use of a MUD or by direct survey—and is recommended to do so. What customers think is important, even where it doesn't match what they do. Branding has to target what customers think, but ease of use must target what customers do.

Feedback is the dynamic driver for refining and improving a website. If you get the feedback loop working properly, then you can start out with indifferent design and a flawed business idea, but quickly refine it so that it improves on a weekly basis. If you have followed the progress of any of the successful websites, particularly Yahoo! and Amazon, you will probably have been surprised by the speed of innovation, both in the design of the sites and in the services they provide. The dynamic nature of such sites is driven by feedback.

One of the joys of having good feedback is that you can generate simple formulae to steer the business. For example, if you know that for every 10 site visitors there is one buyer and that the average buyer purchases $80 worth of goods, then you have a simple formula:

$$\text{Monthly revenue} = \$80 \times \text{Monthly site visitors} / 10$$

It is also very easy to see what needs to be done to improve the level of revenue. There are only three options:

@   Increase the number of visitors.
@   Improve the 10 to 1 ratio of visitors to buyers.
@   Improve the average sales per buyer.

Although very simple this is also very powerful, because on the web you can track all of these areas easily. The bricks-and-mortar store knows neither the number of visitors it gets, or the ratio of visitors to buyers. It may run an advertising campaign that draws more visitors to the store but does not result in significantly greater sales. The conclusion is likely to be that the advertising campaign failed, but it didn't. Either the new visitors were disappointed with the store, or the wrong type of visitor was attracted.

The web allows you to make rational deductions. You can work out very quickly how much it costs to attract new visitors, and if you plan advertising campaigns in a scheduled manner then you can quickly get to know which medium is least expensive and most effective in drawing a crowd. In fact, getting new visitors is relatively inexpensive, but getting them to return is far more important, especially as visitors very rarely buy on the first visit.

Here the web is very obliging, because you are able to know at exactly what point the visitor left the site—on the home page, after browsing the catalog, after searching for a single item, after looking at prices, while trying to place an order, and so on. You can find out where the site is not working and thus it is usually easy to find out why.

It is also important to pace the growth of the site if possible. Visitors who go away unimpressed are more expensive to tempt back at a later date. For this reason, it is important to provide good reasons to return and mechanisms to allow you to relate to the customer. This is where two of the publish–subscribe mechanisms are important: email and the MUD.

With email, you have to be careful to seek permission to email the customer and also to set a level of expectation as to how often you will email them and under what circumstances. There is thus another ratio that you can monitor: the percentage of visitors who register (to become members). It then becomes possible to compare sales to members and sales to other customers.

The level of activity on the MUD is also important and indicative of success. The community has to be useful if it is going to attract users. If you create an active community, the network effect will kick in and the community will attract visitors at an increasing rate, who in turn may become buyers and perhaps members. Again, the ratios can be monitored.

The soft touch

Customization is the best differentiator on the web. This is almost a self-evident truth. Customization is the only tactic that allows you to conceal information or ensure uniqueness. Your prices, your site design, your navigation mechanisms, and every aspect of your website are open to the world and can be copied. These can contribute in various ways to branding, but beyond that they cannot provide you with anything that is unique. Customization can give the customer a unique relationship to your site that no other site will be able to copy.

The loyalty tactics discussed so far correspond to sensible store design and the use of business intelligence, but they will not be able completely to counteract an arbitraging operation. Consider Trip.com, a travel site that uses robot software to go direct to airline websites to find the best fares and then lets you buy direct. Such an operation undermines travel sites like Travelocity and Expedia, but also arbitrages the airlines themselves. So how is it possible to compete with this? The following five customization tactics can make a difference.

Personal pages

Yahoo! invented the idea of the personal page with MyYahoo! and this was immediately imitated. Initially it was not a sophisticated capability, but it was useful, and preferable for many, to the default Yahoo! home page. However, the idea has become more complex with time and now involves companies writing fairly advanced web-based software applications for their customers. Probably the most developed example is MySchwab, the outcome of a partnership with Excite. This is a customizable personal portal for the investor that can include news, weather, sport, shopping, email, and chat. However, it also includes stock portfolio tracking, an advice service, and a link to Schwab's website. You could happily use MySchwab even if you had no interest in stocks.

By constructing a personal page, customers will do something unique in relation to your site. Even if the same capability is provided elsewhere, they will not use it in the same way and are unlikely to use it at all if they have created a satisfactory "mini-portal" via your website. The point of the personal page is that it may become habitual—a personal portal that individuals use as their starting point for web navigation. It contrasts, if you like, with the canned service that some ISPs provide to all their users. However, the idea is still being worked on and seems to be tracking the development of the portals themselves. First there were a few portals and then there were many. First there were a few personal page capabilities and now there are many.

The problem the personal portal tries to resolve is that each one of us navigates through the web in a slightly different way and often with different goals in mind. In this area there is much to play for and there will be further innovations.

Personal bundled deals

One way of defeating the pure market model is to vary the price per individual in a way that defeats the possibility of arbitrage. Individuals can be offered personal discounts according to a varying set of parameters, which can include the amount that customer has spent in a given time, the other products being bought with this purchase, and having passed on recommendations to other customers. Research indicates that price incentives appeal to virtually all customers no matter what their salary range.

A financial incentive to be loyal particularly appeals in relation to certain kinds of purchases such as groceries, where few consumers shop for pleasure and where suppliers will often partner in specific promotions. If discounts are coupled with a site design that genuinely saves time, then shopping becomes habitual. However, individual discounts are difficult to keep track of and manage. Better, perhaps, to introduce your own currency.

Creating your own currency

A very effective way to implement a discounting scheme is to offer "points," "coupons," or "beans," all of which are different names for what is, in effect, a limited-circulation currency. The popularity of such schemes on the web is already very high. Most schemes are themselves businesses that have grouped together a whole series of web retailers. For example, MyPoints has over two million users and 200 web retailers signed up. There are many others: FreeRide, e-centives, CyberGold, Netcentives, and so on. In general, shoppers tend to spend their points on small products such as CDs, books, and movie tickets.

What is useful about such schemes is that "points" can be awarded in small amounts for simple acts such as registering or clicking through on banner adverts, or in large amounts for buying high-value products or services. Experience indicates that points users are far more likely to register if there is a points incentive, and a survey by Forrester indicated that click-throughs on banner ads can be as high as 20 percent if they are rewarded with points.

The actual financial value of such points is simply impossible to determine, even though the business that runs the scheme assigns an internal value to them. For the points collector it is a closed economy—there is no exchange rate outside the points network and points cannot be traded between users. Additionally, participating retailers can use points in special price promotions, or choose to be less generous with the value they allow in any given purchase. They can vary the value to the collector. A further disturbing factor with such schemes is that users don't think of points as currency, but as a bonus that they have accumulated and will eventually cash in.

The points schemes are not merely online. AOL is involved with Supermarkets Online in a scheme that provides electronic coupons for local grocery stores. Single-site points schemes have a tendency to expand because the value of the quasi-currency increases according to its possibility of circulation. The natural area of expansion is into affiliate programs. This is why we have seen frequent-flyer miles schemes expand to include hotel groups and applying to alliances of airlines.

Personal service

Personal service begins with sites such as Point.com, which leads you through an online questionnaire about cellular telephones, helping you to organize your criteria until you naturally arrive at the appropriate product and plan. However, it can go much further. Grocery site Peapod provides a recipe-generation capability that helps you construct a shopping list. The *Wall Street Journal* lets you design a personal newspaper, as do a number of other media sites. Garden.com's garden planner has established it as the current brand leader, simply because the software is so good.

Profiling software can make a huge difference. Andromedia's Like Minds, which is remarkably accurate when properly trained, is the driver behind Moviecritic.com, selling videos. By employing this software Levi's nearly doubled the time each visitor spent on its site and increased the average spend by a third. The advantage of such software is simple: it saves time instead of wasting it.

Amazon was the first site to employ this type of profiling with its recommendations system, which provided the same kind of capability. However, it also combined this with the community effect of allowing readers to comment on books and even succeeded in involving a number of authors in "community" conversations. This, more than anything else, accounted for the site's early success. Personal service works on the web, even if it is completely software driven.

True involvement

The PC manufacturers, particularly Dell and Gateway, have demonstrated a trend that will probably be followed by all other areas of manufacture targeting the consumer. If the customer wants anything other than a standard-spec product, then they will probably get the best-priced deal directly from the manufacturer, not just because the retailer is eliminated from the equation, but also because the manufacturer can build to order.

Dell, Gateway, and a few other PC manufacturers provide online configurators, intelligent pieces of software that guide the customer through the process of specifying in detail exactly what is wanted. The upside to this is that the PC is less expensive and a far better fit to requirements. The downside is that delivery may be later and will certainly not be immediate. Particularly important in the case of the PC is that the software comes fully loaded, tested, and ready to use. If you know what you want then this is clearly the best way to buy.

It also highlights a split in the market. PC retailers are in a commodity business with thin margins, but PC manufacturers are not, because they truly involve the customer. This trend is only in its infancy and will soon spread beyond the PC market into other areas of manufacturing, particularly the automotive business.

MYTHS AND MISCONCEPTIONS

There are a number of misconceptions about the internet that have been commented on at various points in the book and are worth summarizing here. They need to be challenged directly, because they can have the effect of leading businesspeople in the wrong direction.

Internet businesses do not make a profit

This particular misconception derives from two facts and is usually supported by reference to Amazon.com. The first is that setting up an internet business costs money, as does any other business, and thus there is a need for an element of front-funding. Thus in their early years internet businesses make losses while they build infrastructure. The second fact is that wild IPOs deliver a huge gift to a number of businesses—an immense amount of cheap funding. Naturally, these businesses regarded spending to consolidate their position as a higher priority than making a profit. When absurd valuations of the kind we have witnessed are possible, businesses that can take advantage would be foolish to put profitability ahead of acquiring customers. It is simply a matter of the best use of funds. Many internet businesses do not make a profit, but they will when the stock market finally demands that they do.

Eventually, everything will be sold direct to the consumer from the manufacturer

This may happen with some products, but it is a simplistic view of a complex reality. In almost every area of commerce there is a market and a mill. The reality is that many processes must take place for a product or service to be delivered to the customer. You can analyze the situation for any given product by categorizing the processes into manufacturing, distribution, retailing, and so on.

It is true that in any such supply chain a company could attempt to carry out all the processes, but it would then run the danger of weak focus. It might be beaten in the field by a company that focused completely on the market or on the mill. Of course, this does not change the fact that there will be a number of businesses that specialize in customization and thus deliver "straight from the factory."

The large portals, such as AOL, Yahoo!, and Lycos, are establishing a monopoly on internet traffic and will eventually come to dominate all business sectors

These portals are indeed impressive in their capabilities and influence, but apart from AOL, which clearly has a successful ISP and software business, the portals have yet to demonstrate where their long-term revenues will come from beyond advertising. They are retailers, they run auctions, and because of their level of passing business they can get into any business they want. But that does not mean that they will do it well. Also they have a branding problem, because in most cases their brand means "portal."

Wherever these major sites choose to concentrate their attention, they will be vulnerable to companies that concentrate on excellence within a given niche. They may have ridden hockey stick curves, but they have not raised insuperable barriers to entry into their markets.

The large etailers like Amazon have already sewn up whole areas of ecommerce, so there is no chance of competing with them

The large etailers like Amazon and eBay have established themselves as successful businesses that will not melt away like the winter snow. However, it is not impossible to compete with them and beat them. Again, this is a matter of picking the territory on which to do battle and providing excellence in a given niche. Competing directly with these sudden giants is unlikely to be a clever move. Note also that every new change in technology may open up opportunities for competition to get in and eventually challenge the etail giants.

Much of retailing will be reduced to a commodity business where price is everything

Some areas of retailing will not be able to avoid commoditization. However, we need to understand why this is happening. In many instances, it will be because some differentiators have been removed, e.g., geographic barriers, price insensitivity among consumers, personal service being replaced by electronic service, and so on. The ways of differentiation discussed earlier may balance this out. It is worth noting that etailing involves the shopping *experience* as well as the product or service bought.

Brokerage firm Charles Schwab is able to maintain a premium over other internet brokers by using service offerings, maintaining an excellent website, and leveraging its brand. If stocks are not a commodity, then what is?

Intermediaries get disintermediated

This is a wrong formulation and it is often repeated, but refers to a clear phenomenon. What actually happens is that the business process of some intermediaries is automated by the internet and various computer software applications, to such an extent that the price for supplying this service falls dramatically. For example, certain broking activities are automated by the existence of search engines and information made available on the net. However, the search engine and probably the websites that provide this automation will be making money from advertising.

The outcome is that some intermediaries are destroyed because they no longer provide value. The internet also creates some completely new, and possibly unwelcome, intermediaries in the form of arbitrageurs that trade solely in order to equalize prices.

Retailing on the internet is all about one-to-one marketing

There is very little one-to-one marketing on the internet at the moment. Mostly what is going on is mass marketing and a certain amount of segmented marketing. The internet differs from bricks-and-mortar retailing precisely by virtue of its automated nature. There is a distinct lack of person-to-person contact and very few internet businesses are attempting to establish one-to-one relationships with the customer.

Nevertheless, in the medium term the capabilities of software are such that one-to-one marketing will become possible in a way that is not the case with current retailing. It will be possible to know a customer's profile and hence their preferences. As a general picture, there will be one-to-one marketing, one-to-several marketing, and one-to-segment marketing, but the efficiency of profiling will eventually make mass marketing a thing of the past.

In order to build a web business you need a thorough understanding of computers

Knowledge of computers does no harm and for success, it will be necessary to have IT talent on board. However, successful web businesses are run by good businesspeople with good business vision. You cannot have that nowadays without a certain level of computer literacy. In addition, particular requirements are:

@   a flexible business plan and a strong vision;

@   an understanding of how to design, build, and maintain a compelling website;

@   an understanding of your target customers.

On the internet all information has to be given away free

Not so. There are a number of successful subscription sites, such as the *Wall Street Journal* with its successful subscriber service. It charges $49 for a full year's unlimited access, a third of the price of actually buying the paper, and provides a far more detailed set of information than is available to the reader of the paper version. Despite this, the paper still sells.

Perhaps the most popular subscription site on the web is ESPN Sportszone, a US-centric sports site. Apart from providing a comprehensive sports service that covers everything the ESPN sports TV channel covers, it also offers fantasy leagues, highly active discussion forums, merchandise, and just about anything the sports fan could want.

Giving information away free is something that many websites do to attract custom. Information is the easiest thing to give away. This and the lack of microcharging have led to most magazine sites pursuing an advertising model. At the moment advertising is the only practical mechanism to enable charges at the level of one cent or less per page view to be imposed. This will be the case until microcharging technology is deployed and used, and of course there can be no certainty that the consumer will accept it.

English is the language of the internet and non-English websites are at a severe disadvantage

English is the main language of the internet, but all the evidence suggests that people prefer their own language and culture. Local-language websites are the ones that are popular. Those who wish to trade internationally outside the currently dominant English-speaking domain will have to compete with local-language sites set up by people who understand the local economy and culture. It will be difficult to compete with them. Non-English websites will naturally thrive within their own cultural domain.

THE BIG MOMENT HAS ARRIVED

We have described a whole series of strategies, techniques, and ideas for use by various sorts of websites or businesses. You can implement these where appropriate for your business. However, it needs to be understood that all these tactics are for the pursuit of a single goal—to become the *de facto* market leader just as the market passes the point of inflection. If this is not achieved, then a defensive strategy is necessary.

The primary tactic for competing with the market leader is not to compete. Instead, develop a defensible and profitable niche and let other competitors take the gorilla head on. Niches can have their own benevolent hockey stick curves, but only if they constitute a genuinely differentiated part of the whole market. The test for this is simple: Is there a community of interest? As an example, you could build a specialist website for backgammon players that competes indirectly with a general site for players of board games, but you could not do this for every board game. There is a backgammon-playing community, but there is probably no community, say, for the game of chinese checkers.

The hockey stick curve confers an extraordinary advantage on the market-leading website in any sector or subsector. It provides momentum, "the big mo," which boosts profitability and protects the market leader from competitors by giving it time to react. The market leader need only watch what the other competitors do and copy them in order to beat them off. For the market leader, the real enemies are complacency and technology failure. Other competitors are forced to be innovative and take risks in order to compete.

However, genuine leaders, such as Amazon and eBay, have demonstrated that there are far superior tactics for the market leader to adopt than looking backwards over their shoulder. Once in the lead, the market leader can drive the hockey stick effect ruthlessly: investing the maximum amount possible in pulling the crowds and giving them good reason to return again and again. This raises the bar for all the competition, making their operation more expensive and less rewarding.

8

The Alligator Pools

The Everglades in Florida are an area of outstanding natural beauty. Even those who have never visited the area have probably seen photographs of the swamps there, with the trees standing tall on their roots, looking more like a Salvador Dali painting than a natural phenomenon. They may also have seen pictures of itinerant alligators crossing roads or sliding menacingly through the reeds at the edge of a river or pool. These scenes are characteristic of the whole area and a consequence of the local climate.

In the winter months, the water is high and the Everglades are flooded, but in the summer months the area dries up. It is the dramatic change in the water level that causes the trees to stand on their roots as if on stilts. Their bark needs to remain above the water line or the trees will become waterlogged and die. The swamp's slowly moving water gradually washes away the earth between the roots of the trees and the roots dig deep into the earth as the land dries up, creating a twisted and surreal set of legs.

In the rainy season, the alligators spread out across the Everglades, in search of "alligator pools." Clumps of trees surround these areas of the swamp. The trees indicate that the water is deeper than in other areas where only reeds grow. The trees would not survive the dry season unless they surrounded an area that was well supplied with water. As the dry season approaches, the water level falls and such areas become pools.

For the alligator, life in the alligator pool is fairly easy. It has no natural enemies and it is larger than any other natural inhabitant of the Everglades. In the winter it simply eats whatever passes by, usually different varieties of fish. As the summer approaches, food becomes abundant. The water in the swamps gradually dries up and alligator pools form. These pools become the only source of water for much of the fauna of the region. Fish that once swam with relative impunity through the swamp find themselves trapped in the same pool as an alligator and are devoured at will. Mammals and birds that come to the pools to drink are also potential prey. Life depends on water and the alligator owns the source of supply. As the pool gradually shrinks in size, all kinds of prey are forced closer and closer to the jaws of the predator.

If the summer is particularly dry, then some of the alligator pools will dry up and the resident alligators will go off in search of other pools. The alligator knows that if he does not find another pool he will die, and if he does, then when he arrives there, he will have to fight with its owner for possession of the food supply that it represents. In the end, the great predators of the Everglades battle with each other for survival.

The various business sectors of the commercial world can be seen as forming a similar kind of ecosystem to that of the Everglades, with successful corporations playing the role of the alligator. In times of plenty, most companies do reasonably well, some fail, and some just manage to scrape out an existence, but most of them prosper. As some companies fail, others appear and the economic ecosystem is generous to its inhabitants. These are times of expansion and they correspond to the winter season when the Everglades flood. Indeed, it could be said that the business cycle of boom and bust, which seems to follow a very rough cycle that usually lasts between about nine and eleven years, represents a parallel cycle to the one acted out each year in Florida.

The economy also has its generations of alligators that replace each other with time. Once the world economy was dominated by the hunt for precious metals, provoked by the Spanish success in raiding the extraordinary wealth of the Incas. In those days the economic entity was the nation, not the corporation. Later, the world economy became dominated by trading companies that shipped commodities: tobacco, tea, sugar, and anything else that could be grown cheaply in far-flung places to satisfy the European consumer. In the nineteenth century, it was the building and running of railways that created millionaires, excited the investor, and caused the stock market to boom and crash.

Then it was the turn of oil and the car industry, although it was hard to say whether it was the Fords or the Rockefellers that were calling the shots. No matter, that time has passed. Nowadays, the car industry is manufacturing at about 70 percent of capacity and is dominated by a handful of corporations, from the US, Germany, and Japan. The global tire industry operates at a similar level of capacity and is dominated by six companies. The price of oil that was printing money for the handful of giant oil corporations in the 1970s is now on the floor.

The twentieth century also saw the construction and growth of many other industries as a mass market emerged in North America and Europe, and then spread to the Far East, but many of the industries that prospered are now saturated. The usual figure at which saturated markets seem to settle once they have turned into markets that are driven by replacement rather than new purchase is 70 percent of capacity. Similar imbalances currently exist in chemicals, the airplane industry, steel, shipbuilding, and so on.

It is not only in manufacturing where we see the phenomenon of the surviving alligators. It is also there in farming—the production of most crops in the US is under the control of a few major combines and produce is, in any event, in the main sold to just a handful of customers. The same picture is repeated across the world: only a few major grain companies, only a few cocoa, sugar, and coffee providers, only a few oil companies, and so on. If we look at retailing, we see the grocery retailing business being shared between a handful of players in every major trading nation: the US, Japan, Germany, France, the UK, and so on. The pattern is repeated again and again.

And so it is that markets are born and come to maturity. The various competitors in the markets either thrive or die. At maturity, a market tends to reduce to a limited number of players who rarely fail, but who are prevented from outright dominance by antitrust legislation.

Forbes magazine does an annual analysis of the 400 richest Americans. A mere 15 years ago, the list was dominated by manufacturing, oil, and real-estate money. Fortunes from these areas of the US economy made up 60 percent of the list. In 1999, they accounted for only 16 percent of the list, with technology, finance, and media now in the ascendant. Microsoft on its own accounted for 12 members of the list—an astonishing 3 percent, half of whom are billionaires. The world economy is now being driven by information businesses—media, entertainment, software, computing, telecommunications—all of them either the content or the fabric of the internet.

As if by some uncommon freak of nature, perhaps a devastating hurricane, whole areas of the economic Everglades have been uprooted and rearranged. A whole new generation of alligators has been born and they are aggressively taking up position in their alligator pools, shoving aside or completely ignoring the generation that they are there to displace. All too soon, the summer has arrived and is drying up the swamp. It is destroying the food supply for many of the older generation of alligators. Poor things. Were they too blind to see what was happening or too set in their ways to react? Life is going to be hard for them, particularly in the retail and financial sectors.

THE NEW GEOGRAPHY

As must now be abundantly clear, the electronic economy is distinctly different to the paper economy. One of the problems that it will create, indeed has already created, is that people will naturally try to view the new economy through their understanding of the one that is dying.

The paper economy could be easily divided into sectors. All the world's stock markets adopt such a classification system for companies, and as new industries emerge they add to the classification. You can scan the share prices in the financial pages of the newspapers to see it. This, however, is an old map and does not give a coherent picture of the new geography.

In order to gain an overview of the new geography, we can go back to first principles and redraw the map. In doing so, we are inevitably taking a predictive stance in respect of how we believe the electronic economy will evolve. Nevertheless, it is a worthwhile exercise.

Economic sectors can be considered based on the following 10 headings:

1   *The fruits of the earth—mining and harvesting.* This covers all economic activity involved in extracting minerals from the earth or in farming the biosphere. This used to be the major part of every nation's economy, and for the less developed countries it still is.

2   *Building stuff—construction and heavy engineering.* The activities of construction and heavy engineering became the main motor of the indus-

trialized economies throughout most of the twentieth century, but have decreased in importance in recent decades.

3   *Moving things—travel, transport, and logistics.* While transportation technology has varied over the centuries, its fundamental position within the national and international economies has not changed. It is essential as it enables trade.

4   *Infrastructure networks—utilities, telecoms, and computing.* The basic infrastructure of the economy has grown with time until eventually all utilities—gas, electricity, water, and communications—have become extensive networks. The last utility to be networked is the computer and the networking of computers has given birth to the electronic economy.

5   *Services—accountancy, legal, healthcare, leisure, maintenance, education, government, and trusted third parties.* We have classified together all services involving the use of human skill to serve the wants or needs of others in any context. We might think of this as the "professional" sector. It is, however, huge and could be divided further.

6   *Making and tailoring—"light" manufacture.* We have deliberately distinguished between heavy engineering and the manufacture of smaller items, although the boundary is somewhat artificial. The differences reside in the fact that FMCG (fast-moving consumer goods) are mass market, as are some business-only goods, and that one-to-one manufacture becomes possible in this sector.

7   *Immersive retailing—shops, showrooms, malls, and theme parks.* We have taken care to distinguish between retailing in the virtual environment and bricks-and-mortar retailing—they are different and they will diverge.

8   *Electronic retailing—market making, broking, and auctioning.* This embraces all buying and selling done electronically, but only where the goods are physical rather than pure information.

9   *Digital distribution—banking, insurance, securities, info-goods.* This involves trading in goods that are purely informational, such as music, video, electronic games, software, and so on.

10 *Authoring—information and entertainment.* This involves the creation of goods that are purely informational, for any purpose.

In looking at this classification scheme, the first thing to note is that some of these sectors remain largely undisturbed in the transformation to an electronic economy. These are the first three sectors listed: mining and harvesting, construction, and transportation. All will be served better with information and this may in turn boost their productivity to some small degree. The internet will improve many of their mundane business processes to good effect. However, these sectors will not be transformed by the internet, because much of the activity within them remains as it was. This is especially the case for mining, harvesting, and construction.

The transportation sector will be changed by virtue of its level of traffic. Areas of the distribution industry will be stimulated by the need to dispatch and deliver more goods to the home on behalf of internet retailers. At the same time, the electronic economy will make it feasible for people to travel less for business purposes; although they might instead choose to travel more for recreational reasons, so the level of travel is not easy to predict. The electronic economy will increase price competition and put a downward pressure on prices, which may in turn stimulate demand. There will be adjustments, but no great change.

When we consider the fourth sector, the utilities, we can see at once that it will be transformed. Apart from anything else, there will be some significant restructuring due to globalization and deregulation and the further advance of technology. We are already seeing the combination of energy utilities and the movement toward an open market in energy.

In telecommunications, there will be great changes that emanate from the following trends:

@ The internet itself.

@ The rapid growth of mobile communications, including personal mobile internet connection.

@ Internet connection in vehicles, particularly private cars.

@ The trend toward internetworking the household.

@ The convergence of telecommunications and broadcasting, leading eventually to their complete integration.

@ The growth of ISPs (internet service providers) and ASPs (application service providers) as commercial computing is gradually absorbed into the internet.

In the medium term, this will probably lead to mergers between utilities on a geographic basis, pursuing the idea of "one provider per household." There are already many battles in progress that are attempts to own the point of connection or at least own "territory" at that point. Whoever dominates the point of connection has the opportunity to take a percentage of everything downstream of that point.

This battle will become much clearer as the internet matures. It began with the commercial software scrap between Microsoft and Netscape for the browser. However, it has moved on from there as the browser was not the real territory. It quickly became apparent that the ISPs and the portals were the ones that owned the sacred turf. So now we see AOL, Microsoft, Yahoo!, Lycos, and others fighting it out. We also see telecoms companies desperate to establish a presence as ISPs. The media empires are gradually joining in, with Disney and Time Warner both very quick to recognize which way the wind is blowing. The computer games companies that collectively represent an industry of $10 billion, just larger than the whole of Hollywood, have also taken a step in this direction by providing internet access.

In the UK, the giant supermarket chain Tesco and electronics retailer Dixons have both entered the market as ISPs, as have Barclays Bank and Virgin. We are witnessing the beginning of a great area of crossover between economic sectors.

The service revolution

The service sector is extremely broad, embracing a mass of professions and skilled activities. The nature of the internet is such that it demystifies much of the skill that many of these professionals possess. The diagnoses of doctors and vets can be checked. Legal advice can be discussed in chat room sessions. Education can be acquired online, and so on. The professions are suddenly subject to a much higher level of scrutiny from the customer and many of their bread-and-butter revenues will diminish, because the internet will encourage and enable a self-help approach by providing all the required information.

This suggests a culling of the professions, with only the highest levels of expertise guaranteeing a long-term career. Knowledge that used to be absorbed by individuals through many years of training can be stored on computers, and dispensed by them, through the ubiquitous net. At the same time, there is likely to be compensatory growth in many other areas of the services sector. The leisure industry in particular will show a high level of growth and tourism will continue to flourish.

From a technology perspective, many large-scale organizations, particularly educational organizations, social services, the legal system, and a whole mass of governmental and quasi-governmental institutions are due to be undermined and replaced. Nevertheless, all of this will take a good deal of time. Governments will not be willing to participate visibly in the undermining of professions. After all, professional people cast votes. Neither will they willingly participate in undermining themselves, even though many of the services that government provides could be provided extremely efficiently over the net.

In the longer term, the mechanism of funding governmental organizations by taxation and trying to ensure their efficiency by the extraordinarily ineffective method of cost accounting will go into decline. In most instances, it will be replaced by a more direct means of funding where the price and the benefit are more strongly related to each other. Thus the trend in government toward privatization and outsourcing is likely to be encouraged by the march of technology and the spread of the net.

However, no matter how far "free market" economics is pushed, there will still be services provided for the community (defense, policing, fire fighting, and so on) that will necessarily be levied as a charge on the community in the form of taxation. It is worth noting that these are geographic in provision, and hence taxation will have to be levied on a geographic basis.

Immersive manufacturing

Light manufacture can be further divided into two subsectors of:

@ commodity product;

@ tailored product.

Manufacturing companies are likely to produce both, but "immersive" manufacturing will be where growth occurs. Logic suggests that the easiest way to avoid being dragged into a commodity market is to involve and collaborate with the customer. This makes it difficult, if not impossible, for the customer to compare prices, except in a very general way. Moreover, it can also delight the customer and lead to a much stronger supplier–customer relationship. The customer can be involved in the design process and possibly even in the manufacture.

This is not an idea that was born on the web. Andersen Windows, the largest manufacturer of windows in the US, was a pioneer in this area. It built PC software that allowed its customers to design their own windows for quick manufacture and delivery and deployed it in building materials supply outlets. Within a few years, 30 percent of its business was in tailormade product. All that the net does is make such operations easier to run, and allow the level of customer immersion to increase.

Naturally, as the trend toward immersive manufacture increases, the manufacture of commodity product will migrate to areas of the world where labor is cheap. The net will assist this migration, because it will expose any differences in price that geographic distance had once hidden. The commoditizing effect of the internet makes it very difficult for manufacturers of general-purpose product to sell directly to the customer because of conflicts with those in the conventional sales channel.

An illustration of this occurred in 1999 when Home Depot, a major US retail chain supplying DIY, decorating, and gardening products, launched its website. This was a well-laid-out site providing detailed DIY project plans for its enthusiastic customers and an online ordering capability. Before the website was fully implemented, the company wrote to more than 1,000 of its suppliers, including major manufacturers of electrical and DIY tools, threatening to blacklist them if they competed by selling their products direct to consumers over the net. On the surface of it, this may seem heavy handed, but Home Depot is providing showroom space for its suppliers and, whether via the web or bricks and mortar, is adding value for which it feels it has a right to be rewarded.

Clothes company Fruit of the Loom provides a good example of a manufacturer anticipating this problem. It depends on 50 US-wide wholesalers to ship its goods in bulk to thousands of silk-screen printers, embroidery shops, and other outfits. Its strategy was to web enable the wholesalers and leave it to the channel to sort itself out. It set up an ecommerce system, called Activewear Online, to display its colorful catalogs, manage inventories, and process electronic orders 24 hours a day. So far, it has chosen to ignore the one-to-one market.

The area of tailored or one-to-one manufacture is both a manufacturing and a retailing operation. To put it another way, companies that choose to pursue one-to-one manufacture remove the need for a retailer. This is exactly what PC manufacturers such as Dell and Gateway have achieved, although both companies pursued this business model prior to the growth of the net. With the growth of the net there are now many examples, from InterActive Custom Clothes through to General Motors and others we have referred to earlier. From a business perspective, this trend is very significant because the manufacturer suddenly gains control of the customer relationship.

It does not take a great leap of the imagination to see where this could lead. Consider a customer being able to watch the manufacture of their personalized car via web cameras placed at strategic points on the production line. The customer would become deeply involved in the manufacturing of the car weeks before receiving the finished item. From there, we can leap to the idea of the in-car computer that links to the net, but also provides the manufacturer with a means of directly maintaining the customer relationship while the car is being driven. This leads to the manufacturer selling "product enhancements" to the customer on a regular basis and arranging for the building of the customer's next car when required.

Thus consumer manufacturing divides between a tailored, one-to-one subsector and another where general-purpose product is manufactured and sold through online or offline retail outlets, or possibly through auction.

Immersive retailing and the gratification gap

We refer to bricks-and-mortar retailing as immersive retailing because the customer is directly involved in the shopping process. It is a sector where great changes will occur. A number of the current generation of bricks-and-mortar retailers will not survive in their current form because the cost of their operation is too high compared to a commercial website.

Immersive retailing is solidly based on geography and physical space. When a retail chain opens up a new outlet, its decision on where to locate depends on geography: What is the potential customer catchment area? What is the local competition? How healthy is the local economy? How good are the transport and parking facilities? etc.

When it designs its new outlet, it does so on the basis of the building's internal space: How will customers walk around the store? How can we direct them to the goods they are interested in? How can we make them walk past all the goods we sell? Where shall we put the tills? How will they collect and take away the goods they have purchased? Where do we need to place the security cameras? The geographic imperative reaches all the way down to the floor and shelf space: How can we maximize the profit per square foot? How many different brands shall we stock? How much shelf space should be given to each?

Retailing is also intricately related to time: What should the normal opening times be? When should we extend these for late-night shopping? How can we entice customers in at slack times during the day? When should we initiate seasonal sales to entice customers during quiet times of the year? How do we maximize the take during the Christmas rush?

Retailing also profits from the customer's imperfect knowledge, and is able to ask questions such as: How competitive do we need to be? Which products can we successfully sell at a premium? How can we use our brand to differentiate? How can we run down obsolete product lines?

Nearly all of these important retailing imperatives disappear with electronic retailing, although they continue to apply to roughly the same degree with immersive retailing. That will not disappear, but it is unclear how large the immersive retailing sector will eventually be. If you walk through a retailing area of any kind, you can count the businesses that will continue to prosper in a world of electronic retailing. They are the service-oriented ones that genuinely require your presence: restaurants, pubs, clubs and dance halls, hairdressers, beauty salons, health and sports clubs, and so on. Such businesses may have an electronic existence on the web, but will still need a physical "shop."

Beyond this, shops become:

@   convenience stores for instant gratification;
@   showrooms, tied to websites;
@   immersive retail environments.

In the purchase of physical goods there is what can be called a "gratification gap," a lag in time between the act of purchasing and receipt of the goods. The gap varies according to what is bought and how it is bought, but a good proportion of the current bricks-and-mortar retailing outlets provide the possibility of instant gratification, whereas the net can never offer this possibility where physical goods are involved. The cost of instantly gratifying the customer may be high, but the premium the customer is willing to pay for that may well rise significantly.

There are also goods that the customer genuinely wishes to see and experience prior to purchase, and where the cost of inventory is so high that instant gratification cannot be easily supported. Such retail businesses face the problem of the customer visiting the showroom and then buying at a lower price from a different vendor on the web. For these outlets, a linkage needs to be established to make this impossible. Either the goods must be priced identically on the web, or an arrangement has to be made of the type that Home Depot was attempting to enforce. There is good reason to believe that in some areas of retail, a hybrid of web and bricks-and-mortar may evolve. This could happen for fairly large items such as furniture and white goods, where items are normally delivered but the customer often likes to select them in person.

It could well happen in other areas as well. In autumn 1999, a new venture in the UK, Toyzone.co.uk, set up in direct competition to eToys, the large Californian web toy vendor. By coincidence, both vendors entered the same geographic market at the same time with different business models. eToys is a typical web retailer with a pure web-based model. Toyzone's business model is a hybrid. It is linking up directly with a UK-wide toy retailer, Kids Play Factory, but intends to do the majority of its business directly over the web. The Kids Play Factory bricks-and-mortar outlet becomes part of the delivery logistics—you can buy over the web but collect from the shop, or have goods delivered direct.

Finally, there is the immersive retail environment where shopping turns into leisure or entertainment. This is simply a matter of how far retailers can go in changing or enhancing the shopping experience. There can be little doubt, for example, that teenagers buy clothes at boutiques that play pop music and show videos on large screens because they enjoy the ambience. This principle can be extended much further.

As a matter of simple evolution, retail operations that work far better via the electronic channel will gradually disappear from shopping malls and retail villages. These will change in nature accordingly. They will become leisure-oriented complexes, with cinemas, amusement parlors, and bars blending in with showrooms and "instant gratification outlets"—gift shops, curiosity shops, newsstands, and kiosks. Some shopping areas will take on the character of amusement parks, entertaining places to be where money gets spent.

Electronic retailing and the procurement dynamic

If gratification is the spirit of immersive retailing, then procurement is the spirit of electronic retailing. When you buy physical product over the net, you know you are going to have to wait for delivery of the goods. But there are many things you purchase that you will be happy to wait for. These are the things you have to procure. Business-to-business retailing is almost wholly a matter of procurement and we can expect it to become dominated by electronic retailing fairly quickly. The business-to-consumer market is split between gratification and procurement.

With electronic retailing, the price will nearly always be significantly lower, but there will also always be a gratification gap that the consumer has to endure. Indeed, it could be argued that the price difference between the internet and immersive retail outlets will eventually define the value of early gratification. It is too early yet to say what percentage of any specific area of retailing will move to the web. However, wherever a gratification gap exists or showrooms are necessary for the sale of goods, immersive retail outlets will retain a percentage of the market.

A web retail site is open 24 hours and a single outlet is all that is required, although if it attracts a genuine worldwide customer base then local "language and culture" oriented implementations will eventually be needed, which may in practice mean several distinctly different websites. Delivery to the customer's door is an additional expense, but for most products this more than compensates for the costs of property, staff, pilferage, security, logistics, storage, and many other retailing expenses, which diminish or disappear. The great leveling factor lies in "bandwidth." If a bricks-and-mortar retail chain wants to double its revenue, it will need to double its number of outlets. This amounts to an immense investment, probably in the hundreds of millions and perhaps even greater. It will also take a length of time probably running into many years and, of course, there is no guarantee that the expected customers will materialize.

For the online store, the situation is quite different. Twice the revenue will be achieved by twice the level of traffic to the website. There may need to be some investment in logistics and almost certainly a significant upgrade of computer equipment, but it certainly will not take hundreds of millions of investment; it is even unlikely to take tens of millions. Neither will it require a long time to implement. Thus we have many examples, such as Amazon, Charles Schwab, Egghead Software, and so on, where revenues have more than doubled, in fact multiplied tenfold in fairly short timeframes, and yet the infrastructure investment has been low. Indeed, for many of these ebusinesses it is marketing, not infrastructure, that has consumed revenues.

Groceries constitute one very large area of consumer activity that is primarily a matter of procurement. Here the consumer is rarely driven by gratification and a quick review of the cost profile of a supermarket operation indicates that the business is destined to become web based. In the UK, for example, supermarkets exhibit the following cost profile (as a percentage of product price). Typically, fixed overhead is between 4 and 5 percent, staff costs are between 5 and 6 percent, and other operating costs are between 2 and 3 percent. The average mark-up on product is around 17 percent, so the net profit per item typically averages between 4 and 5 percent. The situation is slightly more competitive in the US and Germany, but not significantly different.

On the internet, fixed overhead, staff costs, and operating costs fall, but a delivery cost is added. The result is lower prices if volumes are large enough, which can be ensured by penalizing low-volume purchasers with a high delivery charge. The main part of the grocery business will go on to the web, destroying the immersive retail sector's economies of scale and forcing conventional outlets to add value in a completely different way. The supermarkets will move to the web, but the delicatessens will not, for example.

One of the early movers in the UK was Tesco. It has had an internet ordering capability for quite a while, but only in certain areas. It has now launched cyberzones providing internet access from within its stores, selling books, CDs, and videos, products that it currently sells in small numbers. It also intends to move into the sale of white goods and automobiles, which constitute completely new business lines. In the UK, Tesco is facing web competition from Iceland and Waitrose, both of which have been quick into the market. In fact, Iceland has rebranded itself as Iceland.co.uk, implying a dedication to web purchase and home delivery (a service it already provided).

In the US, the early movers were Webvan and Peapod, but at the moment shoppers get no significant price advantage. However, there is also Priceline.com's WebHouse Club, which offers shoppers the capability of naming their own grocery prices. The company does not deliver, instead the consumer collects from one of the participating supermarket outlets, their credit card being billed automatically. Some shoppers claim to have cut their bills significantly via this service. There is a charge of $3 a month after customers have used the service for three months. The biggest grocer of all, Wal-Mart, has yet to enter the market meaningfully, so the situation is still evolving.

Specialist retail is interesting, because it is a definable area and it will straddle the web and bricks and mortar. Indeed, the term "clicks and mortar" has emerged to describe such situations. Kiteman, a kite shop in Oklahoma (www.telepath.com/kiteman/), and Kites.co.uk are examples of shops that saw an increase in business once they set up websites. Similar examples can be found in almost any specialist area, from antique firearms through to security gadgets. In most such niches there will be competition, but it will rarely be fierce.

The electronic retailing sector is diverse. It includes recognizable retail outlets that roughly mirror bricks-and-mortar businesses. Californian online supermarket Webvan, for example, currently mirrors a traditional supermarket in the groceries it provides. Another good example is Bluefly.com, a clothing site that sells designer brands from an attractively designed website at competitive prices. It provides attractive photographs of the goods and it also offers some added value with MyCatalog, an interactive capability that gathers your profile and makes suggestions about goods that might be of interest.

Amazon is becoming a kind of web department store, selling a variety of goods that would normally be found in separate shops: books, CDs, videos, greeting cards, toys, and more. The selection of goods for sale appears to be determined by a combination of the size of the web market for the product and the logistics of delivery—the site is not in any way like a bricks-and-mortar department store. The company is now also renting "floor space" on its website to other retailers.

A further development will inevitably happen within this sector as websites become more sophisticated. At the moment entertainment is not a significant part of the web shopping experience but it will undoubtedly become so with time. Already Landsend.com gives you the ability to clothe a model that conforms to your own dimensions. It is easy to conceive of adding sophistication to this by changing hairstyle, adding make-up, and so on. When they become sufficiently refined, such developments will be attractive to consumers and may pull customers away from immersive shopping.

It is also worth noting here that the electronic retailer needs to have the underlying capability to deliver. The fact that Webvan and Amazon have made heavy investments in delivery infrastructure indicates that the economy of the US (and elsewhere) was not geared up for the kind of service the web customer requires. Indeed, many purchases from the web involve longer delivery times than customers expect.

Because of this, the real web retailer may not even be visible to the buyer. An example of this is Ingram Micro, currently the largest distributor of computer hardware and software. Traditionally, Ingram was a wholesaler that delivered to PC retailers. With the move to the net, it began to specialize in distribution, so that now it is capable of shipping in single units directly to the customer—and it can make it look like the order came from someone else, usually a website, complete with customized packing slip. To support its operation, Ingram has also built an extranet website to share information with any web-based operation that wants to use its services. Other wholesalers are copying this model in the areas of books, toys, and office supplies.

Thus a number of supposed electronic retailers are really nothing more than agents for the true distribution operation—the real service that the consumer is buying, along with the goods themselves. There are also aggregation operations, such as Letsbuyit.com and Accompany.com, with websites grouping together a set of individuals who wish to purchase a specific item in order to obtain a quantity discount. Such aggregators naturally take responsibility for delivery and hence they compete with the wholesaler/distributor operations.

Finally, it is worth noting that auctions are already proving to be a huge subsector within electronic retail and yet this is still in its infancy. The force of commoditization is far stronger on the web and this leads to electronic retail moving in the direction of various forms of auction or pure market in order to sell goods, in line with the trading model discussed in Chapter 6. Consumer-to-consumer auctions have proved popular, but the area of growth will probably be in business-to-consumer auctions, where manufacturers may discover that the auction process offers them the best channel through which to sell goods. It has the advantage of being a very fast way to dispose of unwanted inventory. Indeed, the whole of electronic retail has the character of reducing the inventory in the distribution channel.

The digital distribution of weightless goods

Digital distribution, the fourth retailing sector on our list, covers a massive area. It covers the whole of the current financial sector and extends to other "weightless" products such as music recordings and videos. In the other sectors there can be debate as to how large the role of bricks and mortar might eventually be in the market for any specific product, but in digital distribution there can be little doubt that the whole of the market will eventually migrate to the internet.

The rapid migration of the market for stocks and shares demonstrates this. In 1994 there were no online brokerages; they didn't get started until late into 1995. By fourth quarter 1998, estimates were suggesting that over 16 percent of overall trading volume on NASDAQ and NYSE was happening through the internet. A Dataquest survey of 550 online investors confirmed the obvious, that investors preferred the web because it provided the ability to access investment data at any time and because it cost less.

It certainly did cost less—a lot less. If you chose your internet discount broker on the basis of price, then a share deal that once cost $200 could cost as little as $10 on the web. However, the hockey stick curve was yet to demonstrate its power. It did so month by month as 1999 rolled forward. By mid-1999, estimates were suggesting that figures for trading volume on the net had risen to above 30 percent. The market was moving to the web at the astonishing rate of over 1.5 percent, perhaps even 2 percent a month. In first quarter 1999, Charles Schwab was declaring that traffic on its website was 10 times greater than in the same quarter the previous year. The total value of trades had been running at about $2 billion per week and it was now above $1.5 billion per day. Schwab had become the market leader with over 20 percent of the internet shares market, and its website was being swamped with traffic.

Insurance and banking have been slower to flower as web-based businesses. Nevertheless, few people believe they will not be sucked into the whirlpool. The online sale of insurance is hampered by the fact that many people perceive it to be a complex product about which they need personal advice—something the web is not yet equipped to enable easily. However, the portals are trying out the concept: Yahoo! has an insurance center and AOL partners with Provident American Insurance. There are also many direct insurance websites and their number is growing.

Although insurance products can be very complex, they are based on a simple principle. The customer pays for the underwriter (insurer) to assume a risk. If the event that is underwritten occurs, then the underwriter pays the agreed amount. Some of the premium for the insurance policy pays for its sale and administration, while the rest is pooled to cover claims from policyholders or goes toward profit. Life assurance constitutes a special case, as life assurance policies may have an element of investment. Here, some of the premium is invested and may provide the beneficiary with a return, even if the death insured against does not occur within the lifetime of the policy. The insurer is expected to provide investment as well as underwriting expertise.

Insurance policies are mathematical equations that model the risk of specific events, based on a mathematical analysis of statistics of past events, and relate this to premiums paid and interest earned. Except for special risks, such as those dealt with by Lloyds of London, an insurance product is a legal contract based on a reasonably well-defined mathematical model.

The insurance needs (or perceived needs) of the individual vary quite considerably, but the insurance industry has tended to provide standard products for common situations (house insurance, car insurance, life assurance, endowment policies, pensions, and so forth). Such policies are easier to sell, easier to administer, and the risk is easier to model mathematically. Despite this simplification, until recently there was a general need for insurance brokers and financial agents to provide advice to assist the buyer.

The insurance industry has traditionally had a four-tier structure of customer, broker, insurer, and reinsurer (to cover exceptional risks). The disintermediation of the insurance broker began to happen before the birth of the internet, with the advent of telephone insurance, pioneered in the UK by Direct Line. The business idea was to concentrate on simple standard insurance products, such as car and house insurance, at highly competitive rates. When the success of this strategy became evident, it was copied across the world. Now in the UK, about 70 percent of insurance is purchased direct. Clearly, the insurance industry had evolved to a point where the commissions the brokers were paid exceeded the value of their advice.

However, we should not suddenly leap to the conclusion that the broking function is now redundant in the insurance market. In practice, individuals have a genuine need for help in managing their insurance and investment situations so that as their circumstances change (marriage, house purchase, becoming a parent, etc.), their portfolio of insurance and investments changes in harmony. As the internet evolves, we can expect a new kind of software-based financial advisory service to emerge, dealing with both insurance and investment.

In consequence, the insurance product itself may change. More complex insurance products are possible. It is easy, for example, to envisage an insurance portfolio being sold as a flexible "single product," the customer having the ability to add or subtract insurance components at any time: life, car, house, possessions, travel, and so on. The broking function would be all important, with the risk associated with each component needing to be placed with the most appropriate underwriter or pool of underwriters. This bears some similarity to the way that Lloyds of London operates, but would involve a dramatic restructuring of the industry.

There is a similar revolution occurring in retail banking. A wake-up call to the banks was sounded when E*Trade, the second largest online stockbroker, announced in mid-1999 that it would buy Telebanc Financial, an online bank, for $1.8 billion in stock. E*Trade was clearly intending to create a broad financial services business. Telebanc was one of the few internet-based banks that only operated online. At the time it had 70,000 virtual bank account holders and E*Trade had one million trading account holders. The merged company offers a powerful set of services to its customers: making trades, paying bills, transferring funds, and applying for loans, all with the click of a mouse. ATM cards and credit cards are available as well as loans and mortgages. The aim is to be a one-stop financial shop.

This is not the only example. In the small-business financial market, OneCore.com is behaving in a similar manner. It is paying small businesses interest on the cash in their checking accounts. OneCore.com pays money-market interest rates on all the money it holds for its customers, but technically it isn't a bank, it's a financial services business operating under securities rather than banking laws.

Consider the awkward situation of the retail banks. The reality they face is indicated by the following: The average cost of a payment transaction through the branch network is 90 cents. The average cost via telephone banking is 53 cents. The average cost of an ATM (automated teller machine) transaction is 27 cents. The average cost via committed computer banking (direct connection of a PC to the bank) is 26 cents. The average cost via the web is 10 cents.

In order to run a web-based retail banking operation, you have to provide customers with access to ATMs and you need sophisticated computer systems to manage card-based services, checking accounts, and all other retail banking products. Much of this can be outsourced and is being outsourced in joint ventures, particularly with banks that have been more active in addressing the challenge of the web. In the same year that internet stock trading began, 1995, Security First Network Bank became the first virtual bank. It had no bricks-and-mortar outlets, and its deposits were insured by the US government just as if it were a traditional bank. There are now many virtual banks, but the march of customers on to the web has not yet become an exodus, even though it is now in the millions. In our opinion, the take-up will be boosted significantly when the "killer" capability of automated bill management and payment is provided.

Although we rarely think of it as such, banking is a broking activity. A bank acts as an intermediary:

@   in its dominant activity of matching borrowers to surplus funds;

@   in the sale and purchase of financial instruments, shares, bonds, etc.;

@   in its foreign exchange dealings.

The bank adds value to these activities by arranging them and administering them, but in reality it is market making or broking. This activity can be run with much greater efficiency and at much lower cost through the web, as web banks such as First-e, OneCore, Telebanc, and others are demonstrating.

The foundations on which banking is based may give us some indication of where this sector is headed. Checking and deposit accounts involve the customer holding money at the bank and the bank using it while it is available. In payment, the bank clears transactions (performs a service) and pays interest, also charging interest if a balance goes negative. Consider the impact of ecash. If I transform my balance into ecash, there is no longer a need to clear transactions on a checking account. In fact, there is no need to write checks at all, just send ecash. There is no requirement to hold this money at a bank at all, it just has to be held securely somewhere on the web. With this the nature of banking suddenly changes, and it changes drastically. The advent of ecash removes the need for the check.

Think this over: A check is a guaranteed short-term loan (usually at a zero interest rate). eCash is money *now*.

Also think this over: If an ISP can guarantee the safety of electronic money held on its computers, then it is a bank. It could also act as an automatic money broker (i.e., a bank).

It is easy to imagine the banking sector diminishing in size dramatically. However, there is a banking service that will need to be provided and in a very secure manner—the banking of information. Information banking involves the combination of a unique ID—perhaps a biometric (fingerprint, irisprint, etc.), maybe held on a smartcard—and a secure place to deposit information. The smartcard validates the identity of the "account" owner and provides access anywhere in the world.

The retailers of other weightless goods—music recordings, video recording, electronic documents, electronic contracts, and title (ownership of stocks, futures contracts, retail incentive points, and so on)—are banks by any reasonable definition. They do not sell goods so much as exchange one currency for another and take a commission for doing so. If an electronic retailer of weightless goods opens an account for you and pays interest when the account is in surplus, is it not also a bank? When it extends you credit, is it making a loan?

Therefore just as banks need to be regulated, so do retailers of weightless goods. There is nothing to stop these retailers extending credit to their customers and holding weightless goods as deposits. The banking systems of the world gradually evolved over centuries, slowly learning how to control the circulation of money and its creation via credit. They now face a challenge that needs to be addressed with some urgency. The whole business of banking is on the move and the regulatory structure needs to move with it—or else one day there will be a financial disaster of supernova proportions.

DOMINANT ENTERTAINMENT

The final sector, digital content, deserves detailed consideration. It is already a massive growth area when you consider that it embraces all computer software, including computer games, and also the movie industry, television, radio, the music business, and the authoring of books. It is destined to grow rather than shrink.

Information as presented through the information media can be classified as belonging to one of three types, or possibly a combination of two or all three:

@ factual;
@ functional;
@ entertainment.

Factual information is self-explanatory. Fact is fact—Washington, DC is the capital of the US, France is in Europe, and so on. Functional information is information that has elements of knowledge embedded in it. Software programs fall into this classification, as do instruction books, lectures, and any kind of organized information that seeks to transmit or implement knowledge.

The final classification, entertainment, is perhaps the most interesting, as it is by far the dominant form of information. Before the advent of the printed word, very little information in the form of entertainment was committed to paper. The novel did not really exist prior to Gutenberg, and there were only a few "classical" works that were primarily entertainment, such as *Beowulf* or Chaucer's *Canterbury Tales*.

Once print technology was established, huge volumes of entertaining writings were produced. To the vast array of books that are aimed at entertaining, we can also add the immense volumes of newspapers and magazines where entertaining rather than informing the reader is the prime motive. Entertainment dominates the publishing industry and it also dominates the media.

The digital content sector regularly invents whole new products, propelled by the simple fact that people like to be entertained.

Consider the following example. In the early days of the Windows PC, the problem of screenburn developed. The PC's display unit is simply a cathode ray tube, which works in a similar way to a television, with a stream of electrons being directed on to a thin chemical film on the inside of a glass tube. If the PC's screen is left turned on with the same image showing for long periods, then eventually the image burns itself into the chemical film. As a consequence, the screen's ability to display a clear image deteriorates.

This is not a huge problem. In reality, most PC monitors are replaced before screenburn makes them unusable. However—waste not, want not—it is sensible to have the Windows software work in such a way that if the PC is not being used, the static image is suddenly replaced by a simple moving image that does not burn the screen. This innovation was added to Windows at a very early stage. Microsoft provided several kinetic "screen saving" options between which the user could choose: flying Windows logos, flying through space, your own typed slogan that regularly drifts across the screen, and a few other options, including the most sensible one, a blank screen. So far, perhaps, a reasonable development.

However, this improvement by Microsoft gave rise to a minor software industry providing fun screensavers. The first product in this area was called After Dark and offered about 30 new options, nearly all of which were more interesting than those from Microsoft. Other screensaver products followed with some very sophisticated options, such as a series of Far Side cartoons. Guinness produced a popular screensaver that it circulated free. Some software companies gave screensavers away with their products. When Pointcast introduced its push information service, it was no surprise that there was a screensaver option that could be configured.

Screensavers have become popular information artifacts. Staff in commercial companies sometimes compete to have the most impressive one. You see them installed on portable computers, which don't have the same screen technology as desktop PCs and cannot suffer from screenburn.

What we are describing here is the very important phenomenon of fascination. Anything other than the simple blanking of the screen makes no sense—but damn it, it's entertaining. The introduction of screensavers damages productivity, although it is difficult to know by how much. You can watch it happening all the time. A screensaver starts up and quite frequently someone will watch it for a while, whether it is on their PC or someone else's.

If we look at other information technologies, for example television, we can see that the tendency to use technology for entertainment is general. Television is completely dominated by entertainment and so is the radio. Edison's phonograph, which was intended as a dictating machine, proliferated entirely because of its use for entertainment. The Columbia Gramophone Company and the Victor Talking Machine Company employed the greatest singers in the world, in order to make records to sell their gramophones—the first international "rock star" was the Italian dramatic tenor Enrico Caruso. As soon as moving pictures had been invented, the greatest entertainment industry of them all was established in Hollywood and it flourished.

There is clearly a human law at work here, which can be stated as:

When a new information technology develops, its use for the purpose of entertainment will eventually become dominant.

A raw new medium

The internet is a new information medium. Historically, technologies have introduced a series of changes in media. First, the book and other printed products supplanted the handwritten word. So did the typewriter and then the wordprocessor. Radio supplanted the printed word for news, but the printed word continued. Then television marginalized radio and the movie business, but did not destroy them. In fact, throughout all these changes the newer technology marginalized but did not completely destroy previous generations of technology. Radio still has an audience and a commercial life. The handwritten word continues to be used, although more marginalized than ever before.

Similarly, the internet will supplant and marginalize earlier technologies. Many newspapers now give away most of their content online and usually post news on the web before they print it, because they can—although one or two are fighting a rearguard action on this. The internet will marginalize television and further marginalize radio, and gradually destroy the activities of video publishing and rental, as well as sound publishing (CDs, etc.).

The internet is already squeezing magazine publishing. According to consultants McKinsey, *National Geographic, Reader's Digest,* and *Family Circle* have lost about 20 percent of their subscribers in the last four or five years. Over 43 percent of the magazines in the US have shed subscribers in the last 10 years. A survey by FIND/SVP in 1997 found that internet users claimed to watch less television and videos and read fewer newspapers and magazines.

There is undoubtedly a switch of medium occurring, for several reasons. First and foremost:

The internet is the first ever medium with a memory.

The importance of this should not be underestimated. Once an information product becomes available on the internet, it will always be available for use by anyone at any time, unless it is deleted by the originator. This is immensely more useful to the user than newspapers and magazines, which are transient by comparison, filled with information that is written to be thrown away. The internet is a far more suitable place for certain items of information, such as consumer reports, price lists, television schedules, and so on.

As sound and video become easily available over the web, either on demand or as scheduled broadcasts, eventually the internet user will prefer to select their own schedule rather than be pushed at. The net will also absorb and marginalize the telephone and all activity associated with it. It will become the dominant medium. Nothing short of a nuclear war will stop it.

If we analyze the nature of this raw new medium, we can see at once that it is extraordinarily broad. For instance, it can usefully cater to the following range of traffic:

@   commerce (interactive purchase of goods and services);

@   delivered electronic product (software, video, sound);

@   interactive product (online games, online software paid according to usage);

@   point-to-point connection services (email, telephony, videophone, electronic data interchange, messaging);

@   collaboration (MUDs, news groups, chat groups, online communities);

@   information push (solicited information regularly delivered: radio broadcasts, news, etc.);

@   push advertising (unsolicited or incidental information embedded in other products);

@   pull information (information deliberately sought: education, research, marketing);

@   live broadcast information (text, images, sound, video).

Some of these categories of traffic are only flowing at a fraction of their eventual volume. Multiple hockey stick curves will combine to determine how they grow. The force of automation will repeatedly reveal new harvests to gather. New media capabilities such as integrated internet telephony, good-quality video, ecash, microcharging, and so on, will push the medium forward.

Information transactions of many different kinds will cease to occur in the world of bricks and mortar and instead take their place on the web. And just like all other media before it, it will be dominated by its use for entertainment.

We could, if we wished, categorize the activities of the individual on the internet according to a scheme like this one:

@ *Passive entertainment*—covering all forms of pushed (broadcast) entertainment, whether words, sound, or video, hence embracing publishing, radio, and television.

@ *Live entertainment*—put in a different category because it sits somewhere between push and publish–subscribe and it will have higher value.

@ *Selected passive entertainment*—the same as the above but provided in a publish–subscribe manner where the user selects interactively.

@ *Interactive entertainment*—interactive software games such as Super Mario, interactive collaborative games such as Quake and fantasy MUDs.

@ *Active information seeking*—where the internet replaces the function of public libraries and a large part of the education system. This embraces collaborative information activities and educational software.

@ *Social activity*—the huge area of social interaction that currently happens over the telephone and increasingly by email, now enriched via the mechanism of the MUD.

@ *Information work*—using the internet to carry out various tasks associated with a particular job.

@ *Shopping*—looking for things to buy and buying them.

@ *Facility*—looking for jobs, paying taxes, voting, and so on.

@ *Advert consumption*—being distracted by advertising or volunteering to receive advertising.

Such an analysis makes it immediately obvious how broad a medium the internet is. It leaves nothing untouched. Nevertheless, this is a bricks-and-mortar analysis, because it assumes that these activities are actually separable. It may be possible to consider them as separate now, but they will weave together with time. Indeed, there are already many examples of them converging.

One of the greatest media triumphs of the twentieth century was MTV, a music/video channel that drew the attention of a whole generation and was nothing more than a continuous stream of adverts for music/video products. In the twenty-first century, the internet's MTV equivalent may show videos with more impressive special effects, but the crucial difference will be the button in the corner of the screen enabling you to buy that music or video at once. The advert and the sales process merge, because they can. Here we need to declare another reality, in case it should be overlooked:

The internet is the first medium that is truly immersive.

One can argue that television is immersive, transforming people into couch potatoes with a single click of the remote, but it is *passively* immersive. The internet is a space through which you travel, *actively* taking decisions on a moment-by-moment basis, assailed by adverts and buying opportunities and often frustrated by an inability to find what you are looking for. The act of surfing can be entertaining, buying can be entertaining, working through this medium can be entertaining, being educated by the medium can be entertaining. Maybe our collective understanding of what entertainment itself is will have to change because of the internet.

There will undoubtedly be a merging of media businesses because of the internet, to form something we can think of as the "content sector." So news services, television, radio, film, the music industry, education, publishing, entertainment and leisure businesses (to some extent) naturally become providers of content. But also the act of viewing (or experiencing) may *be* the advertising process, the buying process, and the consumption process.

COMING SOON!! THE AGE OF ENTERTAINMENT

Anyone who is building a website needs to consider exactly how they are going to delight and entertain their visitors. It needs to be part of the design process. You are either the circus or the sideshow. There are two possibilities:

@   The site visitor wishes to enjoy the visit.

@   The site visitor wishes to transact business and go elsewhere quickly.

If in doubt, assume that the first applies. Even if you know that the second is correct, still attempt to delight the customer.

However, the entertainment dynamic has yet to be properly exploited on the web. There are good reasons for this, some technical, some circumstantial, some simply a matter of immaturity.

The use of color is limited by technology, as is the use of animation and graphics for those web users that have low bandwidth connection—a reality that may persist for quite some time in some rural areas. Few people have a clear idea of the skills required by a web design team and anyone who has enthusiasm can usually get involved. Web design itself demands a technical understanding of software coupled with good graphic design capability. This has to be combined with an understanding of a web user's needs and behavior (in navigating a website), and all of it has to be tailored to the business model that is being implemented. It is not surprising that some websites don't provide a compelling experience for the visitor. There is no profession of website designer. For the moment, we're all amateurs.

The media supply chain can be divided into three, creation, sale, and delivery:

@   *Content creation*—or authoring, regarded as the preserve of individual talent, even if it often involves large teams and massive investment, as in the movie business.

@   *Digital distribution*—already discussed as a sector.

@   *Infrastructure networks*—including broadcasting, telecommunications, and the internet. This comes into the utilities sector in our map.

Historically, this chain tended to be strongly integrated under the control of "publishers." These publishers financed the work of specific authors, took possession of the publishing rights, and turned them into marketable product, sold down a well-established channel. This is true of magazine publishing, book publishing, television, movies, computer games, and to a certain extent computer software.

If we wished, we could take this idea further and insist that an insurance policy is authored by an actuary or team of actuaries and sold on. We might even go so far as to insist that specific products are the creative work of individual inventors, and that manufacturers do no more than package and market the inventor's idea. There is, however, a distinction to be made. Actuarial ideas are not so unique that an actuary could act independently of an insurance company and sell an idea to the highest bidder. An inventor might be able to do so, but the reality of manufacturing is such that the inventor often has great difficulty in attracting any interest at all, and if a manufacturer does appear then there is still significant effort and cost involved in refining and developing the product before even considering its sale.

What distinguishes authoring is that an individual or a team of individuals creates an informational product that can then be marketed. The internet is an inexpensive publishing medium, so the individual or team of authors may be able to publish without the assistance of a publisher. So the question is: *What value does the publisher add?*

This varies from one context to another. The newspaper and magazine publisher creates the whole product and its branding. Any contributory author creates no more than a component. Here the publisher also finances the creation of the product and gathers money in a sophisticated manner that involves both advertising and direct payment (subscription). On the internet the published product is a website, but the means of gathering money is the same— advertising and direct subscription:

@   *Advertising*. This is generally charged per "click-through," with prices varying between 3 and 10 cents a click. Direct internet advertising revenues were estimated at $3 billion for 1999 and are expected to grow at a rate of between 20 and 30 percent over the next five years. But the publishing sites are not the main beneficiaries, as about 90 percent of this revenue is shared between the top 10 sites, which are portals.

@   *Subscription*. There has been huge success in subscriptions among the pornography sites, but it is very difficult to get accurate figures because the whole business area is shady. Beyond this, there have been some successful subscription-based websites, but not many. At the moment web users don't like to pay subscriptions, because they expect a high level of free information, which many retail sites provide. (But remember, they are subsidising this "free" provision.) The non-pornographic subscription revenues on the web are estimated at less than one-sixth of the advertising revenues. However, pay-TV and video rental are yet to be implemented on the web and this will change the whole attitude to subscription. Successful subscription sites include Consumer Reports, The Wall Street Journal Interactive Edition (WSJIE), Lexis-Nexis, and West Group. All of these are straight publishing or aggregation sites.

The revenue model for web publishing businesses is confused by a number of realities. First, very few web-only publishers have become successful. Secondly, microcharging is not yet possible, so paying per page is not an option. Thus for the moment an advertising-funded business model has to be employed, which may not be entirely appropriate. Thirdly, although there are some subscription-based publishing businesses on the web, nearly all are bricks-and-mortar brands.

If we examine the movie business, then it is clear that the large studios also contribute hugely to a successful movie, providing financing as well as the marketing, and possibly also getting involved with merchandising. Movies are usually large undertakings and successful independent movie making is rare. However, *The Blair Witch Project* demonstrated that it is not impossible and that the internet can be used successfully to promote a small-budget movie. The cost of movie making is also falling, which itself undermines the power of the studios.

It is interesting to note that the computer games market is now $10 billion in size and as such overtook the revenues of the movie industry in 1999. However, it is structured in a similar way, with a few major players (Sega, Nintendo, and Sony) controlling the output of various authors. The music industry is comparable—although it offers a possible direction for authoring. Many successful rock stars and bands run their own websites, most notably David Bowie, who experiments with the web and was the first major artist to release a track on the net before it was available in record outlets. Such wealthy "composers" can go it alone if they choose.

There is also MP3.com, which has provided web space to thousands of unknown bands and seeks to become a web music publishing site. Whether it will be successful is difficult to say, but it is clear that very few web surfers are likely to sample music from more than a handful of bands, and MP3.com has not yet come up with a model that will market the more popular groups.

However, the recent development of a software product called Napster may be a straw in the wind. This software enables the playing of MP3 files, but also facilitates chat and helps to create an individual directory of where specific MP3 files are on the web. It could possibly be a precursor to the creation of a catalog that itself might be the electronic equivalent of a publishing model. In other words, the publisher no longer publishes by creating a product, but by adding content and capability and storing the links. It is too early to say whether Napster represents a profitable business idea.

All of this tends to suggest that, except for the superstars in any field who can surely run their own websites, the role of the publisher is not redundant, although it will be changed. It will be web based.

Growth lies in entertainment

If we now consider the 10 sectors of the new economy again, it is clear that only a few of them (infrastructure, electronic retailing, digital distribution, and authoring) offer significant growth opportunities. It is also clear that the internet will destroy jobs in many areas, particularly in the professions and in government—so it is worthwhile asking where the economic growth, and hence the new jobs, will come from.

There is no reason to believe that the trend toward service industries and service jobs that became clear in the advanced economies in the latter half of the twentieth century will not continue, but within this we can expect to see the growth of authoring and particularly its expansion to serve the needs of entertainment. The information age will be superseded by the entertainment age.

We can already see that auctions are popular to some degree because they are entertaining and that internet retailing will enrich the buying experience through entertainment. Those with funds to spare will naturally become speculators in the electronic markets and will do so primarily as a means of entertainment—gambling by other means. And in the age of entertainment, the composer will be king.

If an economy adequately clothes and feeds and shelters its population with a fraction of its gross domestic product, then it almost doesn't matter what else is made and traded, and assigned value, by those who buy and sell. If the past is any judge, the dominant economic activities of the electronic economy will revolve around entertainment in its various forms. It will be "bread and circuses" as usual, just as it was in the time of Julius Caesar. Different bread, perhaps, different circuses, and perhaps a different economic ratio between the two, but bread and circuses all the same.

9

The Aftermath

We have traveled a good distance and we have seen many sights in our odyssey through the electronic b@zaar. We may even have gathered some understanding of what we can do to help ourselves adjust to the altered reality. The new economic landscape is amazing and the changes are profound. To mention just the main ones:

@   All the fundamental business transactions are being automated well beyond their current level—presenting information (marketing, etc.), placing an order, presenting an invoice, making payment, providing customer support, and communicating generally (email and chat).

@   In particular, the buy/sell transaction itself is changing.

@   A huge increase in the availability of information has occurred by virtue of the gang of four publish–subscribe mechanisms.

@   A new medium has emerged that is superseding all others.

@   Paper money is being replaced by electronic money.

We have not yet passed the point of inflection of the curve of the electronic economy as a whole—although at the current rate of change, we may be passing through it by the time you read these words. The change that will solidify the whole situation is when electronic money becomes pervasive, an event that is not easy to predict.

AUDIT TRAILS AND SELF-DESCRIBING DATA

Accounting may not be very exciting, but it is a very intelligent scheme. The idea of a debit and a credit that balance each other and move money from one account to another is extremely sophisticated. It naturally creates an audit trail. You can track where money came from and where it went to, and if the books are properly kept then a complete history of all the changes that have taken place is available to view.

In accounting, data is not changed, it is always added to—and thus there is always an audit trail of what has happened to money. Consequently, auditors can audit the books of publicly quoted companies, examine the money flows, and state with reasonable certainty whether the annual accounts present a true and fair view of the company. Misrepresentation becomes very difficult to achieve.

In this respect, the computer industry has made one very sorry error, by not imitating accountancy in its handling of data, and has also not developed the fundamental technology of data management as far as it could and should have been developed. This double fault is easy to describe and understand. It is as follows:

@   A completely false mechanism has been introduced into software—the update. Data should never be updated.

@   As matters stand, data has no knowledge whatsoever of what it is. In other words, it is not self-aware. We do not have self-describing data.

With the costs of computer resource having collapsed, a full audit trail for all data is not an impractical idea and it desperately needs to be adopted as general practice. Electronically held data is not as reliable as it could and should be. A whole series of undesirable computer phenomena, such as viruses, fake emails and criminal hacking, as well as accidental distortions and loss of data, are possible because data has no enforced audit trail.

Not only does data rarely know where it came from, it also knows almost nothing about itself. This is in contrast to the realities of the paper economy, where many products now contain explicit data about themselves. Packaged food, for example, usually contains an inventory of its constituents.

In a world where computers consisted of islands of information, self-describing data was not particularly important. When a computer program ran against some data, the program knew what the data was and what it could and should do with it, and as it was the only program that had a strong need to know, it did not matter that such knowledge was buried in the software.

We are rapidly moving to a connected world and in the connected world the data needs to know much more about itself so that software on other computers can properly understand what it is. For an electronic economy to be able to work properly, data must know certain things about itself. As a minimum:

@   it must know if it is the prime source of the data it contains or simply a copy;

@   it must know who owns it;

@   it must know what its financial value is;

@   it must know how to decode itself and who has the rights to use it.

In the long term, data will have all of this knowledge about itself, because it will have to. At the moment, computer data in isolation is quite similar to the artifacts that are dug up by archeologists: it is not possible to say for sure what the data is used for and how, just as it may not be possible to say what some artifact from thousands of years ago was used for. At the moment, data has no knowledge of itself and because of this, it cannot properly participate in an electronic economy.

eTITLE TO VALUE

Paper money is nothing more than a "title to value," valid proof that its bearer owns the value described on the note. The establishment of paper money in the seventeenth century was the foundation of a new economics. At that point, value began to be recorded on paper and wealth ceased to be entirely based on actual goods and property.

The introduction of paper title had a dramatic effect on the world that is not so easy to appreciate because it happened so long ago. Paper title separates the value of an object from the object itself. Objects have value in two ways: They have value by usage and they have value within a buy/sell transaction. Paper title separated these two values from one another. Once paper title was introduced, legal ownership became a matter of holding paper title.

It is paper title that has determined the existing "world order." Currently the world is divided into distinct nation states—economic areas, where a specific currency is used to measure "value." The currency is guaranteed by a central bank that manages the money supply, usually in conjunction with the government. The government imposes taxes on the economic activity within its geography and organizations obey governmental dictates. If a government fails in its economic management and the value of a currency steps out of line with the value of the economy that it represents, then the currency markets compensate and the currency increases or decreases in value. This rosy arrangement that the world has become used to will not persist once the move from paper title to electronic title takes place.

It is already a fairly unstable arrangement. The laws that nation states impose on economies do not apply to all organizations, particularly multinationals. Such organizations can choose where to employ staff and where to pay tax, and are excellently positioned to force governments to compete for their presence within a national economy by subsidizing their activities. These organizations collectively represent more than 20 percent of the productive wealth of the world, and as such they have an economic power greater even than that of the United States.

The current economic situation might have been sustainable if the internet had not opened up the same set of possibilities to lesser organizations than multinationals. There used to be very significant barriers to becoming a multinational operation, but now there are not—it is quite easily achieved. This means that many more organizations can choose to arbitrage jobs and taxes and take advantage of subsidies.

Let us make the difference between virtual and conventional businesses abundantly clear. A virtual organization consists primarily of skills, software, and a position within some kind of supply chain depending on the nature of its business. Manufacturing is a fixed activity that is pinned to a geographic area and cannot be moved without expense. Even so, multinational manufacturing companies have happily arbitraged jobs, moving employment out of the advanced economies into areas of dependable, cheap labor. Multinational virtual companies can skip from one country to another and move funds from one country to another. They do not have to move plant and machinery, all they need to do is move the business process and they can do it in record time.

If Yahoo! or TheGlobe or any other such organization that lives on the web decides to operate from Panama, Japan, or Khazakstan, there is nothing to stop it. Thus governments may soon begin to compete to attract such organizations into their geographic areas and the organizations will, surely, be happy to receive the subsidies that will be used to attract them. In turn, this will create incentives for organizations to outsource low-grade activity and make its intrinsic value as mobile as possible between tax regimes and skills pools in different geographies. Thus the wealth of the world will become highly mobile.

An interesting corollary of this is that national currencies have no function in an electronic economy—ultimately, there is room only for a single world currency. Which currency this will be may be decided by market forces or by international agreement, but there will only be one. If there is any attempt to impose more than one, then the more stable currency will drive out the less stable. A national currency will come to be seen as a tax on international transactions and where the tax can be avoided, it will.

The coming of electronic money

The use of paper money is in decline. The figures in the table below show the change in the use of cash in the UK in the 20 years between 1976 and 1996.

Year	1976	1996
% of employees paid in cash	58	15
% of bank account holders	44	83
% of credit card holders	15	65
Annual no. Card Transactions	78 m	2423 m
Annual no. e-transactions	262 m	2613 m

Source APACS and RBR estimates

Clearly, as time has passed, more and more transactions have become electronic. In the UK, cash still accounts for 70 percent of all purchases made by private individuals. For the US, Mastercard estimates that 70 percent of all private transactions worth $5 or more and over 50 percent of the value of all transactions are implemented in cash.

Credit cards and charge cards are widely used for payments over the internet, although this is less risky in North America, where the credit card companies protect the customer against all but the first $50 of fraud and liability laws are different to Europe. Even in North America, people are wary and some people, the laggards, may resist participating in ecommerce until secure electronic transaction technology is well established. There are now a fairly large number of companies across the world that are addressing the market for electronic money in all its forms, including VISA, Mastercard, a large number of banks, and providers of specific technology such as Cybercash, Verisign, Verifone, Certicom, Certco, and many others.

Secure electronic commerce depends on encryption to verify that data is genuine (in the sense that it came from the person it claims to have come from). The process is normally referred to as adding a digital signature, and involves encryption of the data using a public key/private key mechanism. Put simply, this is a cipher with two keys. The private key is the only key that can create the message, but the public key can read it. Thus the sender can lodge the public key with a trusted third party from whom the receiver can acquire it. The receiver can read the information using the public key, but still could not create data in that form, as the private key is required to do that.

In February 1995, Utah became the first US state to pass digital signature legislation. The Utah Digital Signature Act recognized digital signatures as legally equivalent to traditional signatures. This was a step that other states and other countries have since followed. Consequently there are trials in progress involving various banks and digital signature technology from companies such as Verisign and Certco. It is digital signatures that make electronic cash possible.

VISA and Mastercard have been instrumental in defining a standard for SET (secure electronic transactions) and have been running series of test programs for several years now. The technology has been implemented by a fairly large range of ebusinesses, but it still being refined. SET technology covers a whole series of financial possibilities, from electronic charge cards and checking accounts to electronic cash and coins.

Electronic cash works in a similar way to real banknotes. There are different schemes, but the following process is typical. The electronic cash of a certain value is issued, with a unique serial number and in an encrypted form from the issuing "bank," and the customer's account is debited. The cash can be held on a PC, in a computer network, or on a smartcard. When it is used at a website to buy something, the website checks the validity automatically with the issuing bank (trusted third party), which verifies that it is unspent money and registers it as spent. The bank then settles the transaction.

The money cannot be lost because the bank keeps a record of what was issued, so if a PC were to be destroyed or smartcard lost, the money could be reissued. But that is not cash as we know it. It is not anonymous. It would be possible for the bank to know who spent which money on what, when and where, if it examined the data that it held.

There is a mechanism implemented by CyberCash that allows people to issue their own electronic money with their own serial numbers against withdrawal from an account at the bank, which the bank authenticates by digital signature. The mechanism involves sending a "blank note" to which the bank adds the amount and the signature. Encryption of the serial number prevents the bank from tracing the origin of the money, but it can still accept payment because it can validate the digital signature as genuine.

Apart from this there are other "intermediate" payment schemes that are helping to enable ecommerce, prior to the advent of true electronic money. The Lawson chain of convenience stores in Japan solves the payment problem by conducting the transaction through a local store. The customer uses a kiosk in the store to browse an online catalog and order the products. The kiosk produces a paper payment slip that the customer uses to pay the store. The store arranges payment and accepts delivery of the products, with the customer collecting the goods from the store. This is an interesting model because it removes the third party from the loop, and may represent a sensible technology for the internet bricks-and-mortar store. There are also schemes for adding items purchased over the internet to telephone bills.

Micromoney

Checking accounts, charge cards, credit cards, and electronic cash all suffer from the problem that the mechanism is too expensive for payments below a certain amount. Many new web business models would flourish if they could levy very low charges to customers for the service or information they provide. Certainly, many web users would not object to tariffs of a few cents a page, and might perhaps prefer this to being exposed to banner advertisements. The ability to implement microcharging is thus very important.

One way of implementing micropayments is by cooperation between multiple sites. A company that provides technology for this is the Clickshare Service Corporation. Clickshare can track movements as users jump to multiple unrelated sites, manage multiple-site subscriptions, and settle charges down to 10 cents per transaction. The way it works is that a user registers with a single site that supports Clickshare, providing the site with enough information for account billing. The user can then be charged for access at all sites that support Clickshare. In practice, when the user first logs on, they have to register that they are starting a "clickshare session." They are authenticated by the central Clickshare site and from then on, individual page visits (clicks) can be charged for. Account information is sent on a daily basis to the web user, on request, and personal information is blocked for any usage other than billing. Member websites in the scheme can also reward each other for posting links to each other's sites.

There is a micropayment system called MilliCent that can deal with the lowest imaginable charges and it comes from the digital division of Compaq. This system is based on electronic tokens called "scrip," which can be purchased through a number of brokers. You can buy scrip using a credit card and it is automatically placed in your MilliCent wallet. which is in reality an intelligent program. It takes care of online payment automatically as you click, paying the website that is being used in scrip. It also deals automatically with foreign currency.

In addition, MilliCent can keep an eye on spending habits. You can use it to set yourself a web spending budget and it will warn you if you are about to exceed your limits. You can tell the wallet how much you'd be willing to spend per click, per day, per week, and per month. So you could tell it to warn you if you exceed 10 cents on a single click, $25 in a day, $100 in a week, and $300 in a month. If you don't exceed any of the limits then the wallet pays without notifying you, but if you reach one of your spending limits, the wallet asks for authorization on each purchase.

MilliCent supports single-click purchases as small as 1/10th of a cent and is also able to accept credits into the wallet for websites making promotions—thus it would be able support "frequent clicker" loyalty schemes.

You've got bills

The invoice is one of the hallmarks of the paper economy and it is a very inefficient way of moving money around. The customer buys something—the vendor sends a bill—the customer arranges payment—the vendor accepts payment. Obviously, this is far less efficient than the customer buys something—the vendor accepts payment. However, the invoicing arrangement has the virtue that it can be used to cover a strong customer/vendor relationship, with the customer making many purchases over time and the vendor sending regular statements. In particular, it documents the history of transactions for both sides of the relationship and thus various discount schemes can be driven from it.

What the invoice does is separate the point of exchange of goods or services from the point of payment for them. This has its downside. In reality, there is a loser in this arrangement as money is always earning interest. If the customer pays first and then waits for delivery, he loses. If he pays later, he wins. Naturally, this only applies where there is no agreement to cover the cost of "interest" for the time between delivery and payment, which is the norm. And obviously, it leads to strategies for delaying payment by one side or another, because the simple act of delaying makes money. A whole sector of the financial industry, factoring companies, exists precisely to cover this situation. They pay you instantly for invoices issued, collect the money on your behalf, and you pay a percentage for the service.

Factoring companies are probably doomed in the long run, because invoicing is going electronic. There are various schemes: AOL/Netscape Communications plans to offer web-based ebilling software, as does

Transpoint, a joint venture of Microsoft, First Data, and Citigroup. The Integrion Financial Network, a consortium of financial and technology companies including Checkfree, IBM, RSA Data Security, and VISA, is preparing a pilot with Bank One.

There are different ideas being tried and it is by no means certain which will dominate. One idea is simply to send invoices in a specific processable email format, so that customers running particular accounting systems, or even bill-paying software like Intuit's Quicken, could process them automatically. If a *de facto* standard emerged then all accounting systems would fall into line.

Another possibility is to post invoices and a rolling statement on a secure customer page on the website, enabling electronic payment at the click of a mouse button. This is very publish–subscribe, as the customer might be allowed access to other useful software and data from the vendor, helping perhaps to integrate the supply chain. It would be attractive for vendors, because although they might be running an account for the customer, they might be able to outsource the financial support of that account to a bank that could charge interest on outstanding amounts and grant interest on surplus monies in the account.

However, the customer might prefer all bills to be held in one place. Cyberbills.com offers a consumer service that sends customers all their bills electronically. There are distinct advantages to this, especially if the customer retains the information in a searchable format. Then the customer can do direct price comparisons from their shopping history. If all the bills are held in one place, then software will undoubtedly emerge that will help individuals manage their money automatically.

MILESTONES ON THE EROAD

There are three main trends that are still in progress and that will drive the growth of the electronic economy further:

@   Internetworking of all computer systems.
@   Integration of business processes.
@   Embedding of intelligence.

259

The first trend is clearly visible as all organizations gradually connect their computer systems to the internet and all individuals become connected. The impact of this is slightly less obvious than the trend itself. Most organizations were surrounded by "manual boundaries." While they may have automated many of their internal business processes on computers, they rarely automated their relationships to their suppliers, partners, and customers; these were usually handled person to person. The simple act of connecting to the internet naturally creates spaces in which the force of automation can act and inefficiencies in these relationships can be removed. A great deal of the initial impact of the internet came from the fact that a mass of information was suddenly available and searchable. A secondary impact is that a mass of computer processes are now available and shareable.

The second trend is less obvious because it has not yet started to have much of an impact—but it will. Once there is guaranteed electronic connection between organizations, then it becomes far more possible to sell an automated business process as a product. Organizations will naturally start to take advantage of the fact that a number of common business processes are automated and available for use over the internet, and a large amount of virtual outsourcing will begin to happen. With the passage of time it will become possible to create a new company by creating a new business idea and simply linking it up with other necessary functions over the web: hiring processes, personnel processes, accounting processes, logistic processes, and so on—a genuine virtual enterprise.

The final trend involves the embedding of intelligent devices in objects. The reality here is that manufactured objects have a fairly low level of embedded intelligence, a level usually implemented by a mechanical technology. The automobile industry is already driving as much intelligence into its products as it can and most other manufacturing industries will follow. The embedding of intelligence provides two major gains: a product can be made more functional using software; and the product can become connected to the web and report its status back to the manufacturer or, if desired, to other web users.

If we take a long-distance overview of the trends in computing, we have witnessed the distribution of computer capability away from the centralized mainframe to PCs. We are now witnessing a vast movement in the opposite direction, as all the intelligence migrates back into the network. Yet at the same time we are still distributing intelligence in the form of embedded devices in manufactured products, and in the future we shall see the same kind of migration of intelligence from these devices back into the network.

Constraints to be overcome

A number of constraints will gradually be overcome as the internet matures. The removal of each of these will provide an impetus to specific sectors of the electronic economy or to the economy as a whole. They are the milestones on the electronic trading highway, the eroad. There is no way of knowing in exactly which order or the timing of when these constraints will be overcome—although the technology already exists to remove almost all of them.

Availability of video-capable bandwidth to the household

Currently, websites are constrained to use word and image because the majority of internet connections run at a low speed. There is a race among the world's telcos to provide high bandwidth as fast as possible. Once this happens, websites will be able to employ sound and video as a matter of course and this will alter their nature, especially retail and entertainment web sites.

Integration of broadcasting and the internet

At some point beyond the availability of high bandwidth, the broadcasting industry will be absorbed into the internet. While there are high hopes in many quarters for digital television as a way into the internet, it is unlikely that it will have much impact. Broadcast television will continue, but only for live event or live entertainment. The rest of television will be by the selection of "video products" from appropriately designed websites. Beyond that, it is unlikely that people will surf the net from their sofas. Primarily this is because the internet is fundamentally absorbing—it is a "lean forward" medium—whereas television is fundamentally entertainment—it is "lean back." Surfing the net isn't something that is done in groups. The natural outcome of this is that the entertainment dimension of television will be amplified and the rest of it diminished.

Integration of telephony and computing

Because of the protocol that allows computers to become part of the internet, computers have IP addresses that can also double as physical telephone numbers. The integration of the telephone network and the computer network is currently taking place and it promises much. In particular, it is worth reflecting on the fact that a website is a very "inhuman" environment. No matter how well designed and easy to use, the user is still interacting with a computer and it feels that way. The integration of telephony with computing (sometimes referred to as voice over IP or VOIP) naturally leads to the potential for being able to contact individuals directly through the website. This is already possible using messaging software, but once telephony is available voice-to-voice contact will dominate. This will also change the nature of the website.

Integration of video and computing

The exploitation of the capabilities of video is in its infancy and very few possibilities are open on the internet at the moment because of bandwidth restrictions. Currently there is camera output and animation. The special effects capabilities for altering camera output have been confined to Hollywood and television. In the computer domain, the technology for animation has only been used in games and in a limited number of simulations. There are great possibilities for this technology, especially if combined with sound and software, particularly in the field of entertainment.

Centralization of databases

At the moment most of the world's information is duplicated many, many times. This is particularly true of information about individuals and organizations. Even small companies have databases that they try to keep up to date at significant cost in order to stay in contact with their customers and suppliers. The consolidation of these disparate databases will naturally occur as the internet matures and this will in turn simplify and speed up internet interactions and transactions. In particular, the frequent need to enter the same information time and again to register for specific web-based services will disappear.

General adoption of electronic money

Government economists the world over have shown scant realization of the inevitability of electronic money, and there would almost certainly be strong resistance to any attempt to formally replace paper money with electronic money. The general adoption of electronic money is also held back by the double errors of computing: the lack of an audit trail for data, and the fact that data has no knowledge of itself. Thus electronic money does not know that it is electronic money and its movements cannot be traced. In order to implement electronic money, the possibility of forgery has to be eliminated completely and thus these problems have to be resolved. Nevertheless, as we have already discussed, the technology already exists to resolve most of this and all that is required is an internet banking structure that trails the use of electronic money.

Availability of micromoney

Micromoney is simply a further extension of electronic money. The problem for micromoney is that the transaction costs of actually exchanging the money have to be very low before charging at a very low rate for, say, viewing a page on a website is viable. At the moment, advertising is acting as a substitute for micromoney and it will continue to do so until the use of electronic money is established. After that, micromoney will become an option and will enable the sale of small electronic objects.

Availability of video-capable bandwidth to mobile devices

The popularity of cellphones took most of the world by surprise. The point that mattered was that the cellphone number gets you to the individual, whereas a telephone number of any other kind only gets you to a location. If there were no cost difference, then it is doubtful whether most people would use fixed phones at all. Interestingly enough, this is a trend that has a strong cultural emphasis. Mobile phones are extremely popular in Hong Kong, Italy, and Scandinavia, and are far more popular in Europe than in the US. However, PDAs (personal digital assistants or, if you like, small computers) are highly popular in the US.

It is difficult to know exactly how important the use of the internet via mobile devices will become, but it is quite clear that it will eventually be the dominant means of access and this may happen very quickly. Its expansion is constrained by the availability of high bandwidth to mobile devices and this is in the process of being addressed; once this obstacle is removed, more business opportunities will emerge, many of which are already being discussed among the excited proponents of WAP.

And also...

Finally, there is one constraint that deserves more than a few paragraphs, because it forms the basis of any electronic economy. This is electronic identity. The facts are simply this: In order to process information and relate it to the world of things, every item represented within a computer system needs to have a unique identity. If we bring all of the computer systems in the world together, then everything needs to have an absolutely unique identity.

Electronic signatures

Every person has a unique identification tag, stamped out by their collection of genes. While scientists may debate about whether characteristics like intelligence and sexual preferences are transferred down the family tree, there is no debate about the proposition that the genes completely determine the initial characteristics of the physical body. With the minor exceptions of twins, triplets, and other combinations of descendants from a single egg, the genes stamp out unique patterns all over the body.

They deliver unique fingerprints, unique palmprints, unique patterns in the iris of the eye, and so on. If you record a voice and measure its use of tone, volume, and frequency, you get a unique voiceprint. If you accurately measure the distances between key points on the face, say from the point of the nose to the corner of each eye, and from the eye corner to the lower and upper point of the ear, and to the corners of the mouth and the point of the chin, and so on, hold these as ratios and you have yet another unique pattern for each person. If you did the same measuring exercise on each individual ear, you would have yet another unique stamp.

More remarkably, if you use an infrared camera to detect and record the temperature gradients in the flesh immediately beneath the eye, then you discover yet another unique identifier that never varies, no matter if the weather is warm or cold. Even our actual signatures are impossible to forge if they are measured in terms of the speed of writing the signature and the pressure on the paper at specific points in the process of writing it. All of these are referred to as biometrics, and some of them will even separate twin from twin.

Biometrics are the only dependable means of authentication and they are reliable—far more so than passports and driving licenses, which are often used as validations. You simply cannot forge someone else's body. Biometrics are going to become important in the electronic economy, because they prevent fraud with an efficiency that defeats the thief.

The British police claim that tens of thousands of credit cards are stolen every week across the world without the owners knowing. An electronic reader that can read the strip on a credit card costs less than $50 and is easy to obtain. In situations such as restaurants where your credit card disappears from view, it is a simple matter to run the card through a reader and quickly make a physical imprint. This information is then, the police say, sold to credit card factories in Hong Kong, which then sell newly minted credit cards that can be used with impunity until the owner of the card receives the next statement of account.

Smartcards could make this kind of scam far more difficult to pull off, although biometrics would stop it dead. With smartcards, coded tokens can be passed with each transaction. It would be much more difficult, but not impossible, to forge a smartcard and if it were done the useful life of the card would be very short.

Dataquest estimates that smartcards will reach production levels of 1.32 billion by the year 2001. This is clearly a "nonsense trend," as currently the number of smartcards being issued in Europe exceeds the continent's population by a factor of three. In the long term, everyone will want to carry a single smartcard rather than multiple cards, so there will be a period of consolidation as cards take on more and more functions.

Clearly, there are good reasons to carry a smartcard. An example is provided by the KidzKard now being issued in New York City. This initiative was started by Mark Basile, whose child was rushed to hospital for emergency treatment but could not be treated until information about the child's allergies was obtained. He decided to do something to prevent such dangerous delays and his efforts launched the KidzKard, which holds vital medical information about a child. The smartcard makes a very good all-purpose key and we can expect it to be used extensively in this type of application for a while, but in most cases it will be superseded by a simple biometric reading.

Biometrics are also becoming affordable because the price of cameras is falling so fast. Fingerprint readers can be obtained for about $70, but they have the drawback of being only 98 percent effective, as some fingerprints are not distinct enough to read easily. Iris cameras seem to achieve 100 percent effectiveness, but they are more expensive. In any event, it is clear that the technology is coming into place and one of the prerequisites for the electronic economy, foolproof authentication of individuals, is being met.

Once people have a unique, authenticatable ID, then organizations can have one by associating the organizational ID with several of its officials. Once such IDs exist, then ownership of anything is simply represented by linking the unique ID of the owner to the unique ID of the object that is owned. The transaction that changes ownership also becomes very simple, far more simple than it is now. This is electronic title.

How many Sgt. Peppers to the dollar?

In February 1997, rock star David Bowie offered a $55 million dollar security against his future royalties for sales of his back catalog (his previous 25 albums). The bond was "A" rated, paid 7.9 percent interest, and it was snapped up within five days of offer by the Prudential Insurance Co. of America. David Bowie's music clearly has value and he has been able to realize this value via a financial mechanism. There is nothing unusual in this, other than the fact that the bonds were "A" rated even though the future royalties from any recorded music are not necessarily guaranteed at all.

The international music business is currently in a state of upheaval due to copyright theft. Music is far too easy to copy and for a while there is very little that the music industry can do to prevent it. With the passage of time, copying technology has got better, cheaper, and more available. We have now reached the situation where recordings are digital and copying technology is digital, which means absolutely no loss of quality. CD recording devices retail at minimal prices and the price for a blank CD is negligible. DVD has made no difference to the situation, it has simply spread the problem from the music business to the movie business. And at any given time, there are estimated to be about 2,000 illegal jukeboxes in cyberspace. Unless something is done, we can assume that 2,000 or more illegal cinemas will come on line, once the bandwidth allows, each playing perfect digital copies of the latest movies.

However, something is being done. Technology exists to apply electronic watermarks and locks to the digital signals that make up an item of music and video. There is a battle going on between hackers who try to find ways around any new security mechanism, and software companies that invent new mechanisms. The general idea is that you put an electronic lock on the electronic object (music, video, text, or whatever) and the buyer buys the right to play the item in the form of an electronic key, which grants the ability to play music once, a certain number of times, or for ever.

From the legal perspective, and for all practical purposes, there is now very little difference between counterfeiting a currency and music copyright theft—although the law is not yet chasing the hackers who write software to permit electronic counterfeiting. If an electronic object can be copied perfectly or even so well that most listeners cannot detect the difference, then the product is debased, just as a currency becomes debased if counterfeiting is easy. This problem will be solved, because it has to be solved. What is more, the point at which it is solved and the usage of electronic objects proliferates is an important point. In my view, it marks the ending of the period of inflection, the period through which we are passing prior to the rapid take-off of the electronic economy.

Once the internet is fully enabled in this way, there will be many electronic "titles to value" passing between computers. Undoubtedly, tickets for airlines, trains, musicals, plays, sports events, and so on will eventually become electronic and must be guaranteed against forgery. With the further passage of time, all title of ownership will come to be held electronically and almost certainly this too will be tradable electronically.

We need to understand that all of these electronic items—software, music, images, video, electronic forms of text, tickets, bonds, stocks, memberships, air miles, and so on—will only be electronic. They will have no paper existence at all. They will be distinctly interesting items within the electronic economy, because they will be their value. They will also be tradable, and where markets do not already exist in these items, pure markets will form.

So while the electronic economy will have the effect of gradually retiring some currencies that will cease to have a role, it will create a vast number of other items that are currencies of a kind—that have a value and that will be instantly tradable. Will such electronic items have prices or exchange rates? How many *Microsoft Encartas* to the pound, how many *Apocalypse Nows* to the deutschmark, how many *Sgt. Peppers* to the dollar?

EMBEDDED INTELLIGENCE

According to Les Belady, head of Mitsubishi Electronic Research Laboratories in the US, the amount of software code embedded in appliances has been doubling every year for the last four years or more. Two-thirds of the programmers in the world now work on this type of software; five years ago it was only half. Embedded processors are already big business.

There are two types of embedded processors: microcontrollers— purpose-specific chips that already have their function etched into the silicon— and microprocessors—CPU chips that run software programs and that therefore can have their function changed, simply by changing the programs they run.

In 1998, about 4.6 billion microcontrollers were shipped and under 300 million microprocessors shipped. Market projections suggested that the micro-controller market was growing faster, at around 20 percent compared to around 12 percent for microprocessors. Microcontrollers are the chips that go into dig-ital watches and calculators and act as sensors in cars and airplanes, doing lit-tle more than measuring temperatures or fuel levels. They are general-purpose components in the sense that the same chip may be used in many different devices, but they are single-function devices that require a program to carry out their function. Fairly recently, the fitting of airbags in cars led to a huge (in the tens of millions) new market for a microcontroller that could properly time the explosion of the airbag.

A typical house today contains 50 or so microcontrollers in various household devices such as stereos, televisions, washing machines, and so forth. A typical car contains between 50 and 100 microcontrollers, and ships and airplanes are littered with them. The disadvantage of microcontrollers is that they have a fixed function that cannot be changed. Their advantage is that they are very inexpensive, with some costing no more than a few cents.

By contrast, microprocessors are far more flexible. They are used primarily in computers of various types, from PDAs to mainframes, and the programs they run vary dramatically. Until fairly recently there was no attempt to build a processor that was network dependent, loading its software from a computer network rather than a local device such as a disk. This changed with the invention of Java by Sun Microsystems, a computer language designed specifically for distributing and running programs over a network.

What is now happening is that the software industry is standardizing on the use of Java, primarily because it is a viable technology for running programs over the internet, but also because it is a step toward programmable embedded processors. From a business perspective, the benefit is simple: embedded processors that can have their functions upgraded.

With the coming of networked embedded processors, we shall see the integration of devices and device functions. There will be two parallel trends. One will be the consolidation of devices. Thus the mobile telephone becomes the PDA, the personal music center, the mobile web access device, and so on. Similarly, the television becomes the web telephone, the networked computer, and the music center. The second trend will be the adding of further intelligence to devices, so that, for example, a refrigerator can know what is in it. Ultimately, all sophisticated devices will carry full information about themselves, their possible functions, and their current state.

In the home, all devices will be networked together and be able to share information. All connections to services (gas, water, electricity, communications) will also be networked for easy management. Prototype projects along these lines are already in progress and early technology is available. The same goes for vehicles, whether cars, buses, ships, trains, or airplanes.

With vehicles, there is already the capability to receive and act on navigational information. There are over five million navigational units installed in cars across the world connected to the satellite-based Global Positioning System (GPS). General Motors has been particularly successful with its OnStar product, which can be fitted to existing models as well as being provided on new ones. OnStar uses GPS, but also integrates with security systems, airbag sensors, and so on, automatically summoning the appropriate help if the car is stolen or involved in an accident. Its subscription is between $17 and $33 per month, depending on the services chosen, and General Motors will be adding in-car voice-activated internet access by the end of 2000, via the OnStar communications link. The company expects to have a million subscribers by then, giving it substantial potential revenues as an ISP. Other car manufacturers are pursuing similar developments.

It is not implausible to think of an individual carrying a "personal area network" with GPS connection that links together biological sensors and an all-purpose PDA. IBM developed a technology several years ago that allowed the body to be used as an information circuit, so that when two people shook hands information could pass between them via devices that each of them wore. With biometrics, they could check each other out automatically and invisibly. Information exchange could also be done directly between devices.

The proliferation of embedded processors may also bring unexpected changes. The next generation of products that are movable will probably use GSM directly. Thus a device could phone you to inform you of any attempt to move or open the case of your PC or any other similar device, such as a television or stereo system, or your camera or PDA. It does not take much imagination to realize that theft suddenly becomes very difficult to pull off. Devices could even check regularly that they have the right owner. We can thus contemplate a line of technology that might make viable the "white bicycle" idea discussed in Chapter 2. Properly designed embedded processors with communications capability would make the bicycles safe from theft.

THE INFORMATION VALUE PARADOX

There is a vast amount of information now available for free on the internet, much of which was assembled at minimal cost.

This massive resource of free data includes information of the highest order and greatest possible qualitative value. The *Encyclopaedia Britannica*, which once used to sell in print form for thousands of dollars, is now available free on the web. There is even a website that provides the text of a large number of books, including most of the classics, for free. It is being assembled by Project Gutenberg (at www.promo.net/pg/) and currently includes more than 2,400 titles with 40 titles being added every month, most of which are not protected by copyright.

The value of information is difficult to measure and not easy to pin down. In some areas it responds to the dictates of the market, but even then it is not a simple supply-and-demand relationship. In other areas there is a distorted market because manufacture and distribution are heavily subsidized. To add to this, there are many people who are quite happy to make their information available for no charge. Of all the markets that exist, the market for information is the most distorted, subject to government interference, laudably generous, and open to massive abuse.

At the start of this chapter we listed the main changes that the net has introduced, but we declined to mention two of them:

@   The value of information is in flux.
@   People are being empowered (by the publish–subscribe mechanisms) and hence are changing in ways that will bring about political change.

In examining these issues and their possible resolution we will realize, surprisingly perhaps, that they also harbor economic change, and alter the economic picture in an unexpected way. We will first consider the nature of information and its ownership.

Information artifacts and the information spectrum

As a product, information has some unusual characteristics. The cost of reproducing it accurately is usually very small and can be almost negligible. The same applies to the cost of its distribution. For example, the cost of a television broadcast is the same whether only one viewer or millions of viewers tune in.

The base cost may be significant, but the incremental cost for the additional viewer is almost nothing. This is also true of the cost of the internet itself.

To add to this, the means of reproducing information of various sorts is widely available and becoming less expensive with time. Thus the cost of stealing most information products is low and the chances of being caught for the crime are minimal. However, this is something that will change.

The value of some information products is difficult to assess without actually possessing them. But to possess the product is in many cases to consume it. Consider some examples.

Money

This is a very important example of an information product, because it illustrates some important points about information. First of all, money cannot be replicated, except by the government that prints it, so it is subject to an indefinite copyright. Where it is possible to copy it (i.e., forge it), then its value starts to deteriorate as the information product is distributed. However, if it is not copied then it is only possible to distribute it by dividing it. There is a very definite supply and thus the demand determines the value. The purpose of this product is simply to have value and to store it.

A piece of music

A piece of music has to be heard to be appreciated, although we may believe it is good because we already admire the performer and composer. Once we have acquired this information product, on a CD or equivalent medium, we may get a great deal of use out of it. We will not wear it out quickly, but we may tire of it after a while and its actual marketable value may decline over time if demand for the product diminishes. From this viewpoint, we could liken this information product to a fairly robust object such as a well-made chair. The big difference is that the cost of manufacture of the information product (rather than its content) is very low.

A novel

In normal circumstances, a novel differs from a piece of music in that it is usually only consumed once. Thus it is an information product that cannot really be tested by the buyer, only recommended by a third party and then purchased and experienced. In fashion terms, it is similar to a piece of music, in that its value may decline. A paper novel can be compared to a physical product that wears out fairly quickly and has a specific amount of usage, such as a candle— although there is some residual value once it has been read. If held in an electronic form, it does not wear out and is more like music or a video, in that it can be sold on to others.

News

News is an information product that wears out very quickly indeed. Like food it has a sell-by date, after which its value drops very low—almost to zero. It can also be passed by word of mouth at no charge. The more fascinating news is, the higher its immediate value. It is also the case that live entertainment and live sports events have the character of news. Their value diminishes quickly with time, but the immediate value can be very high. Such information products could be compared to, say, a meal, which has no value once consumed.

A hot tip on a horse in a race

This information product has a very specific use and has the same quality as paper money—the more it is "copied," the lower its value becomes, as more people will take advantage of the knowledge, bet on the horse, and reduce its odds. It also ceases to have any value whatsoever after the race has started, so its value does not degrade but reduces directly to zero, rather like a stock option that expires. It is valuable and highly perishable.

An advertisement

An advertisement resembles a tax that the consumer pays on an information product. It usually detracts rather than adds to the value of the product in which it is embedded. It delivers value to the publisher and the advertiser. While the information an advertisement contains may deliver value to its consumer, as they may have a genuine need for the product advertised, it may also simply be noise.

An idea

An idea is an information product that, in many instances, has no marketable value whatever because it cannot be turned into a product by itself. If an idea is complex enough it can be patented in a design and then it can have value, but if the idea is already in the public domain it cannot be patented. However, an idea may have massive value in use—just like, say, a hammer. The fact that some ideas can easily be borrowed or stolen is the basis for the belief that information should be free. Humanity has yet to find a means of preventing ideas being plagiarized. There are no physical products that resemble an idea.

A law, standard, or brand

A law is an information product that is pushed. A standard such as a unit of measure may be imposed and hence have the same characteristic, although sometimes the market dictates a standard, as happened with standard units of measure or with VHS as a video standard. Education constitutes a country's information "standard" up to a certain level and is both pushed and heavily subsidized in an attempt to achieve a basic standard of knowledge.

What is interesting about this kind of information product is that its value is cumulative but follows an exponential curve rather than a straight line, like the value of telephones or other networked products. The value in the use of this information is that it reduces transaction costs, pure and simple. A brand is an information product of this type and it can have great value, as illustrated by BMW's purchase of the Rolls-Royce brand for $60 million. The value of the brand comes from public acceptance.

We have looked at the whole spectrum of information and in doing so we can see that:

In general, information products are similar to physical products.

The main factor that makes information products different is that their manufacturing and distribution costs are now very low in most areas—and continuing to fall.

All manmade objects contain implicit information. A simple cup, for example, embodies both the knowledge of how to retain liquid in a useful way, and the knowledge of how to turn clay into pottery. With the growth of the paper-based economy, commercial products gradually became far more information explicit, with information being published on the packaging. This evolved to the point where almost all purchased devices were accompanied by a significant amount of paper-based information.

The most extreme example of this is the commercial jet. No modern commercial jet, not even a jumbo, could take off if it had to carry a paper copy of all the information manuals that accompany it, because of their weight. The sale of passenger jets is subject to a massive set of international regulations, with a particular emphasis on safety. This means it is necessary to know where every wire runs and to document it. The situation is further compounded by the fact that almost every plane delivered is different in one way or another, so even innocuous components have to be documented as they may be unique to the plane.

Human artifacts all embody knowledge. Some of them now come with a certain amount of information, which itself may aid the understanding of the knowledge they embody. Additionally, some of this embodied knowledge may be owned by patent—a legal registration on the ownership of knowledge for the sake of its commercial value.

Data ownership

Patents came into existence in the seventeenth century and were necessary for the economics of the Industrial Revolution, an era characterized by the embedding of knowledge in machinery. Manual tasks were replaced by mechanical automation and with the passage of time power sources were added to the equation: water power, the steam engine, the internal combustion engine, then electricity. Ultimately, the design of the machine was where the value lay and if this was not protected then innovation would be discouraged, so the idea of the patent was born. The patent was and is a paper title to intellectual property.

Patents only provide protection for 17 years. Officially, in order to be patented an invention must be novel, useful, and not of an obvious nature. Patents can be taken out on algorithms as well as designs, and recently it became possible to take patents out on plants. The number of patent applications has increased inexorably over the years and has reached the level of hundreds of thousands per year. In the US alone there were 163,209 patents issued in 1999 (compared to 28,096 in 1949). A patent is not free, and keeping an invention's patents in force over their 17-year lifetime is likely to cost as much as $250,000 in legal bills, filing fees, and other costs. However, the potential advantage that a patent may confer has led to the patenting of simple business processes and the much debated patenting of genes. In reality, what is happening is the attempt to patent any kind of information pattern that may have value, no matter what it is.

The patent is closely related to copyright, which is free. Copyright applies to a fully defined information artifact, where the exact form is what is protected. With patents an idea is protected, no matter the form in which it is expressed. Awkwardly for the computer industry, computer software falls somewhere between a fully formed set of information and an expression of knowledge, hence it is subject to much confusion and legal action. Software is naturally protected by copyright, but it is easy to mimic software to produce the same result without using the same form. Thus various algorithms used in software have been patented in an attempt to protect ownership under an alternative set of laws.

Today, most major nations follow the Berne copyright convention and thus all writings created privately and originally after April 1, 1989 are subject to copyright, whether they carry an explicit copyright notice or not. This applies to images too. It also applies to information posted to usenet groups and to email. By law, nothing is in the public domain and such information only goes into the public domain if it is explicitly put there by its author, or 70 years after the author's death. The situation can be summarized as follows:

@   Information products or artifacts such as writings, recorded music, and images are owned by copyright for a lifetime plus 70 years.

@   Information about the design of a process is owned by patent for 17 years, but if it is embedded in software, it is owned by copyright.

@   Company names, trademarks, and domain names are owned by registration.

@   The ownership of all these things can be transferred by sale.

@   Information that is in the public domain is freely available for anyone to
    use.

There is a mass of information that is not covered by this summary. It includes
a great deal of information that already exists and the immeasurable amount of
information that has yet to be created.

For the sake of the freedom of the press, some information is naturally
deemed to be in the public domain, such as an individual's image and voice.
When a specific image is captured by a photographer, the image becomes the
property of the photographer. Additionally, an individual has no rights over
recorded or accurately reported conversation. This can be made valuable by
journalists if it is interesting enough to a particular audience. Information relating to any criminal, immoral, or even unusual behavior is in the public domain,
and often highly valuable if the individual is famous. However, an individual's
personal information is protected.

Small extracts of a written work may be reproduced under "fair use"
exemptions of commentary, parody, news reporting, research, and education,
none of which needs any permission from the author. Although email is not
copyrighted, it is not deemed to be secret, so it may be quoted from within
reason.

Derivative works also fall under copyright, with all rights reverting to the
original author unless permission was explicitly granted by the copyright holder.
Thus you cannot borrow characters from an author or creator. Everyone from
Wallace and Grommit to Batman is covered by copyright, although there is a
small loophole—parodies are permitted.

Some MUDs have "acceptable use policies" specifying, and hence
restricting, the types of activities allowed on a system or network. In general,
such policies declare to participants the limits in the sysop's liabilities, the property rights to posted items, the usage rights and fees, and privacy protection
responsibilities. What would generally happen is that users would register and
electronically declare that they accepted the rules of the MUD. From that
point, the contributor's copyright depends on the policy of the MUD.

Trademarks

Company names are guaranteed uniqueness by registration and protected by law against impersonation. Trademarks are protected in a similar way to patents, by registration, although the actual use of a trademark is normally sufficient to establish legal rights to it in some countries. There is a generally applicable restriction in that it is not possible to register a word in common use as a trademark. This is in conflict with the registration of domain names on the internet, where there is no restriction on words in common use.

Consequently, although the most valuable brand in the world is Coca-Cola, the most valuable domain name is probably www.sex.com. If you are interested in chess, say, you will probably enter the domain name www.chess.com without even consulting a search engine, just to see what is there, and you will discover to no great surprise that it is a chess merchandising site. As "sex" is the most searched-for word on the internet, it follows that sex.com is the most valuable domain name. Sites with obvious self-describing domain names get more random traffic and they have also managed to turn a common word into a *de facto* trademark that has value, as the URL is owned.

Woody Allen, Tony Blair, and Monica Lewinsky have all had their names registered as websites by organizations, sometimes referred to as "warehousers," who make a hobby or a business of registering domain names. Warehousers hope either to sell the domain names at a vast profit or to use the recognition factor to draw web users to their site. Woodyallen.com, for example, is a pay-per-view porn site entitled "A Tribute to Oriental Women."

However, you cannot usurp an existing trademark or company name via a URL. In the US, the law ruled on the side of trademark holders in 1996, and a 1998 test case in the UK reached the same conclusion. As a name is not a trademark, the legal point is also being tested in respect of names. Jim E Salmon, a Californian, registered 400 domain names of famous individuals, including 27 country music artists who have jointly filed a lawsuit. Salmon has used the names to front porn sites, so it is not surprising that the individuals have objected.

He is not the only player in this game. Companies with the names Naughtya Page, Friend to Friend Foundation, and QConnection have all registered famous names. QConnection sells them for prices between $2,000 and $10,000. Anecdotal evidence suggests that when such domain names are used misleadingly, they are used to sell one of three things— pornography, politics, or religion—with pornography being dominant. You might buy one just to have a prestige email address— JohnDoe@JohnWayne.com, perhaps.

The ownership of web links is also subject to a legal dispute that has yet to be properly resolved. Universal Studios attempted to set a legal precedent by suing Movie-List to prevent the site from providing links to Universal Studio's content. Movie-List was providing a comprehensive set of links to current film trailers, a logical thing for such a site to do. As such, it was providing a service to its own visitors and also providing a service to the film studios in terms of increasing their exposure. However, it was also circumventing the Universal Studios home page, thus preventing Universal from presenting other information and possibly adverts to the web user. Rather than fight the superior financial muscle of Universal Studios, Movie-List backed down and redirected its web links accordingly.

In a previous case that was settled out of court, Ticketmaster complained that Microsoft's Sidewalk.com site linked directly to low-level pages. Microsoft backed down by agreeing to link to the home page only. It looks as though individual links are the property of the creator, who has the right to deny usage to others. Nevertheless, this doesn't help us with the matter of who owns the chain of links that may constitute an "item of knowledge."

Data protection

In 1980, the Organisation for Economic Cooperation and Development (OECD) issued a set of guidelines for data protection, and these have been widely adopted by many countries. Roughly, the principles are that data relating to a citizen and held by an organization:

@   should be accurate and, where necessary, kept up to date;

@   should be accessible to the individual and correctable by the individual, but also surrounded by proper security;

@   should be obtained and processed fairly and lawfully and only held for lawful purposes that are openly declared (in an official register);

@   should be adequate, relevant, not excessive in relation to the purpose for which they are held, and held no longer than is necessary.

All the countries in the European Union have specific laws based on these principles that govern the use of data held on computers and the ownership of that data. These derive from the OECD principles and were harmonized with effect from 1999. Under legislation enacted across Europe, data are not deemed to be processed fairly unless data subjects are informed of the identity of the "data controller" and the purposes for which the data is to be processed.

How this legislation will be applied is yet to become clear, but the general thrust is very similar to that in force in the US. Data protection in the US stems from the Privacy Act of 1974 and a number of later additions to the act, which originally only dealt with wire tapping. In May 1998, Vice President Al Gore proposed an "electronic bill of rights" to protect US citizens. In his opinion:

> *Citizens have the right to choose if personal information is disclosed, the right to know how, when and how much information is being used, the right to see the information and the right to know that the information is accurate.*

There is a problem here as to where the ownership of personal data resides, because there is a natural conflict between freedom of information (i.e., people should not be censored) and data protection (i.e., we have a right to data privacy). Legislation and legal precedent seem to lean toward data protection, especially where the conflict of interest is commercially based. Public opinion naturally seems to side with data protection where marketing is involved.

Thus in January 1991, US consumers openly revolted against a CD-ROM called Lotus MarketPlace, a database that was to feature detailed personal information on 120 million American consumers in 80 million households, information that had been collected by credit agency Equifax. The CD-ROM was intended for businesses that might want to customize their mailing lists from a vast, sortable registry of names, addresses, incomes, and buying habits. US consumers decided that they were not going to put up with that level of information about them. In a short time, more than 30,000 people had contacted Lotus and demanded that their names be removed from the database. The CD-ROM was scrapped.

Thus, it is a political truth that consumers own their own data, irrespective of the law, but at the moment the law favors them in any case.

TRACES OF THE INDIVIDUAL

The electronic consumer meanders from site to site leaving traces as he or she moves through the web. With every click of the mouse, some organization out there learns something about the consumer's preferences or intentions. Each search engine can target individual users by dynamically posting an "appropriate" banner advertisement relating to the word being searched for. Try it and see. Search for "gardening" and see what comes up. The exact content will vary from week to week as different companies buy the word "gardening" at different times from the owners of the website.

There have been calls for new laws that grant each of us "ownership" of all the transactional information generated as we move around the web—our information traces. This would mean that any interaction with advertisers would have to be explicit, so that we contracted to be a customer for their advertising content. Such a scheme is entirely feasible and would allow a separation between those who do not want advertisements pushed at them, and therefore might prefer to pay ecash for information, and those who would prefer to experience the advertising and pay with their attention. Once microcharging becomes a reality, then we can expect technology that allows the user a choice. Either you have dynamic billboards on the highway or no billboards, but you pay a toll.

By considering the area of web advertising we can estimate a value for the information on web pages. If, for example, banner adverts are 5 percent effective and cost 4 cents per click, then an ad-worthy web page is worth one-fifth of a cent. However, consider the following.

As illustrated in Chapter 2 using the info pyramid, there is a hierarchy of information that moves from low value to high value, from data (information without context) to information (simple facts) to knowledge. Tim Berners Lee's brilliant idea to link together all the online information in the world via electronic addresses parallels the transformation of information into knowledge. To all intents and purposes, a web link to quality information is as good as the information itself—we might even argue that "the link is the information." Similarly, a whole series of coherent links can constitute knowledge—we could say that the knowledge is the collection of links.

The information-gathering behavior of intelligent individuals could easily be very valuable, because it might trace out useful knowledge. It would be easy to store and distribute such knowledge. As such, the web behavior and web history of some individuals might be very valuable indeed. It would be even more valuable if they were to record their electronic knowledge paths and then revisit them later to eliminate the noise and amplify the signal. According to Paul M Romer of the University of California at Berkeley, an economist who has studied the information economy in some depth:

Ideas are the instructions that let us combine limited physical resources in arrangements that are ever more valuable.

True indeed, but even more importantly:

An idea can be represented by a collection of web links.

Most of the information required to educate the world already exists on the web. This goes beyond the idea of a virtual school or university. Such establishments already exist—for example, Athabasca University in Canada has no campus and its MBA program is delivered over the internet. A very effective means of educating children or adults could be obtained simply by aggregating the web behavior of the fastest learners.

This could be put another way, by saying that a proportion of the collective knowledge of the world's web users could be collected, analyzed, and synthesized. The web is gradually accumulating intelligence—but who owns it? Who *should* own it? Who can be trusted to own the knowledge that is now embedded in what is becoming the collective nervous system of humanity?

10

A World Turned Upside Down

What political change could the technologies of the electronic economy bring about? The technology of the printed word pulled down the old power structures of Europe, undermining forever the secular power of the Catholic church, tearing down the monarchies, and gradually establishing democracies across the planet. The publish–subscribe mechanisms of the electronic economy will lead to a new emancipation.

Consider the situation of John and Jane Doe, average citizens in the average democratic nation with a developed economy. They are valued by those in positions of power primarily for their ability to follow. And so they are cajoled, bribed, persuaded, manipulated, invited, and even inspired into "following" by a sizable population of organizations and individuals with a particular ax to grind—politicians, advertisers, marketers, evangelists, and philosophers. Indeed, the list could include any group or individual with an agenda, whether altruistic, malevolent, or simply neutral. Wherever possible, such organizations and individuals use the mass media as channels to attain their goal of lining John and Jane Doe up in support of their agenda.

The Does and their ilk have, for many centuries, been fed information through the prevailing media, which were weighted in favor of the interests of the powerful and the wealthy. They have been subjected to "push media," which are very corruptible. For the first time in history, then, they are being offered a publish–subscribe mass medium with the capability of leveling the relationship between those who have something to sell and those who might like to buy—whether the goods in question be dreams, ideas, or Coca-Cola.

John and Jane Doe will no longer be so easily controlled. Information shared is power shared—and power shared is power lost.

BIG BROTHER UNDER SURVEILLANCE

The decline in centralized power was a prevailing theme of the twentieth century. The ideological victory of the West over Communism was a triumph for the technologies of information distribution over those of information control and suppression. The technologies of information distribution make it increasingly difficult to foist a lie on a credulous public. This has made life very difficult for despots and, also, for all those who might wish to control information content and distribution.

The demise of President Richard Nixon in the Watergate scandal had the hallmarks of a Greek tragedy. In order to perpetuate Nixon's presidential reign, his henchmen attempted to bug the Democrat National Committee at the Watergate office complex in the run-up to the 1972 election. Nixon won the election, but as details of the scandal unfolded, the finger began to point more and more toward the heart of government and many of Nixon's lieutenants resigned. In May 1973, the Senate Select Committee on Presidential Activities began televized hearings and startling revelations followed. John Dean "sang like a canary." He testified that Former Attorney General John Mitchell had ordered the Watergate break-in and that a cover-up was in progress. Nixon was now in deep trouble and his fate was sealed when White House aide Alexander Butterfield told the committee that Nixon had ordered a taping system installed in the White House to automatically record all conversations—Big Brother was bugging himself.

Some tapes were subpoenaed, one of which had a mysterious gap of 184 minutes which experts eventually determined was the result of deliberate erasure. More tapes were subpoenaed and they revealed, among other disturbing things, that Nixon had attempted to thwart the Watergate investigation. In late July 1974, the House Judiciary Committee approved three articles of impeachment, and President Nixon was informed that, if it came to a vote, the vote would go against him. Nixon resigned on August 9. In 1974, in the wake of Watergate, amendments were added to strengthen the Freedom of Information Act.

Nobody remarked on it at the time, but the Watergate scandal demonstrated something very important. George Orwell was 180 degrees wrong and the nightmare vision of 1984 was not becoming a reality at all—indeed, the opposite was happening. The would-be "tyrant" had been laid low by the medium of control. With the passage of time, other events of a similar kind occurred. In June 1988 in Victorville, California, six sheriff's deputies were caught on video as they "subdued" a Latino party. A four-minute segment of the video caused uproar when shown to the local Latino community. It resulted in a lawsuit that in turn led to a ruling against the sheriff's men and an award of $1 million to the victims. This videoing of police behavior was later parallelled in the Rodney King beatings and in other events around the world.

Information recording and distribution technologies have made it difficult for all organizations, including governments, to hide oppressive behavior or "sensitive" information. The fax machine and the telephone are ubiquitous informants that the secret police cannot arrest or torture, but neither can they operate without them any more. The camcorder is an ever-present guardian, defending freedom wherever it is under attack.

The net has added to the whole battery of information weapons that make oppression very difficult to sustain. It has become an instant distribution mechanism. If anyone tries to suppress information that appears on the net, then a spontaneous campaign of disobedience erupts—and travels round the globe three times in the space of 10 minutes, crying "catch me if you can."

POWER TO THE AGGREGATOR

Consider the following simple proposition:

Power belongs to the aggregator.

This is not a sophisticated idea. We are simply using an unfamiliar word to create a different perspective on power. It is self-evidently true that kings, emperors, presidents, dictators, industrial magnates, and union leaders draw their power from the collection of individuals and "economic units" that they represent, no matter whether their followers have been coerced or the economic units have been acquired by unfair means. We can view such individuals as aggregators.

We use the word "aggregator" because all the publish–subscribe mechanisms perform an aggregation function that allows an individual to interact with many people at once. Thus it is now more possible than ever for individuals to become aggregators in their own right, to increase their personal power.

We could view the downsizing of large corporations in recent decades and the decline of empires from the British Empire to the Soviet Union as separate phenomena, but in a way they are not. They have both been brought about by information technologies. We could even predict with a high degree of confidence that the decline of the current Chinese empire is inevitable because of information technology. So is the further spreading of more democratic government across the globe, even if we still see democracy overthrown by force of arms occasionally. If we wish to stop the despots and prevent such eventualities, then we should not send in the troops, but the ISPs.

The previous new world order

In the immediate postwar years the world was not prosperous. The infrastructure of Europe had been destroyed and food was scarce. Memories of the Great Depression persisted and anxiety about the world's economic future was high. In Europe, capitalism was still considered to be a rocky American experiment and few commentators, if any, foresaw the economic boom that began in the 1950s in the US and spread across the world in the decades that followed.

In 1946 a new economic order was established. The Bretton Woods agreement gave birth to the International Monetary Fund and the World Bank, and set up a system intended to provide exchange-rate stability between the main trading currencies. At the Geneva Trade Conference in 1947, 23 nations signed the General Agreement on Tariffs and Trade (GATT) treaty. This created an international forum dedicated to the expansion of trade and the settlement of international trade disputes. Since then, many more nations have accepted the treaty, with 96 nations, constituting all the major economies of the non-Communist world, becoming signatories by 1988. At regular intervals, new rounds of tariff reductions have been introduced, progressively diminishing the barriers to free trade.

These were the foundations of the modern global economy and they delivered prosperity to the leading countries via the mechanism of capitalism, which competed with and eventually defeated its communist adversary. Capitalism simply proved more effective in its ability to generate wealth. But who managed to aggregate and control this wealth? Not the leaders of the capitalistic nations.

While the communist dictators had direct and unchallenged control of the wealth within their geographic domains, the leaders of the "free world" did not. It was owned and created by the large corporations. In the capitalistic economies there are organizations that are larger than small countries. Most of them are not owned by any nation, or even by a group of citizens from any nation. They are multinational.

At the beginning of the 1990s, when the internet came into being, just over a third of the top 500 multinationals were headquartered in North America, just under a third in Europe, and a further third in the Far East. As a group, their economic growth since the 1970s had been phenomenal. Their revenues had risen from $721 billion in 1971 by about 700 percent to reach $5.2 trillion in 20 years, a compound growth rate of just under 11 percent. This was more than double the growth of the world economy as a whole over the same period. The multinationals' combined revenue of $5.2 trillion amounted to approximately 20 percent of the world's gross domestic product— a full fifth of global output.

The top 500 multinationals dominate world trade. Figures from 1991 show that they were responsible for 80 percent of international trade in technology and management services, 75 percent of trade in commodities, and 33 percent of trade in manufacturing. In 1991, in the US alone, 40 percent of US exports and just under 50 percent of US imports were international intra-company transfers by the top 500. Figures for other advanced economies were similar. A huge amount of international trade is actually the transfer of assets or the movement of work in progress within multinationals.

The economic power of these companies does not derive from efficiency, although they may be efficient in their operation. It derives from their size and their ability to carry out arbitrage. Multinational corporations have been able to take advantage of commercial opportunities that are not open to smaller companies. International trade was less competitive in the years prior to the internet, simply because it involved so much expertise and basic cost. These constituted very high barriers to entry, diminishing competition and creating commercial opportunity.

Unfortunately for the multinationals, the barriers to entry are now collapsing. A whole series of factors are driving this, but the trend started well before the birth of the net. It began with financial deregulation in the 1980s, which at first worked in favor of the multinationals. The volume of foreign investment across the world more than tripled during the 1980s, reaching $2 trillion. International banking loans quadrupled from 1980 to 1991, to reach $3.6 trillion, and foreign exchange trading totalled more than $1 trillion per day by 1991. International trading in stocks, bonds, and other financial paper also accelerated, and most of this international activity was handled in one way or another by the top 50 banks.

However, international trade was ceasing to be the preserve of the large corporation. The first breach in the wall was, strange as it may seem, the provision of credit cards that could be accepted worldwide. This meant that international payment was possible for small transactions without having to go through the tortuous and expensive process of applying for a letter of credit. The credit card process is so easy that nowadays some exporters prefer to break payments into, say, $5,000 parcels and use a credit card.

For small items, the problem of international delivery was solved by the expansion of DHL, FedEx, UPS, and other delivery services. By 1994, the internet was taking shape and these two factors, credit card payment and secure international delivery, made international ecommerce viable. By 1996 ecommerce was up and running, and international trade was no longer the preserve of a select club—it was open to anyone. The power of these economic aggregators had been shared out.

How the tigers got their teeth

In 1975, the average American family needed 18 weeks of earnings to buy the average car. In 1995, the cost was 28 weeks of income. In real terms either the price had gone up or the wages had gone down; actually it was the wages that fell. In the US from 1989 to 1994, output rose by 10 percent while wages rose in real terms by only 4 percent. So why wasn't the productivity gain reflected in wages?

There were several contributing causes, but the main reason was that some of US manufacturing activity was exported. The figures say it all. In 1993, US workers could make a shirt in 14 minutes while a Bangladeshi worker took 25 minutes. But the US wage was $7.53 per hour, whereas in Bangladesh it was 25 cents per hour—one-thirtieth as much. Similarly, a US worker produced steel at the rate of 3.4 hours per ton, whereas in Brazil a worker took as long as 5.8 hours to produce a ton, but the US wages were $13 per hour whereas the Brazilian wages were $1.28 per hour.

Multinational corporations do not protect home jobs and have no legal responsibility to do so. For example, General Electric more than tripled its revenues and profits while it shrank its workforce from 435,000 to 220,000. In its worst years, IBM was shedding US jobs at the same time as it was expanding employment in Japan—eventually it eliminated more than half its US workforce, and more than 50 percent of its total workforce are currently employed outside the US. From 1988 to 1993, the Japanese began moving assembly work out of Japan to combat the effect of the rising yen. In Europe, the Germans moved manufacture into the Czech Republic and other low-wage areas of Eastern Europe. The picture was the same everywhere.

The export of manufacture may cause dismay, but the alternative would probably be worse. At least when manufacturing is exported there is a rump of local workers who retain some chance of staying employed. The results of not exporting manufacture can be seen in the shipbuilding industry, where the once traditional shipbuilding countries such as the US, UK, Germany, France, Finland, and Sweden lost jobs to Japan and then Korea, both of which are now losing jobs to Brazil, China, and Taiwan. Manufacturing is nomadic in nature. It moves where the labor is cheap, and it does so because the multinational corporations arbitrage the labor markets of the world. They dispose of expensive employees and acquire cheap ones.

And this, of course, is how the Asian tigers got their teeth. In 1970, Asia had only eight cities with more than five million inhabitants, but there are now 30. There have been massive increases in the number of roads and railways and in electricity production across the region. In a single lifetime, millions of Asians have escaped destitution and many can be accurately described as middle class. From 1971 to 1991 in Malaysia, GNP rose from 13 million to 123 million ringgits, a multiple of 10. Per capita income rose from $410 to over $3000, and life expectancy increased from 62.3 to 70.5 years. Incomes in South Korea have quadrupled in the last 20 years. The story was similar in all the tiger economies.

The Asian way was to blend capitalism with a kind of socialism. Public housing and various forms of income support were provided in exchange for controlled industrial wages and either token or no unionization. For the sake of prosperity, human rights were sacrificed in some areas, just as they were in Europe during its industrial revolution. Employees in the factories were quick to learn, yet earned remarkably low wages, and governments strained to keep wages low in order to encourage inward investment.

The treasonable nature of capital

In Joseph Heller's *Catch-22*, Milo Minderbinder sets up a deal with the Germans for the American Air Force to strafe and bomb its own airfield. The economic logic is impeccable. The Germans would attempt to attack the airfield anyway, but the Americans could do it at much lower cost, not having to travel so far. So Milo Minderbinder sets up a win–win deal, where he and everyone else makes a profit. This ruthless satire merely points out the completely amoral nature of capital.

Capital chases a good risk/reward ratio and that is all it cares about. Capital only becomes moral when politicians or activists (politicians by another name) enforce morality on it. Capital shunned South Africa in the apartheid years because activists altered the risk/reward ratio by drawing attention to organizations that invested there and protesting against them. Capital will happily invest in dictatorial regimes and, when it is allowed to, it travels abroad the moment that its home nation is in economic distress. It cares nothing for the Stars and Stripes or the Union Jack or the Tricolore.

So who are the evil capitalists that flout our values and sneer at our patriotic impulses? By and large they are you and me, most of the citizens of the modern economy. There is a very large pool of investment capital spread out across the world economy. It is added to daily as individuals save money and make it available in one way or another to the pool: directly by investment in mutual funds, bonds, and stocks; indirectly by pension contributions, or any other financial instrument. All of this capital seeks an adequate risk/reward ratio and thus it moves from place to place. Where an investment is perceived to be undervalued, the capital moves in and the price naturally adjusts. Similarly, when an investment is perceived to be overvalued, the capital moves out.

This is the nature of the paper economy. It is simply the pull of the market, but politicians sometimes get upset about it, wishing that it would work in some other way. For example, Dr. Mahathir Mohamad, Prime Minister of Malaysia, addressed an audience of international financiers and civil servants at an IMF–World Bank meeting in Hong Kong in 1997. Pointing out that foreign exchange trading is 20 times larger than the trade in goods and services, he stated that it should be stopped as it was "unnecessary, unproductive, and totally immoral." He described currency trading as "secretive and shady" and claimed that market turmoil in the region at the time was a "move by western industrialized nations to keep Asia poor." By the same logic, the previous decades of western investment were, presumably, a fiendish plot to make Asia immensely wealthy.

The destruction of the value of sterling in 1992 was a demonstration, if any were needed, that governments can no longer control foreign exchange flows. In an attempt to remain within the European Exchange Rate Mechanism (ERM), the UK government tried to resist the flight of capital into other currencies and ran out of funds in two days flat, squandering billions in the process. Governments, it seems, can no longer stop capital flows of any kind, they can only encourage them.

Economic power has passed to the great economic aggregators—the multinationals, not the capitalistic nation states. It is they who find it necessary to hedge against the decline in the value of any currency, and thus it is they—acting in their own interests—who can destabilize a currency and bring down a national economy. The governments of nation states have economic power only by virtue of their ability to tax, and this itself is not under their total control. If governments tax too heavily or borrow too heavily or set interest rates too low, then the multinational organizations naturally take defensive action. After all, they are obliged to act primarily on behalf of their shareholders. So the capital flows through the international financial markets punish the government that moves too far out of line. If it persists, the currency is destabilized, stock markets collapse, and investment dries up.

Throughout the final decades of the twentieth century, governments across the world pandered to the multinationals in the hope of attracting investment. They offered lengthy tax holidays, exemption from import duties, and various employment subsidies. Such benefits were usually only granted for a period of five or ten years, but could often be extended by negotiation, especially if another inward investment were hinted at.

They had good reason for this. The statistics suggested that each new manufacturing job created just over 4.22 other jobs. This explains the intense competition to attract investment, especially from manufacturing companies, and the price paid escalated year on year, as the following figures from the US show:

@   Tennessee gave Nissan $11,000 per job for a plant in Smyrna in 1980.
@   South Carolina gave $79,000 per job to BMW in 1992.
@   Alabama paid $200,000 per job to DaimlerBenz for a plant in 1993.
@   Kentucky broke this record later the same year by paying $350,000 per job to a Canadian steel producer.

But inward investment is by no means permanent, as is regularly illustrated. In 1999 a Siemens silicon chip plant in the North of England closed down, despite that fact that it had received over $400 million in grants for its establishment in 1995. In 1996, John Bruton, then Taoiseach (Prime Minister) of Ireland, publicly complained about some foreign investors with the words:

> *One Japanese company is worth three of any other kind—once they are here they don't leave. For others it's just an excuse to settle in the short term before moving on somewhere marginally cheaper.*

In 1996, multinationals invested $350 billion in productive assets outside their home countries. This is a remarkably large figure, nearly half of which (47 percent) was accounted for by flows in and out of the US, with $78.1 billion flowing in and $85.6 billion flowing out. In all probability, most of the investment decisions were taken by US executives attempting to satisfy their shareholders in providing the best possible rewards for their investment.

In search of productivity, multinational companies have arbitraged the national economies of the world: they sold employees in some economies and bought employees in others, they moved funds between economies to minimize the taxation burden, and they negotiated for the best possible grants in order to subsidize their investment. And we, the capitalists of the world, applauded them when they did this—it was, after all, our pensions that were being funded by the escalation in the value of their shares.

All of this activity has undermined the power of national governments to control the behavior of the multinationals and thus to exert control over their own economies. We might even have been happy to accept such a situation, given that multinational corporations only represented one-fifth of the world economy and are rarely malevolent in their behavior—but this was not going to last long.

The internet appeared and quickly it became possible for small companies and even individuals to become multinational. The publish–subscribe mechanisms were beginning to do their work. Suddenly, the privileged economic position of multinational corporations was being opened up to everyone. The power of the aggregators was being undermined. The cat was right in there among the pigeons.

Three sides to human nature

In the nineteenth century, Karl Marx could happily think in terms of capitalist factory owners and the working class, because the working class owned very little and was usually dependent on the factory owners to provide employment. Things have changed—profoundly. While there are individuals with wealth that runs into billions whom some might think of as capitalists, and also individuals with no significant personal wealth, the worker/capitalist duality is no longer meaningful in the advanced economies.

A number of features of the modern economy ensure that the majority of the population are capitalists in some way. Almost all individuals have life assurance and contribute to a pension, and most individuals hold money in a bank. They may also have some direct investment in stock or in a mutual fund, even if the amount is not huge. The money allocated in this way is capital, and most of it will be invested to provide the maximum return according to some policy of risk/reward. So we are all capitalists now, and thus *our interest will only be served if those who act on our behalf provide us with the best possible return on our investment.*

Except for the wealthy few who do not need to work and no longer choose to do so, most of us are also employees in some form. We must all answer to someone, whether it be to a manager or shareholders or, if we are self-employed, to our customers. The constraint that employment places on us varies. Some of us may have to appear at the factory or office day after day, arriving and leaving at specific times, while others may have a looser arrangement. In any event, as employees we will naturally want to have the best remuneration. *Our interest will only be served if we are paid the highest possible price for our labor.* We are thus at odds with our capitalistic selves, who would prefer our wages to be pushed down.

In addition, we are all consumers of products and services. As such we care that the products and services we receive represent true value. They must be of sufficient quality and be priced fairly. *Our interest will only be served if we pay the lowest possible price for a known quality of product.* As consumers, we are in conflict with our capitalistic selves who yearn for higher margins, and with our employee nature that yearns for higher wages.

While this situation may seem paradoxical, it is probably good news rather than bad. At least we are in a position where we can understand the results of any excessive movement in favor of any one of our three financial aspects: capital, wages, and value. The movement into an electronic economy helps us and also hinders us. It helps us because it makes it far simpler to become involved as a capitalist and an employee and a consumer. What we have described above only really applies to a relatively small proportion of the world, even if it applies to a fairly high proportion of the population of the advanced economies. The electronic economy will change this, as it applies arbitrage to all the world's economic institutions and economies.

Consider first the *capitalist*. Institutions and wealthy individuals have for years traded through electronic facilities and received advantageous discounts, whereas the small investor has had no choice but to buy and sell in an expensive way, through brokers to market makers and specialists who execute trades at spreads. As a result of the net, the small player can now be almost as well informed as the large investor, and can trade at more economic rates using the same mechanisms.

Perhaps the best example of a company making a difference in this area is Wit Capital. It breaks into the magic financial circle on behalf of the small investor, not just by offering very low dealing rates, but by providing access to stock from IPOs (initial public offerings) at the offering price, to venture capital investments, and to high-quality private placements. Wit Capital is also providing access to a digital stock market for its customers—in effect making its own market by allowing its customers to trade directly with each other. The outcome of this kind of operation will naturally be to pull more investors into the market, because the cost of participating is falling. It will also undermine and possibly destroy the institutions that do not follow this lead.

The *consumer* also participates in partially rigged markets. These are rigged at a national level, but also by the tendency of the producer and vendor to keep the consumer in a state of ignorance, as far as is legally possible. Despite this, within an advanced economy the consumer is not poorly served. However, the net introduces a much higher level of competition. It lowers transaction costs and thus prices, and it improves the consumer's knowledge dramatically. Consumers will eventually be able to participate in electronic markets that were once denied to them for all kinds of goods. They will be able to track their own spending patterns and, with greater knowledge of their requirements, order forward in bulk, just as is done in the commodity markets. Suddenly, consumers are endowed with knowledge of their own behavior—knowledge that they will be able to exploit for their individual benefit.

Of the three subpersonalities, the *employee* is probably the most important, because it is political and has the vote. Capitalists and consumers may be influenced by political ideas and campaigns, but it is usually the employee part of our nature who puts the X on the paper. John and Jane Doe cannot possibly entertain the prospect of an investment portfolio or the joys of consumption unless they can first entertain the prospect of gainful employment.

295

Like the capitalist and the consumer, the employee has also participated to some extent in a rigged market, although the rigging may be done for or against them, depending on context. It may have been rigged by unions or professional associations or employers. It may also have been rigged by national governments or natural geographic barriers. The bar is being lowered in all these areas, nevertheless, and the ability to rig the market is diminishing. Perhaps more importantly, the whole employment market is in a state of flux, as it was throughout the twentieth century.

According to research by Stanford University professor Stephen R Barley, the share of the US labor force whose jobs involve manual work (laborers, farm workers, industrial workers, and craftspeople) or non-professional services (hotel workers, distribution workers, retail workers, and so on) has fallen by more than half, from 83 percent in 1900 to an estimated 41 percent in 2000. Those who work primarily with information will have grown from 17 to 59 percent. They are the majority now.

But even among the "information workers," job security is not so rosy. In general, organizations are downsizing by a gradual process of restructuring, removing management layers on the one hand and outsourcing functions on the other. Between 1979 and 1994, the number of people employed by America's biggest industrial corporations fell by nearly a third, from 16.2 million to 11.6 million. According to studies by the American Management Association, management supervisory jobs are currently being eliminated nearly twice as fast as they are being created, while professional and technical jobs are being created about 50 percent faster than they are being cut. The old career path is gone and jobs for life are now as rare as hen's teeth.

The market can be classified in terms of knowledge workers (professionals with genuine and sophisticated, knowledge-heavy skills), managers (organizers of others; nowadays often project managers rather than line managers), and the rest (skilled or unskilled workers occupying subsidiary roles). There is a very large movement in progress here. According to Peter Drucker, the amount of labor required to produce an additional unit of manufacturing output fell by about 1 percent per year from 1900. After the Second World War, the amount of raw material needed for each unit increase in manufacturing GDP began to fall at about 1 percent per year. Then from 1950, the amount of energy that manufacturers required per unit of additional output began to fall at about 1 percent per year. Again, according to Drucker, since 1900, the number of educated workers employed by the average company has been rising at the same 1 percent per year.

This, then, represents the march of the knowledge workers, who are collectively driving out manual work, pushing down the cost of production, and squeezing more out of every industrial unit of energy. It is a ratchet effect, leading to a cumulative compound improvement in productivity. Knowledge is displacing jobs in many areas and creating other jobs as it does so, and most of the population can do nothing more than adjust to the world as it changes. Only the knowledge workers are immune—or are they?

There is a market for knowledge workers and most knowledge worker tasks can be carried out from anywhere—by teleworking. The raw materials for a knowledge worker consist of a good brain, a good education, and a connection to the web. The jobs of manual workers were happily exported to the poorer regions of the world by a process of arbitrage; the jobs of knowledge workers will move in the same direction, pushed by the same force. This could only be stopped by economic barriers put in place by the most political of the three aspects of modern humanity, the employee. But the web dislikes economic barriers and routes around them.

JOHNANDJANEDOE@NEWWORLD.COM

The electronic b@zaar will be visited daily by electronic consumers who are monitored as they pass from stall to stall, from website to website. As the net develops, every click of the mouse will be captured, because most consumers will have eagerly exchanged the right to monitor their behavior for loyalty discounts given to them by one of several large consortia of electronic retailers. The web will thus be inhabited by intelligent software agents that gather data and pass it to large data warehouses, to be sorted and sifted and then analyzed by intelligent data-mining software that will reveal in depth the behavior of each individual consumer.

It will uncover every trend, large or small. The giant electronic stall holders of the b@zaar will hold data on you, will know your preferences, and will be able to predict your behavior before you have even decided what your behavior is. Excellent sales targeting will mean that products and choices in which you have no interest will never be presented to you. The traders at the b@zaar will offer you an excellent and remarkably sophisticated service, for which you will be financially grateful. They will provide you with exactly what you need at a price that you can afford whenever you need it. Right?

Wrong.

That imaginary scenario is based on push, and such a scenario would never take hold in a publish–subscribe world. If it seemed to be developing in this direction, then one of two things would happen. Either individual web users would adopt completely false identities, or legislation would be enacted to preserve the identity of an individual from attempts by any organization to discover it. The idea that "whoever has economic knowledge of you has economic power over you" is going to gain currency.

Individuals may be willing to trade knowledge of themselves for value, but they will not be happy to give it away in perpetuity—only to lend it.

And so a completely different set of possibilities arises.

The personal server and the avatar

John Doe has a charge card and the information relating to it is managed by American Express. He also has several other cards—a loyalty card from the supermarket, a petrol card, and a debit card from his bank—and the information relating to these cards is held by the associated organizations. Jane Doe has a similar set of cards, including a store card that she uses occasionally, and her information is also held by the organizations issuing the cards.

Since they were children, John and Jane have both suffered the odd illness and they have regular medical check-ups, so medical data is held on them by some health organizations. They have both been through the education mill and thus there are records pertaining to their education, and they both have driving licenses. John's career has been patchy and thus his CV has quite a few entries, but the majority of the data relating to his employment is held by the organizations he worked for. Naturally, the government also has records in relation to this and the taxes he has paid.

Jane is similar, but there is also the complication that she had time out to give birth to their son, Joe, and there is a mass of registration data surrounding that event. In her youth, she committed a minor misdemeanor and somewhere in the US law enforcement agencies there is a record of it. She has traveled outside the country, so passport data is kept somewhere. She is also a frequent flyer because of her current job, so additional data is held somewhere relating to her travel behavior, the hotels she stayed in, and the cars she hired. And so it goes on.

We could continue to amass examples of the data belonging to John, Jane, and Joe Doe that is kept on their behalf. We could add details on telephones, cars, and the house. And in each example we would be able to think of one or perhaps several organizations holding information on the Doe family to which they themselves have no easy access, and some of which could be quite wrong.

By law this data belongs to the Doe family—or does it? This depends on where they live. In matters of national security, the data belongs to the nation. In matters of business, the data may well be traded without asking any permission, and it often is. For example, information about traffic offenses committed in the US is sold to US insurance companies, leading to higher premiums for offenders. Technically, the organizations that hold data on the Does are either holding it on their behalf or it is being shared between the Does and the organization so that a better service can be provided—but in every case, the organization has possession of the data, and possession is nine-tenths of the value.

This would not matter too much, were it not for the fact that the Doe family does not actually possess data on itself. When the Does surf the web, the electronic b@zaar holders may be able to monitor their surfing patterns and deduce useful knowledge from them, but the Does do not have organized software that can do this. They know less about themselves than others do.

Each member of the Doe family needs a personal database to collate all the information on them, in fact they need a *personal server*—a coherent personal computing capability that lives on the internet and is available to them whenever they connect.

In reality, this is easy to envisage and technically quite possible to achieve. Imagine that each member of the Doe family has a PC and that all their information is kept on their PC—educational records, health records, titles to ownership, and electronic possessions, such as music, videos, and so on.

Now move the software and the data to a safe place on the web where it cannot be destroyed or damaged. We can think in terms of putting it into an "information bank." If we have the right key (a foolproof biometric such as a fingerprint, voiceprint, or whatever), then we have complete security. So now John and Jane Doe's software and data live on the net and if they wish to use it, they can access it via a network computer, a web telephone, or any web access device.

This is not a fanciful idea, it is simply the logical extrapolation of a set of already existing trends. Individuals who have websites keep them on another computer, possibly with an ISP or a web community such as Geocities. This is their data, but it lives on the web. Users of free email services such as HotMail or chat software such as ICQ have applications and data that live on the web. With time, more and more applications will become web centric and live on the network.

If we look at another aspect of personal computing, personal financial software such as Quicken or the various personal organizer software programs and other applications such as email collectively assemble a set of personal data. It is not inconceivable to think of a whole personal system that provides a coherent collection of all personal data. Thus just as organizations have computer systems, there is no reason that individuals should not have comprehensive personal computer systems. This is nothing more than the typical march of the application of technology: from government to large organizations, to small organizations, until finally it is cheap enough to be made available to the individual.

Whether it is first provided by a credit card company, a bank, an ISP, or some new type of ebusiness, there can be little doubt that the personal server will come into existence. It can be expected to emerge as soon as most of the web security issues have been satisfactorily resolved. The idea can be developed further simply by defining exactly what the personal server is likely to be. It will be a coherent software application that provides access to, manages, and runs all of the following items:

@   Personal identity information for security purposes, including an elec-
    tronic passport and a foolproof security capability.

@   A store of personal data, including health information and records, and
    a cumulative personal history, including education and job history.

@   A store of data relating to all relationships with providers of any kind,
    such as the electricity company, the telephone company, various retailers,
    and the government.

@   A store of transaction history data, showing what was bought, when,
    and how it was paid for.

@   A collection of personal applications bought from software suppliers,
    including email and personal financial management software.

@   A store of electronic possessions, including videos, music, publications,
    computer games, and so on.

@   A store of electronic titles, including ecash, stock, loyalty points, title to
    property, title to possessions.

The idea of a personal server has massive implications, because it puts the individual citizen in control of their own data and their own electronic store of value.
It turns the world wide web into an electronic looking glass in which many of
details of the real world can be viewed—a true virtual world, with virtual citizens, virtual schools and hospitals, virtual businesses, and virtual governments.

We could think of the personal server as a personal website that allows
individuals to interact with other individuals or organizations within the electronic economy. In fact, we could think of it as a secure website that will only
reveal the information it chooses to reveal to whomever visits it. In computing
terms it will behave the same way as an extranet site—in human terms it will
behave as if it were a virtual individual. And thus we have the possibility of a
secure avatar.

An avatar, as we mentioned in Chapter 2, is an electronic identity generally used in MUDs, which can be used to conceal the identity of the user. In
practice, it is nothing more than a false name. It would allow John Doe to
appear on the internet as John Wayne or even Jessica Rabbit. With a personal
server and the help of a trusted third party, we can create a secure avatar that
reveals only the data its user wishes to reveal. We can even associate

permissions with every electronic organization or individual with which we deal and control the data that is exposed on a one-on-one basis. A secure avatar will allow an individual to realize their ownership of their data, and it will also allow them to meet other entities in the electronic b@zaar and interact with them in the same way that people act—revealing some things and concealing others.

Valuing John Doe

There are many good reasons for the development of personal servers, one of which is that they are very economic in terms of the amount of data that needs to be stored. While we can think in terms of storing videos, music, data, and so on, in practice this need not be done. It is enough simply to store the *link* to the video, music, data, and so on, and the *permission* to be able to use the data. This would mean that instead of creating millions of electronic copies of, say, a hit movie, it is only necessary to create a few, and millions of copies of electronic permissions. This is simply an application of the idea that "the link is the information."

In effect, this means that the link, together with the permission to use it, is also a title to value. If you have bought permission to play a particular movie once, then it can be delivered simply as a link and a permission, and if you don't actually play the movie there is no reason that you should not be able to sell the link and the permission to someone else. The link and the permission thus have a definable value.

Envisage now that the personal server contains all of John Doe's electronic titles to value, electronic references to everything he owns of any significant value. This could include quite an array of things: memberships of various clubs, yet to be used tickets from airlines or theaters, holidays bought but not taken, property, possessions from his lawnmower to his car, stock, insurance policies, a pension, and so on. To this we can add all of his liabilities, the payments he regularly has to make such as electricity bills, telephone bills, taxes, and so on. The server would also include a complete history of John Doe's economic activity from the moment he made his first significant purchase, and his complete economic history.

Such a set of information makes it possible to put a very precise value on John Doe. This can be done by using relatively simple financial formulae and metrics to calculate the current value of all his possessions and apply discounted cashflow formulae to his assumed future income, allowing for his spending habits and insurances he has taken against future disability or death. It will thus be possible to reach a very accurate credit rating for John Doe and lend to him with complete confidence. Such a capability would reduce the risk of lending money and hence the cost of low-risk loans.

This set of information also makes it possible to tax John Doe very accurately, and, remarkably, to do so without even identifying him. For example, taxation could be carried out by John Doe's passing the data concerning his value but not his personal details to a tax authority, which could send back a tax bill and a secure electronic proof of assessment. John Doe could select always to trade in this anonymous fashion, or could choose to expose his data to receive some compensatory benefit from a vendor.

The complete personal health records from the personal server could automatically be available for any medical assistance that John Doe receives and prescriptions for drugs could be checked against his records. His exact measurements could be used by his tailor and his personal cobbler, and potential employers could check the truth of his employment records and his educational and professional qualifications.

Another capability that a personal server would deliver would be the ability to trade your possessions quickly if you wanted. It would simply be a matter of transferring titles to value (links and permissions) and then transferring the actual goods. For goods that are or could become completely electronic (videos, music, games, software, airline tickets, holidays not yet taken, next month's supply of coffee, and so on), it would be possible to create pure electronic markets. Speculators might be willing to trade in air tickets between New York and London, or tickets to the latest Andrew Lloyd Webber musical. This may seem bizarre, but trading in pork belly futures always seemed bizarre to me.

Have smartcard will travel

An important aspect of the idea of the personal server is that it is completely mobile. With current technology, all you would need to use it anywhere in the world that had an internet connection would be some personal validator, such as a biometric (and means of reading it), a smartcard, or even a well-thought-out password capability. This would have particular relevance to the likes of Jane Doe, our imaginary web user whose work involves a great deal of travel.

There is a fairly large international industry based around travelers, both tourists and the business executives. Officially world tourism accounts for 8 percent of the world's export market and in recent years it has been growing faster than any other sector of international trade. There are over 20 million hotel rooms across the world and the numbers are growing by over 10 percent annually. However, it is clear from the facilities of the major hotels in the main business centers that a good deal of this trade is generated by business rather than the ubiquitous tourist.

Businesspeople nowadays have mobile existences. Many only occupy their offices for about 70 percent of the time, and others don't have offices, but simply "hotdesk" when in the office and telework from home or from hotel rooms. According to Peter Cochrane of British Telecom, in fewer than eight years over 10 percent of all telephones have become mobile. He notes that in the days of lesser mobility there was a 98 percent chance that someone would be at their place of work, and a 90 percent chance that they would be at the site of their fixed telephone. Call and rental charges were much higher then and calls shorter and fewer. So there was only about a 10 percent chance that you would receive an engaged tone, no reply, or non-availability. For over 80 percent of the working day, you could contact the person of your choice, and in most cases someone would answer the phone, talk to you, and take a message. Nowadays, a contact window of lower than 35 percent is not uncommon.

There are several contributory reasons for this, but mobility is a significant factor. The technology and infrastructure to support the peripatetic Jane Doe are firmly in place: hotels, car rental, mobile phones, faxes, copiers, laptop computers, and above all else the internet. If we add the personal server to this battery of technology, Jane Doe can carry the largest imaginable business toolbox with her wherever she goes and it will weigh absolutely nothing. So the question arises of whether the amount of traveling will continue to increase.

With the advent of videoconferencing systems, one-on-one and group meetings occur via the internet and the absolute need to travel—as well as the requirement for office buildings—diminishes quite dramatically. This enables teleworking as never before, but it is unlikely completely to replace face-to-face interactions or meetings of peer groups. In many cases, it may not come down to cost, just to a matter of whether Jane Doe prefers to travel or would rather stay home.

Another consideration enters the equation. At one point only the large multinational organizations could gain business advantage from arbitraging between countries. Thus jobs were exported to the geographies where labor costs were low and profit was, to some degree, exported to the geographies where taxation was low. The web offers the possibility of international arbitrage to smaller multinational organizations, and provides the incentive for companies to become multinational simply for the cost advantages. So, with the advent of the personal server and greater mobility for individuals, a certain number of Jane Does will almost certainly locate themselves in the most financially advantageous place.

In time, we will see governments competing to attract populations in the same way that in the past they have competed for the inward investment of multinational manufacturers.

The lumpen PONA

The acronym PONA stands for "person of no account." It connects the idea of not having an internet account with the idea of being worthless, and it is a useful because it will eventually be the case that persons of no account will be severely disadvantaged. Someone with no access will be increasingly marginalized economically, educationally, and even socially.

Cyberspace already has a population above 200 million, heading quickly, at the time of writing, for 300 million. This is greater than the populations of all but a few countries. Geographically the net spans the globe, but its population is concentrated among the prosperous citizens of the prosperous nations. It still has a little of a "white middle class" flavor with a dash or two of academic, but it is quickly becoming cosmopolitan. However, like every nation, it has its political activists, its academics, its merchants, and its criminal classes.

The criminal classes are of particular interest here. In *The Communist Manifesto*, Karl Marx refers to them as the "lumpen proletariat." He describes the proletariat as an organized force of workers whose relation to production is established through its productive role, while the lumpen proletariat are those who have been forced into a position of non-productivity where crime is often the only way, or at least the best way, to survive. Actually the lumpen do more than survive—in recent times some of them have done rather well for themselves. Marx regarded the lumpen proletariat as untrustworthy to the cause of communism, whereas most people would just regard them as untrustworthy.

Although this is rarely referred to by economists, the criminal classes make a very significant contribution to national economies and the global economy. They introduce high costs in certain areas of activity and distort the behavior of markets. The examples are many and varied. Pilferage from shops, whether by staff or customers, has to be paid for, and ultimately it is paid for by John and Jane Doe. Governments across the world introduce various welfare schemes that are designed to assist the poor, but the claiming of such welfare payments involves an ongoing battle to combat fraud and raises the cost of providing the benefit. The growing of drug crops distorts the agricultural activity in producer countries. Drug supply encourages criminality, whether in the form of prostitution or simply theft, to obtain the money for the habit.

Collectively, illegal trading of all kinds constitutes a significant percentage of the economy—estimates of 5 percent are often quoted, but clearly it varies from country to country. At some level, the "dirty" money that is acquired through criminal activities in the black economy needs to be laundered—in other words, it needs to be introduced back into the real economy so that the lumpen proletariat can spend it legitimately. It is estimated that criminals launder around $500 billion per annum through the world's financial systems, the vast bulk of which is drugs money. This is far too much money to push through casinos and other businesses; it needs to go through the banks.

There are 61 offshore financial centers that are poorly regulated and whose banks have access to the rest of the world's financial system. These tend to be where much of the money laundering takes place. Indeed, many banks there are believed to belong directly to drug barons. The same sort of laundering operations are now happening on the web, via internet banks and casinos. There has even been police speculation that some ISPs are owned by drug barons, so that tracing of incriminating information can be controlled. This would be no surprise, as it is not that expensive to establish an ISP.

To add to this, we also have the fact that there is a healthy and growing international drug trade that now takes place over the web. In the UK, the local drug pushers are being disintermediated by websites selling cannabis direct from the Netherlands and Switzerland, countries with more liberal attitudes to the use of soft drugs. Commander Andy Hayman, a spokesman for the UK's Association of Chief Police Officers, was quoted in *The Independent on Sunday* as saying that the internet trade in drugs is almost impossible to tackle.

The problem lies in the fact that companies selling drugs over the web run well-thought-out and efficient operations. They do everything possible to protect their merchandise and their clients, using PO box numbers rather than real addresses and changing website address regularly. They also only sell in amounts of 10 grams or less, thus supplying a quantity that defines the receiver as a user rather than a dealer, should they be caught in possession. Buyers can buy reasonably anonymously and untraceably through cybercafés and can also use PO boxes. Alternatively, they can have goods delivered to a false name if they share a flat or house. In the UK the police tend not to prosecute cannabis users, only the dealers, and such a policy will no longer contain the use of cannabis at all.

It might seem that the net is a great boon to the lumpen proletariat, but quite the opposite is true. As the net matures, the audit trails that help to prevent the counterfeiting of electronic money will drive the criminal classes out of cyberspace. Their money laundering will be confined to the paper economy. The lumpen proletariat will become lumpen PONA—people of no account. Electronic purse schemes such as VISA's leave an audit trail, and even ones that don't—such as the Mondex card, backed by HSBC and NatWest—are currently fixed at low amounts (under $1,000), which makes money laundering far more difficult. If the criminal classes are driven from the web, then money laundering will become a more and more tricky operation and some of them may lose their livelihood. They may face unemployment and retraining. It's a grim prospect.

THE FLAMING OF THE WINTERPALACE.GOV

Technology changes bring economic changes, which bring social changes, then political changes. We can attribute the end of slavery to the progress of industrialization, which began to make slavery uneconomic. It was much easier to advocate the end of slavery when the economic fallout became minimal, so the machines allowed the slaves to be free. Similarly, the contraceptive pill promoted female equality. Women controlled their fertility, improving their employability and economic power, which then brought social change and political change.

The internet follows the same cycle. It is technology change that is heralding economic change, and social and political change will follow in its wake. In this chain of cause and effect, the social and political changes are not easy to predict.

The web has its political quarter, inhabited by the followers of virtually every political ideology ever invented, and, unsurprisingly, most of them seem to have the opinion that the web will advance their cause more than that of those who oppose them. There are sites that merely encourage participation in politics, such as the National Political Index, a non-profit, non-partisan organization that seeks to improve the availability of political information, or the Greyhawkes Aerie, which has a page—greyhawkes.com/ps/parties.html—that lists nearly all political websites in America. There is also the World-Wide E-Democracy Projects Page—www.dar.cam.ac.uk/e-demos.html—which promotes democratic connections between the internet and the local community, and many others.

Naturally, all the main political parties in the major democracies have websites and there is a whole multitude of new or reborn political movements, with sites including the Active Reformist Party, Workers World Party, Communist Party of the USA, Libertarian Party, National Socialist White People's Party, among others. Although much concern has been expressed about the number of hate groups online, there is likely to be no real cause for concern. In all probability, the internet will simply expose the nature of the political crank more thoroughly than society currently can and these sites will be drowned in a flood of disinterest.

The only true web-based political movement seems to be the Electronic Frontiers Foundation (www.eff.org) and this appears to have only one political aim, to protect basic civil rights on the internet. To this end, the EFF runs the Blue Ribbon Campaign and opposes virtually all attempts at restrictive legislation. There are other sites pursuing similar goals, usually concerned with the First Amendment to the US Constitution and free speech, including the Freedom Forum On-line (freedomforum.org) and the American Civil Liberties Union (aclu.org). What seems remarkably absent from any of this is any burgeoning political movement based on globalization—on one world. This is ironic, because the web naturally undermines national governments.

For all of our lives, no matter which country we were born in, we have been subject to a government—a monopoly organization to which we have paid very significant amounts of money and from which we have received services, with some of which we may have been happy and others not. Most of us don't choose our citizenship, it is thrust upon us, and with it a taxation framework and a set of laws with which we may not wholly agree. What would happen if one day, suddenly, we all had a choice?

Publish–subscribe politics

The original "gang of four" were the four politicians, including Madame Mao and Lin Piao, who tried to take control of China in the 1960s, but failed. The latest gang of four, the publish–subscribe mechanisms, are also deeply political, and this gang of four won't be stopped.

The trappings of a nation state include government, army, police force, individual currency, central bank, stock exchange, customs authority, taxation authority, and a complete body of national legislation. These are the attributes of the national monopoly, imposed by the rule of law. There is no standardization in this and so different nations have different laws—and some of these laws are fundamentally undermined by the internet. Consider, for example, the two areas of pornography and gambling, both of which are already causing concern to some governments:

Gambling

There are a large number of casino sites with obvious domain names, such as MonteCarlo.com and Nevada.com. Many are based in the Caribbean region in countries such as Antigua, Costa Rica, and Belize, where anyone with a few hundred thousand dollars can set up a casino, with few legal restrictions and no tax to pay. Internet gambling is big business. Christiansen/Cummings Associates, a research firm, estimates the revenue for 1999 at $1.2 billion and has forecast that the worldwide revenue could grow to $2.1 billion in 2001. Most countries have some legal restrictions on gambling that the internet circumvents.

It looks likely that most of the world's gambling industry is not going to reside in the US. There has been much toing and froing over legislation, but there is little doubt about the direction in which it is heading. The US will either use existing legislation as a means of outlawing online gambling or it will implement the Kyl Bill, which will have the same effect. In contrast, UK gambling laws are not so draconian, but the government imposes a betting tax, which UK gambling organizations are avoiding by setting up in the Caribbean, Gibraltar, and other untaxed areas. At the opposite end of the spectrum, Australia is bidding for the gambling market by legitimizing the industry through regulation and legislation. This will boost internet gambling as the established bricks-and-mortar gambling organizations build an officially sanctioned industry in Australia. It will be the first country in the world to offer internet gambling licenses.

Pornography

The internet is littered with pornography sites. Censorship of pornography in the Scandinavian countries is minimal and there is no possibility of preventing access to websites based in these countries, even if it were possible to close down pornographic sites in all other geographies. Surprisingly perhaps, many pornographic sites are run by the Swedish Post Office, which offers a popular and efficient ISP service. The laws in the US are slightly more restrictive, and those in the UK and other areas of Europe are significantly more stringent. Nevertheless, the attitude to pornography in Scandinavia is becoming the general law for the whole of the electronic world.

Who is in control?

There have already been two precedent-setting cases, one on each side of the Atlantic, that provide a clue as to how the world may eventually impose control over the internet.

The first was a US case concerning gambling. New York State attorney general Eliot Spitzer's Internet and Investor Protection bureaus brought a case against the New York-based casino WIGC. According to Spitzer's office, the casino was "selling shares in the casino gaming business for $10,000 each" as well as accepting wagers. WIGC's defense was simply that it never fell within New York state's jurisdiction gambling laws because its server computers are located in Antigua. The New York state Supreme Court ruled that a casino with servers in Antigua nonetheless violates US law if it accepts wagers from state residents. Justice Charles Edward Ramos ruled specifically that:

> *It is irrelevant that Internet gambling is legal in Antigua. The act*
> *of entering the bet and transmitting the information from New York*
> *via the Internet is adequate to constitute gambling activity within*
> *New York State.*

In a judgment similar to that of Justice Ramos in New York, Judge Christopher Hardy at the Southwark Crown Court in London dealt the British pornography industry a crippling blow when he ruled that US porn sites are subject to British law. The ruling was against Graham Waddon, a man described by the newspapers as "Britain's biggest internet porn operator." Waddon had set up porn sites in America that included torture and bestiality content, which is indisputably obscene under British law. The websites were subscription sites for which he charged $40 a month and which were said to be paying him over $2 million a year. Waddon offered the defense that publication occurred outside British jurisdiction, but it cut no ice.

The legal position in both cases is identical and remarkably ineffective. It reduces to the simple position that "the citizens of our jurisdiction can buy but they cannot sell." They can subscribe but they cannot publish. This is the same position that many police forces across the world take in respect of drug supply: only the pusher is guilty. If it were possible to download narcotics over the internet, then we could confine the drug problem to Columbia, the Golden Triangle, and other areas of the planet where the crops are farmed. Given the trend to internet drug trafficking in Europe, this may actually start to happen unless someone intervenes somehow.

There are other similar issues. In the UK, it is illegal to provide information that can be used to carry out terrorist acts, such as recipes for homemade bombs, but this information is freely available on the web—there are no US laws censoring it and, even if there were, the origination of the information would relocate. Information is also available relating to narcotics manufacture and hacking, which would be censored in the UK. There is also fairly extensive violation of copyright that cannot be easily dealt with because of the laws of the country where the violation is taking place.

It is difficult to think of any way that the local laws on any of these matters can be imposed without taking control of either every web-access device or every ISP. This is something that cybercitizens will not trust governments to do and, in any case, it is not at all practical. And so the situation will persist—for better or for worse, the rule of law will be defied.

Employment and taxation

Let us now consider Jane Doe's employment. Governments exert control over employment by controlling the employer. This is their route to ensuring a degree of accuracy on tax returns, controlling illegal immigration, and many other matters. But if an organization contracts with one in another country for the supply of services, then the government of the first country will not be and cannot be concerned. It is not within its jurisdiction and the import of services happens all the time in many different ways. So if Jane Doe can be employed as a teleworker by a foreign company, she can choose to appear to be located in any country that takes her fancy—obviously, she will choose the country that offers her the lowest taxation rate.

As if on cue, EOCnet.com was launched in 1999 as a Bermuda-based ecommerce operation providing virtual offices to allow companies to sell goods globally under the Bermuda tax regime, which has a distinct lack of corporate taxes. EOCnet.com plans to offer thousands of esuites, which will be legal Bermudan entities for global etrading. Granger Whitelaw, chief executive of

EOCnet.com and a New York investment banker, said that US-based companies taking esuites could classify offshore businesses as foreign sales corporations, providing them with tax advantages on overseas earnings. He also noted that EOCnet.com was the first overseas company to qualify as a safe harbor under EU data protection laws. And this, of course, is yet another legal point—the EU has data protection laws that are different to those of the US and that favor the owner of the data.

The implications of this are obvious. Jane Doe can now set up in Bermuda as Jane Doe Inc. and have a foreign bank account, be paid in any currency that takes her fancy, and use her bank account exclusively for web purchases. If she chooses to bank in a country where banking secrecy is a legal right, then it is unlikely that details of her financial activity will ever be discovered. The various offshore facilities available to expatriate workers can now be exploited by Jane Doe without her ever moving abroad.

Nevertheless, if she does this she will be breaking the law—an open-and-shut case of tax evasion. But what if Jane Doe sets up a company in Bermuda and also pays herself a small salary in her country of residence, but pays herself a large bonus on top of this in Bermuda where the taxation is low? First, she will only be doing what some multinational corporations do—organizing her financial affairs across national boundaries in order to avoid tax. Second, she may not be doing anything illegal, depending on exactly how it is achieved.

We can extend this idea as much as we please by assuming that individuals will be able to behave like multinationals in every way. They could take advantage of tax holidays or become eligible for generous grants, simply by choosing to incorporate in a particular region. This is beginning to sound fanciful—but is it really?

Consider the possibilities. Just as advisory companies help some individuals to take advantage of offshore tax avoidance, so some will soon specialize in enabling cybercitizens to arbitrage between different taxation regimes and take full advantage of the anomalies of cyberspace. Such services will be available at the click of a mouse and be possible to implement in hours. Knowledge of these services will spread quickly. Some governments will be happy to introduce legislation to attract inward ebusiness investments, and create special development zones where normal taxation laws do not apply, because they will have nothing to lose and everything to gain in doing so.

Just as some organizations "get the idea" and transform themselves into ebusinesses, so some governments may "get the idea" and transform their territories into ecountries, offering clear financial incentives to knowledge workers in order to attract them, either virtually or in the flesh. The obvious inducements will be to reduce all forms of income tax to zero, either generally or in some well-defined tax-free zone, and to sell passports at a reasonable price, but one that is high enough to exclude the poor and the PONA.

It is clear that governments are losing their mandates as the internet encroaches on the commercial transactions that are their lifeblood. The internet has not yet begun to reduce the taxes that governments collect, but it will do this and it may do so at bewildering speed, at a far faster pace than the machinery of government can move.

In search of the lost mandate

In analyzing the buy/sell transaction we identified five categories—the negotiated deal, the brokered deal, the retail sale, the auction, and the pure market. However, there are six. We can refer to the sixth transaction as the "tax-based sale," or simply tax, and it is the favored transaction of monopoly organizations. They merely name their price and you pay it or you refuse to participate in their market. However, it is slightly unrealistic to talk in terms of a market, because monopoly is anti-market. The monopolist does not make a market—it destroys one. In exchange for your money, the monopoly provides goods and services and chooses its profit level. In short order, the motivation for efficiency and change melts away like the winter snow.

All governments are monopolies within their geographic mandate, no matter whether they are benign or despotic. They set the rules for national economies by the creation of regulating institutions—trusted third parties, of which the central bank and the legal institutions are the most important. If it occurs at all, the regulation of government itself happens by one of three mechanisms: democracy, revolution, or interference from other governments. Governments impose tax and assume responsibility for the infrastructure of the economy for which they have a remit. They also impose laws that affect economic behavior directly or indirectly.

Most governments obtain their mandate by virtue of the "democratic deal." This was tried out first in Ancient Greece and revived as an idea during the Renaissance. As a system, it was tried in the UK by Cromwell after the monarchy had briefly been toppled, and it was retained as a protection against monarchic excess. It became the inspiration for the founding of the US, and it gradually spread across the world in the nineteenth and twentieth centuries. Here's the deal:

@   We provide all the services to allow law to be maintained and society to function smoothly.
@   We will charge you whatever we like via tax and you will pay, because you have no choice.
@   You get to vote.

A democratic government is really nothing more than a monopoly that acts under the influence, but not the control, of its population. The tax transaction involves the complicity of the citizens that are subject to it, a complicity that is achieved by the vote. Even the staunchest defenders of democracy would never claim that any of the various systems of voting is perfect. Democracy is intellectually defended on the basis of being the best mechanism from a series of options. Nevertheless, it imposes a monopoly—and the web undermines this monopoly.

The democratic deal is not going to hold—it is going to change.

There is a possibility that the web will transform governments into competitive organizations that offer a specific set of services for a specific fee. It invites governments to compete and if they are forced to compete, then some of the things on which they now spend money may no longer be viable. So the question is: What would citizens be willing to pay for if they had a choice? So far, nobody knows the answer.

Perhaps we could ask another question:

> **What if you didn't vote for a government, but simply purchased its services according to your perception of their value?**

Such a situation could come into being, but if it did, it would bring a very real problem with it. Governments have always been distributors of wealth via the mechanism of taxation. They have a communal responsibility. If a government's ability to distribute wealth were undermined, then money would flow naturally to the wealthy. This, in turn, would bring economic hardship and eventually provoke a political backlash.

However, the internet has the ability to transform the basic mechanism of democracy—the vote itself. Until now, the vote has been a very rough mechanism for instructing government. In most democracies its maximum reach of power is to swap one government for a single alternative. It varies depending on the system, but in general voters only get to vote about 20 times in their lifetime. In very few countries do voters have the ability to express an opinion in respect of specific policies. They are relatively uninvolved in government, so in most democracies the government is run by professional politicians.

This will change with the internet because it allows voters to be consulted inexpensively about almost every issue. Thus the internet is deeply political—far more so than any commentator has yet suggested. At the moment we live under democracies that are based on push, but in the future they will be based on a publish–subscribe principle where the behavior of government is more closely controlled by the voter. This is easy enough to grasp, but exactly how it will happen is not.

Following a presentation I gave in Amsterdam late in 1999 on the political issues of the internet, I was approached by a young Dutchman. He never gave me his name and he left no business card. Because of the circumstances I did not have much time to chat to him, but I remember the incident well, because he said something that surprised me.

"We are setting up another country," he said.

I blinked.

"All you need is a small amount of territory and five million citizens and you can get a seat at the United Nations. We can attract and register citizens quite quickly over the internet. We can issue passports. We can make our own laws. Maybe we can buy an island somewhere or maybe we'll just anchor a ship outside territorial waters. We have a website," he said.

A few days later I logged on to the address he gave me. All I got was a blank screen. If that was his website then it was under construction. I went to the United Nations site and could find no reference to five million citizens, only that UN membership required a vote by the general assembly. Setting up a new country may not be as simple as it was described, but if you speak for five million people, then you have a voice whether or not the world officially recognizes it.

It was just a straw in the wind. Like it or not, a revolution of some kind is brewing. The introduction of the printing press led to a paper-based economy, but it also led to new political ideas from the quill pens of Jean-Jacques Rousseau and Thomas Paine. The second economic revolution will be no different. Indeed, we shall almost certainly see the same pattern emerge.

First came the technology to enable the new economy, then came the new economy, and then came the political writers and finally the political earthquake—the monarchies were torn down and replaced in the main by democratic republics.

Something similar will happen again, but who can predict the outcome?

THE MARCH OF THE CYBERKIDS

The average child under 10 has spent more time online that the average adult over 50. As the Baby Boomer generation gives way to Generation X, the phenomenon of technophobia will melt away. Technophobia is a psychological or skills problem of the aging Baby Boomers and their parents. Generation X is the generation that grew up with computers. As children they had electronic toys and they played on games computers before they were eight years old; now, as they are slipping into gainful employment, they are completely conversant with the technology.

According to a 1998 survey by ZD Market Intelligence, Generation X outscore the Baby Boomers in their actual use of the web very significantly: in playing interactive games, reading online publications, downloading software, interactive chat, use of MUDs, use of email, and online shopping, whether to buy or just to find out about products. The only activity in which the Baby Boomers are more active online was in utilizing financial services, particularly share trading.

The education of Generation X was not driven by the web, in fact it did not involve the web. But Generation X were exposed to software as a natural part of their environment and have grown up with it. To a child, a computer game is a remarkable thing—it is software for software's sake. The child plays the game with some goal in mind (kill the aliens, reach the next level, and so on), but the reward for playing well is actually visual stimulation. And so Generation Xers learned that software was entertainment and the first kind of software they used set them problems to solve. They were rewarded with nothing more than visual stimulation, but this was a big deal. For them, software was, and is, a challenge.

Some of them even educated themselves in the process. For example, in the very popular computer game Sim City, the player becomes the Mayor of Sim City, a new development, and he has the power to create and grow residential, commercial, and industrial zones. He can locate power plants and build various roads and highways. As the city grows, problems arise in terms of crime, pollution, and so forth, and the mayor tries to solve them. The player is limited by his financial budget and the simple process of the passage of time. The results reflect on the mayor's chances of re-election and if you don't get re-elected then the game is over. Sim City is not a game. It is a sophisticated lesson in town planning with the addition of a little bit of politics. It is education by other means.

There have been other such games, including one called Civilization that cast its net wider and covered the development of the world from the dawn of civilization up to AD2020. At one point the US Secret Service began to believe that some games were subversive, which of course they are in a way. It took a specific interest in a game called Cyberpunk, which it suspected of teaching child computer enthusiasts to hack into real computers, but the game is not that realistic. It only encouraged children into hacker role playing.

The authors of computer games do not sit around designing educational experiences for their customers or ways of subverting the youth of the world—

they design fascinating and exciting audiovisual experiences for their customers. In doing so they inject their own humor and ideas into the game and the game player picks this up. Computer games are subversive in the same way that the *Simpsons* or *Ren and Stimpy* are subversive, and the creators of such information products have had considerable influence on Generation X.

However, Generation X is not the generation that will treat the web as its natural environment. The new bunch of cyberkids who are playing with their first mouse at about the time you read this sentence are those who will inherit the electronic world. For them, it is not Sonic the Hedgehog but online Quake that defines computer gaming. Their education will be threaded with trips into cyberspace to inhabit virtual classrooms or visit the cyber playgrounds of different educational communities across the globe. Their homework will be nothing more than the assisted exploration of a worldwide learning space. To them, *Webster's Dictionary* and *Roget's Thesaurus* will be electronic search capabilities. In their college years they will attend remote lectures given by the illuminati of the day and they will attain their cyberdegrees from the complete archipelago of educational environments across the world.

These cyberkids will grow up in an electronic world, meet new friends in electronic communities, shop in the electronic b@zaar, and earn their living in cyberspace. It is they who will write the poetry and make the music of the new age. I can see them now as teenagers, inspired by some political idealist who has posted a new formulation of the rights of man to the doors of the internet. I see them talking excitedly in cybercafés and exchanging views in political chat rooms. The wires are buzzing with their emails. I see them in a huge procession, carrying virtual message boards emblazoned with slogans. They are marching down the eroad behind the ghost of Tom Paine.

Bibliography

Most of the source information for this book came directly from websites, with many of the domain names being provided in the text. The following bibliography lists books or articles on relevant topics that were read while this book was in preparation.

The 500-Year Delta, Jim Taylor & Watts Wacker, Capstone, 1997.

Blur, Stan Davis & Christopher Meyer, Capstone, 1998.

Brand Building on the Internet, Martin Linstrom & Tim Frank Andersen, Hardie Grant Books, 1999.

"The coming of the new organization," Peter F Drucker, *Harvard Business Review*, Jan–Feb 1988.

The Control Revolution, Andrew L Shapiro, Public Affairs and the Century Foundation, 1999.

Crossing the Chasm, Geoffrey A Moore, HarperBusiness, 1999.

Data Smog, David Shenk, Abacus, 1997.

Digerati, John Brockman, Orion Business Books, 1997.

The Digital Economy, Don Tapscott, McGraw-Hill, 1997.

Digital Nomad, Tsugio Makimoto & David Manners, John Wiley, 1997.

The Elements of Banking, F E Perry, Methuen.

A History of Economics, J K Galbraith, Pelican, 1991.

Inside the Tornado, Geoffrey A Moore, HarperBusiness, 1999.

Intellectual Capital, Thomas A Stewart, Nicholas Brealey, 1997.

The Internet & World Wide Web, The Rough Guide, Angus J Kennedy, Rough Guides, 1999.

Media Virus, Douglas Rushkoff, Balantine Books, 1996.

Modern Banking in Theory and Practice, Shelagh Hefferman, John Wiley, 1996.

New Rules for the New Economy, Kevin Kelly, Viking, 1998.

One World, Ready or Not, William Greider, Touchstone, 1997.

The Pinball Effect, James Burke, Little Brown, 1997.

Retailing, Consumption and Capital, Neil Wrigley & Michelle Lowe, Longman, 1996.

Release 2.1, Esther Dyson, Penguin, 1998.

Retail Management, Roger Cox & Paul Brittain, Pitman, 1999.

Tips for Time Travellers, Peter Cochrane, Orion Business Books, 1997.

Unleashing the Killer App: Digital Strategies for Market Dominance, Larry Downes and Chunka Mui, Harvard Business School Press, 1998.

Index